MW01121162

Debating Hate Crime

Law and Society Series
W. Wesley Pue, General Editor

The Law and Society Series explores law as a socially embedded phenomenon. It is premised on the understanding that the conventional division of law from society creates false dichotomies in thinking, scholarship, educational practice, and social life. Books in the series treat law and society as mutually constitutive and highlight scholarship emerging from interdisciplinary engagement of law with fields such as politics, social theory, history, political economy, and gender studies.

A list of recent titles in the series appears at the end of the book. For a complete list, see the UBC Press website, www.ubcpress.ca/books/series_law.html.

Debating Hate Crime

Language, Legislatures, and the Law in Canada

ALLYSON M. LUNNY

UBCPress · Vancouver · Toronto

23 22 21 20 19 18 17   5 4 3 2 1

Printed in Canada on FSC-certified ancient-forest-free paper
(100% post-consumer recycled) that is processed chlorine- and acid-free.

Library and Archives Canada Cataloguing in Publication

Lunny, Allyson M., author
Debating hate crime : language, legislatures, and the law in Canada/Allyson M. Lunny.

(Law and society series)
Includes bibliographical references and index.
Issued in print and electronic formats.
ISBN 978-0-7748-2959-5 (hardcover). – ISBN 978-0-7748-2961-8 (PDF)
– ISBN 978-0-7748-2962-5 (EPUB). – ISBN 978-0-7748-2975-5 (MOBI)

1. Hate crimes – Law and legislation – Canada.   I. Title.
II. Series: Law and society series (Vancouver, B.C.)

KE8905 L85 2017   345.71'025   C2016-907196-0
KF9304 L85   C2016-907197-9

Canada

UBC Press gratefully acknowledges the financial support for our
publishing program of the Government of Canada (through the Canada Book Fund),
the Canada Council for the Arts, and the British Columbia Arts Council.

This book has been published with the help of a grant from the
Canadian Federation for the Humanities and Social Sciences, through the
Awards to Scholarly Publications Program, using funds provided by the
Social Sciences and Humanities Research Council of Canada.

Printed and bound in Canada by Friesens
Set in Stone by Marquis Interscript
Copy editor: Stacy Belden
Indexer: Heather Ebbs
Cover designer: Gabi Proctor

UBC Press
The University of British Columbia
2029 West Mall
Vancouver, BC V6T 1Z2

www.ubcpress.ca

Contents

Acknowledgments

The beginnings of this book started with a teaching fellowship at the Centre of Criminology at the University of Toronto, where students of mine engaged and challenged ideas of the course and lead me more deeply into the affective study of hate crime. I thank Rosemary Gartner, Marianna Valverde, and my Woodsworth students for their generous support. My colleagues at York University have offered me intellectual comradery, mentorship, and friendship. I especially would like to thank Annie Bunting and Richard Weisman for their support in this book and for so much more and Miriam Smith and Amanda Glasbeek for their guidance with the book's proposal. My research assistant, Brianna Bertin, did a remarkable job of collecting these debates and making them accessible to me digitally; her engagement with, and curiosity about, the materials made my job easier. Thank you to Ryan Dyck at EGALE Canada for offering clarification when asked.

A heartfelt thank you to Randy Schmidt, senior editor at UBC Press, who went beyond his duties and responsibilities as a publisher.

Thank you to my anonymous reviewers who pushed the parameters of the book and offered direction about how to do this; your encouragement and support are very much appreciated. This book, like any other intellectual work, would not have been possible without an intellectual community of gifted scholars. In particular, I would like to acknowledge, not only the academic work, but the personal support of Leslie Moran, Barbara Perry, Brenda Cossman, Gail Mason, and Bruce Ryder. I would like to thank York

University for the generosity of the Liberal Arts and Professional Studies Minor Research Grant and the granting of a pre-tenure sabbatical.

To my loving support system – Diane Lunny Smith, Greg Lunny, Erica Towle, Dena Demos, Nael Bhanji, Lorraine Baker, and Lin Wayne – each and every one of you mean the world to me. And to you, Numila Alvarez, who has come into my life at the right time.

Debating Hate Crime

Introduction
The Political and Affective Language of Hate

> It [psychoanalysis] is therefore a "hermeneutic" form of enquiry that
> explores how meanings are constructed and come to wield power
> within the psyche. For that reason it, too, lends itself to a rhetorical
> approach to politics.
>
> – JAMES MARTIN, *Politics and Rhetoric: A Critical Introduction*

The language of debate in Parliament is a curious thing. It is literally a sign of the times, indexing and standing in for not only contemporaneous political currents and sensibilities but also larger and more abstract notions like the limits of national identity and the affective undercurrents of political economies. *Debating Hate Crime: Language, Legislatures, and the Law in Canada* explores, through critical discursive analysis, the federal legislative debates and parliamentary committee hearings regarding Canada's "hate crime" laws, those laws being hate propaganda and its significant amendments, the repealed section 13 of the *Canadian Human Rights Act* (*CHRA*) that prohibited the telephonic communication of hate messages,[1] and the enhanced sentencing provision of the *Criminal Code*.[2] To date, the language and argumentation of debate regarding Canada's "hate crime" laws have received scant attention, if any at all.

Responding to this lacuna and to the vivid tropes and scenarios articulated by the opponents and proponents of these laws, *Debating Hate Crime* reveals and interrogates the meaning and social signification of the endorsement of, and resistance to, hate law. In its identification and analysis of major and often recurrent concerns and anxieties articulated by federal legislators and committee witnesses about hate and the legislative response to it, the book offers a historical and analytical account of some of Canada's most passionate public debates on victimization, rightful citizenship, social threat, and moral erosion. In a sense, these parliamentary debates and committee hearings are a rhetorical microcosm of an affective economy of hate that exposes larger political tensions, ambitions, trepidations, and fantasies of the national and legal subject. *Debating Hate Crime* attends to the denaturalizing of these arguments, locating them within power relations and exposing their affective materials.

Debating Hate Crime diverges significantly from other hate crime scholarship in that its preoccupation is with language and the signification of political speech and not with hate crime *per se*. Having stated that my interest lies in the analysis of debate and political excess, this is not to say that the topic of hate is insignificant or coincidental. Hate, and its legal manifestations as hate crime and hate propaganda, are the signifiers around which these debates and witness testimonies were generated and structured. In so far as hate is itself an index of affect and visceral emotion, it is no surprise that its invocation, as in the call for hate's censorship, further inspires affective responses, namely patriotism, liberal inquietude, moral outrage, and social anxiety. In this context, hate crime and hate speech are the topics around which political parliamentary passions swirl, sticking to some bodies and objects, as Sara Ahmed would say, and slipping away from others.[3]

It is these passions that, revealed by heated speech, raucous engagement, and radically divergent opinion, have piqued my curiosity and engagement. To cite Kendall Thomas's analysis of the figural and metaphorical language of the Supreme Court of the United States, rhetorical instances of dissonance, defensive posturing, and linguistic excess signify beyond the literal.[4] Such rhetorical excesses, if read closely through the lens of a critical interpretative methodology like psychoanalysis, affect theory and post-structural semiotics and betray and reveal unconscious elements and irrational desires, not only at the level of the subject but also at the level of discourse. My inquiry is informed by, and relies upon, the methods of interpretation inherent in post-structural semiotics, critical Freudian psychoanalysis, and queer and affect theories. This inquiry examines both the literal and the figurative. It is rooted in historical context and is textually evidentiary while, at the same time, being open to displacement, disorientation, and slippage. It attempts to make meaning, to make sense, while simultaneously resisting "closed" meaning, metaphysical "truth," and unified, coherent subjects. *Debating Hate Crime* is an engagement with, and an inquiry into, the ways in which legislative debates have represented and reproduced hate within the affective undercurrents of Canadian political identity.

Reading "Hate"

Semiotics can be defined as the study of signification or the study of the meaning of sign systems. It cannot be "separated from the human subject who uses it and is defined by means of it, or from the cultural system which generates it."[5] Adhering to the most basic Saussarian and Peircian tenets of semiotics, signs are arbitrary and derive meaning relationally and by way of difference. That is, a sign is meaningful only in that it is positioned against something else, drawing meaning from its arrangement to other signs and to what it is not. These arrangements organize by way of similarity – that is, paradigmatically and by way of contiguity and syntagmatically or by way of sequence. Semiotic interpretation analyzes the choice and arrangement of signs, and, importantly, the present absence of those signs not chosen, and makes meaning from such structures. Post-structural semiotics continues the work and interpretation of linguistic sign systems but breaks with a tradition that is purely linguistic.

In this tradition, we have Emile Benveniste's[6] shift away from structuralism's object – language – to that of discourse and Roland Barthes's recognition of a second-order semiological system, one that shifts signification of the sign laterally from language to "myth."[7] Reverberant of both Freudian unconscious materials and neo-Gramscian theories of hegemony respectively, Barthes remarks that "the myth hides nothing: its function is to distort, not to make disappear" and that the very principle of myth is to "transform history into nature."[8] Norman Fairclough, a seminal figure within critical discourse analysis, notes that the critical work of discourse analysis is to "denaturalize" such naturalized "myths" or ideologies.[9] Thus, the interpretative work of post-structural semiotics as a discursive methodology is not restricted to reading linguistic codes and structures but, rather, is compelled to engage beyond the linguistic sign and to account for the demands of history and its ideological forces. It recognizes that discourse is generated by competing networks of historically located social agents in an unstable field of power relations and that discourse is constitutive, reproducing both subjects and knowledge, and thus power relations, through language and other semiotic systems of representation.

To the degree that post-structural semiotics is a study of sign systems, with an adherence to reading signs relationally, it is also a method of interpretation that recognizes that, as Jacques Derrida noted, "meaning is never anything but a slippage or displacement from one term to another," an escape from authoritative or transcendental meaning, an endless play and abeyance of signification.[10] Insofar as this is a problematic for interpretation, which others like Umberto Eco[11] have struggled with, I am aroused and vexed by such a possibility but, nevertheless, seek to make some meaning of these affective debates about hate and its sociolegal propositions.

Another interpretative strategy that I procure is that of critical Freudian psychoanalysis. I use the adjective "critical" to signify that psychoanalysis is used neither as a science nor as a cure. I use it as a tool of interpretation. My engagement with psychoanalysis as a critical tool rejects the notion that psychoanalysis provides a truth about the subject; rather, it suggests a "reading" of a subject – one among many. This engagement with psychoanalysis is also "critical" in that it is highly cognizant and rejecting of the misogynistic and heterosexualizing imperative of Freud's Oedipal logic. Critical of these failings of Freudian psychoanalysis, I nevertheless marvel at Freud's theory of the unconscious, which would include, in part, his claim that all psychic activity is an impulse to avoid unpleasure (psychic excitation often in the form of tension, anxiety, and so forth).

According to Freud, the unconscious works to control or diminish tension by way of a number of psychical operations including that of defence. Unconscious materials, including instinctual and forbidden desires, find disguised expression consciously when the repression of those materials fail. Freud notes several ways these materials express themselves – through dreams, parapraxes (slips of the tongue or pen), jokes, and neuroses (obsession, hysteria, and paranoia). Thus, the manifest sign secretes unconscious materials, which are primarily forbidden or unbearable desires. The disguise of the unconscious signifier works by way of displacement and condensation, seeking expression through other signifiers bound to it by way of relationality and signification. The work of analysis, then, is to read the manifest signifiers by unmasking their cathexis (psychic attachment) to unbearable materials. Although the unconscious can never be truly "known," psychoanalysis is a method of interpreting disguised and resistant signs of the unconscious.

Commonalities between psychoanalysis and semiotics are numerous. Both are theoretical methods of the interpretation of signs. Both view the signifier (the manifest symptom in psychoanalysis) as the first term of the system of signification and the signified (the latent meaning) as the second term of signification. Barthes writes of these shared commonalities, noting that Freudian theory and analysis, like semiotics, postulates a relation between two terms and that each is "no longer concerned with facts except inasmuch as they are endowed with significance."[12] Both methods of interpretation theorize that, although meaning is structured upon relationality, there is not a one-to-one relationship in signification. Rather, meaning may be disguised, displaced, deferred, negated, and denied. Noting the debt of semiotics to psychoanalysis, Kaja Silverman remarks that semiotics "achieved maturity only when it was consolidated with psychoanalysis."[13] In so far as my engagement with semiotics is poststructural, it also impacts the engagement with critical psychoanalysis by highlighting the displacement and slippage in my analytic observations. Thus, my psychoanalytic observations are not end products of a scientific truth or a meta-physical transcendental signified ("truth") but, rather, signs of possibility and speculation.

One distinction that I draw between post-structural semiotics and Freudian psychoanalysis is the place of ideology. Clearly, Freud positions psychoanalysis and the constitution of the subject within the social and the symbolic, as evidenced by his Oedipal theory and his work on civilization and taboo. However, from my reading of Freud, the normative and hegemonic aspects of the constitutive power and demands of the social and the symbolic on the subject are not openly challenged or critiqued by him. For my purposes here, a useful aspect of post-structural semiotics, particularly one that was influenced by Barthes, is the political critique of ideology in the constitution of the subject and the cultural systems to which it is subject and in which it is embedded.

The Affective Economy of Hate

As defined by the *Oxford English Dictionary*, the noun "hate" is "an emotion of extreme dislike or aversion; detestation, abhorrence, hatred." The transitive verb "to hate" means "to hold in very strong dislike; to detest; to bear malice to." It is understood to be the opposite of love. Struggling with the subjective nature of hate and noting its wide range of diverse emotions, the Supreme Court of Canada legally defined it in *R. v Keegstra*, noting that, with respect to hate propaganda, hatred was "restricted to the most severe and deeply felt opprobrium."[14] Different schools of thought have attempted to theorize hate. Classic Freudian psychoanalytic theory, Fanonian phenomenology and affect studies commonly find hate an engaging and dynamic psychic and emotional affective state. Classic Freudian psychoanalytic theory names hate as an extreme reaction of repudiation by the ego-instincts to a perceived threat.[15] The object of hate is seen as an intrinsic threat to the self that must be destroyed in some sense, psychically as in the repudiation of the hated object and physically as in the destruction or annihilation of that threat.

In *Black Skin White Masks*, Frantz Fanon appeals to psychoanalytic theory and Hegelian phenomenology as a means to comprehend the dynamics and power of racialized hate. This affective field takes form through the white racist's declaration "Look, a Negro!"[16] In the Hegelian dialectic, the utterance both produces and destroys, protects and repudiates. "My body," Fanon writes, "suddenly abraded into nonbeing."[17] Here the utterance, as a marking of radical ontological difference, is uncannily similar to the cry of Joseph Conrad's colonial agent Kurtz who exclaims, "The horror! The horror!"[18] This utterance by a white colonial subject is the exemplar from which Fanon illustrates the "anomalies of affect that are responsible for the structure of the [racist] complex."[19] To the white racist, the black (male) body is a "hated" object, "a stimulus to anxiety."[20] The utterance at once hails Fanon, marking him as "Negro," and sticks to his black body, identifying him within a historico-racial schema as a "corporeal malediction."[21] The result – that is, one possible result – is a kind of annihilation of another's subjecthood, a radical reduction to otherness. Another product of this racist utterance, following Fanon's engagement with the Hegelian dialectic, is the shoring up of whiteness, of marking it distinct and safe from blackness – an irrational impulse satisfied; a fragile ego protected.

Insofar as psychoanalytic theory posits hate as a fundamental defence against injury, its dynamic manifests ambivalently as both a turning against and a turning towards. In Sara Ahmed's discussion of hate and the politics of racial hatred, she notes that racist discourse is often both a story of hate and a story of love, a repudiation of the hated and an affirmation of the self. Examining the ways in which the role of hate "shapes bodies and worlds," Ahmed notes that hate works in both fantastic and material ways.[22] Through the rhetorical work of justification, persuasion, and reversal, white supremacist diatribes reproduce the "white citizen" as the one who is hated and who is threatened and victimized by the law and the polity. By constituting the racist's other as being dangerous, hateful, and threatening, emotions of rage, retaliation, repulsion, anger, fear, and loathing appear justified and are a measured response to a fantastic and immeasurable threat. In this particular narrative, the white supremacists' call to arms is a response of defence and protection of an imagined communal self. "Whiteness" itself, as an imagined identity, is under attack. "The emotion of hate works to animate the ordinary subject, to bring that fantasy to life," remarks Ahmed, "precisely by constituting the ordinary as in crisis, and the ordinary person as the real victim."[23]

However, hate is not the only emotion circulating in this affective discourse; love too circulates. Love of "whiteness," of the "white race," is produced alongside hatred for the "threatening" other. The work done by the racist discourse simultaneously produces a "shared 'communal' visceral response of hate."[24] Ahmed's recognition of multiple subjects and communal affective responses in the circulation of emotion between signs and objects shifts her understanding of affect to something more than merely psychic and as something more than a circuit between the subject and his object. "Where my approach involves a departure from psychoanalysis," she writes, "is in my refusal to identify this economy [of emotion] as a psychic one (although neither is it *not* a psychic one)."[25] In a move that dislocates the singular subject as the origin and destination of this affective economy in the circulation of hate, Ahmed argues that emotions do not positively inhabit anybody or anything but, rather, circulate among objects and social subjects, sticking to some things and subjects and slipping away from others. For her, affective economies, like that of hate, are "social and material, as well as psychic."[26]

Notable hate crime scholars, Barbara Perry, Mari Matsuda, and Gail Mason, have also respectively engaged in the theorization of hate and its affective field. One of Perry's major contributions has been her analysis of the psycho-social dynamics of a hate crime – that is, the constitutive effects on identity – something she has coined "doing difference."[27] Her conception of doing difference aligns quite closely with both Ahmed's and Fanon's engagement with hate's affective field and its psychic/social constitution of identity. For Perry, the perpetrator of the hate crime feels that, as a hegemonic subject, his or her material or symbolic interests are being violated or challenged by a non-hegemonic subject in such a way that presents as threatening. For the xenophobic hate crime perpetrator, this may take form as losing out on a job competition to a new immigrant; for the homophobic hate crime perpetrator, this may be an encounter with someone who transgresses sexual and/or gender norms.

Like Donald Black's theory of self-help, the act of violence is the perpetrator's extra-legal attempt to rectify violation, threat, and social disorder.[28] "Hate crime provides a context in which the perpetrator can reassert his/her hegemonic identity and, at the same time, punish the victim(s) for their individual or collective performance of identity," Perry writes, "in other words, hate-motivated violence is used to sustain the privilege of the dominant group, and to police the boundaries between groups by reminding the Other of his/her 'place.'"[29] Notice that Perry's conception of hate crime's dynamic is both at the level of the interpersonal and at the level of political and social community. It is an observation that is well grounded in hate crime studies.

Early hate crime studies have noted the powerful effects of hate-motivated violence, not only on the victim of violence but also on the larger social community. For example, James Garafolo and Susan Martin, commenting on the disproportional harm of hate-motivated violence, argue that hate crimes attack the very identity (or perceived identity) of the victim.[30] In so far as hate crime targets identity – or, to be more accurate, perceived identity – the profound impact of such an assault disrupts the very ontological security of the victim. Moreover, they remark that this kind of violation is not only profoundly damaging to the self, but it also has a secondary effect of victimization, a kind of magnified or "ripple effect" that impacts the victim's (perceived) community, potentially even impacting the nation itself.

Both Mason and Matsuda respectively engage these ideas regarding hate's constitutive effects on identity by looking specifically at the language used during the commission of a hate crime. In *The Spectacle of Violence*, Mason explores the symbolic function of anti-lesbian violence and epithets through what she names "interpretive repertoires."[31] That is to say, Mason analyzes the "linguistic and contextual patterns" found in the incidents of violence described to her by a number of lesbians whom she interviewed.[32] By examining the kind of language perpetrators regularly use and the types of violence in which they engage, she remarks that this has allowed her to "highlight the kinds of sexual and gendered assumptions that transform the words and actions of violence into a statement about lesbian sexuality."[33]

Her analysis of the epithet of "dirty lesbian" is particularly insightful to the symbolic quality and affective constitutive power of hate crime. Drawing on a wealth of critical theory that theorizes corporeality, including Julia Kristeva's theory of abjection and Elizabeth Grosz's analysis of the conception of female bodies as leaking, boundary disrupting, and disordering, Mason argues that the expression "dirty lesbian" has the effect of producing lesbians as the abject and a dangerous contagion to proper social order.[34] Accordingly, in order to maintain security, this particular body and identity is to be reviled and "excluded from legitimate social and political spheres."[35] Insofar as this may be the intent of the perpetrator and an effect of debasement, Mason remarks that violence operates through language performing, not only oppressively but also productively.

Drawing on the Foucauldian notion that power is generative, the violence of homophobic language has the potential to reconstitute its victim into an agent of resistance and self-worth. Here again, Ahmed's affective economy of hate re-emerges in this theorization of hate. For Ahmed, the affective circulation of hate sticks to some bodies and slips away from others – it may have unintended effects and produce unexpected responses and identities. For example, what if in Fanon's example, the racialized subject fails to recognize himself in the hail of "Look, a Negro!"? What if he rejects the hail or reformulates it as empowering? Mason offers these possibilities and demonstrates that the affective economic circulation of hate is simultaneously analyzable and predictable while, at the same time, completely unforeseen and unpredictable. It is a claim that follows closely the ideas of Judith Butler in her essay "Critically Queer," which ask: "How is it that those who are abjected come to make their claim through and against the discourses that have sought their repudiation?"[36]

For Matsuda, there is no such redeeming potentiality to racist speech. Nevertheless, her argument about the affective value of hate speech bears noting. Critical race scholars have long argued that hate speech – not only hate-motivated assault – produces material and concrete harm at the level of identity. Identifying these harms as a kind of "spirit murder," Matsuda has pointedly named the profundity of this ontological trauma.[37] Through her study of First Amendment protections, she argues that racist speech and hate propaganda are oppressively performative. In an argument that hints at the ideas of Fanon and the phenomenological power of the racist utterance, Matsuda argues that uncensored hate speech has the power to reduce the minority citizen to the very ontological status of the assaultive racist invective. It is an attack upon identity; it is a blow to the self.

The effects of hate speech are over-determined psychologically and are symbolically crippling. "As much as one may try to resist a piece of hate propaganda," she writes, "the effect on one's self-esteem and sense of personal security is devastating ... the victim becomes a stateless person."[38] In so far as identity is attacked and laid waste, Matsuda suggests that political-legal identity – that is, citizenship – is also ripped from the subject. Being a "stateless person" connotes a radical ontological displacement at the level of the political-legal. An advocate of hate crime laws, Matsuda argues that state intervention with respect to hate crime and hate propaganda laws has the potential to reinscribe the victim within the state.

Leslie Moran's work on the emotional investments inherent in the political calls for enhanced penalty and his work with Beverley Skeggs, Paul Tyler, and Karen Corteen on the politics of violence and safety reimagine the study of affective emotional response in this area of hate crime studies.[39] Drawing from the work of Wendy Brown on the dangers intrinsic to an emancipatory politics infected with reactionary and conservative political agendas, such as enhanced penalty, Moran prudently questions the desire for the violence of law: "The demand for the violence of the law

[is] informed by the very emotions [hatred, anger, retribution] that it seeks to condemn."[40] Seeking debate and reflection on the emotive appeal to law articulated and demanded by gay men and lesbians in response to hate crime, Moran and his colleagues seek to alert their readers to the perils of pursuing an emancipatory politics – a politics seeking freedom from both legal regulation and violence – by way of vengeance and retribution. Emotional and affective resonance is found, they note, in the demands for new law and enhanced penalty.

Careful not to condemn gay and lesbian demands for state violence in the punishment of hate crimes as a simple alignment with a conservative law and order agenda, they warn that such emotions, nevertheless, are a "disavowed" presence in the violence of institutional punishment in which "punishment as law-bound practice is celebrated as impersonal, tempered, calibrated, measured, and reasonable."[41] He cautions that this normative characterization of law's violence as a kind of redemptive violence, measured and restorative – a sign of social (re)order, not disorder – necessarily negates the unruly, irrational and emotive aspects of criminal law. As they note, these may include fear, anger, hate, vengeance, terror, and pleasure. The desire to be heard, to be inscribed as a citizen within the state, and to demand a legal response to targeted violence produces multiple emotive and affective responses. Moran and his colleagues' work on hate crime, law, and emotion shift the discussion of affect from the dynamic between perpetrator and victim to the dynamic between victim as rights bearer and the state. This consideration, measured with Ahmed's injunctive that we should be "listening to the affective life of injustice, rather than establishing the truth of law," offers thoughtful guidance and awareness to my project of analysis.[42]

Indebted to these engagements with hate and its affective economy, my analysis of legislative debates about hate are affectively rich for hermeneutic mining precisely because they are about hate, hate crime, and hate propaganda. These parliamentary debates and committee hearings are, in a sense, a rhetorical microcosm of an affective economy of hate that exposes larger political tensions, ambitions, trepidations, and fantasies of the national and legal subject. Literally, of course, these governmental forums are not the scene of hate crimes, but they are the scene of passionate exchanges, heated engagements, and often bizarre fantasies of the citizen subject that revolve around the signifier "hate" guised in a civilized form of democratic debate. *Debating Hate Crime* explores the ways in which political and legislative arguments about citizenship, nationhood, and otherness are framed through emotional orientations and economies of affect.

My departure delves not into the language of hateful speech or the affective states of social movement politics but, rather, into the affective language of parliamentary debate and committee witness testimony about hate. The tropes, metaphors, and other unique linguistic signifiers used in these debates expose particular concerns, trepidations, and anxieties of Canadian lawmakers and those expert witnesses called before their committees. These concerns range from the consistent and dominant concern of the protection of free speech and democratic liberty to the vilification of racial and other minority groups, as well as elaborate and twisted arguments regarding equality, religious rights, and the protection of traditional marriage and women's sexual security.

The generic convention of the parliamentary debate as an adversarial and hotly political forum also holds a significant place in my analysis of these arguments for and against hate speech and hate-motivated laws. Notably, the confluence and abuttedness of such diverse opinions index a point of entry into these debates that shift their analysis from one of strict legal interpretation and literal meaning to one of affective analysis. To use one of Ahmed's phrases, the "emotionality of texts" enhances the national and social narratives by reflecting and revealing affective states as well as the unconscious elements of the body politic.[43]

Often much greater than the liberal concerns over freedom of speech and expression, these parliamentary debates articulate and imagine risk and threat beyond libertarian concerns. The rise of anti-Semitic pamphleting in the 1960s, for example, motivated the Canadian Jewish Congress to urge government to create specific laws criminalizing hate propaganda. At the heart of the debates on free speech that followed was an ever-present spectre of a post-Holocaust, modern technological world in which the power of rationality over the persuasive power of mass media was questioned. Nearly forty-five years later, parliamentary debates on a proposed amendment to add "gender identity and gender expression" jointly to these laws and to the *CHRA*, in an effort to offer protection for transgendered and transsexual citizens against hate speech and hate-motivated offences, raised bizarre scenarios of rape in public washrooms by men guised in women's clothing and the need for government to refuse the amendment in order to protect women's sexual security.

The Call for Law

Hate crime scholarship – from victim survey studies to provocative tomes questioning the place of identity politics in the creation of legal reform – recognizes that hate crime is fundamentally structured on identity. We see "identity" in hate crime's symbolic dimensions, such as the perpetrator's epithetical nomination of his hated object: "faggot!" "Identity" also appears as the lynchpin of the social and political mobilization of hate crime. The seminal work of Valerie Jenness and Kendal Broad as well as of Jenness and Ryken Grattet on the organizational politics of hate crimes stresses the importance of the construction of the "legitimate" hate crime victim to the institutionalization of hate crime as a socio-legal category.[44] The hate crime movement in the United States, for example, mobilized to frame victimization of the last twenty-five years as a social condition deserving of social empathy and institutional and legislative response.

Using a social constructionist model, these scholars argue that legitimate victimization is a status conferred onto injured parties, denoting a transformation from a merely harmed status to a status connoting innocence and harmed by forces beyond the individual's control, a status worthy of social concern and deserving of political and legal assistance and redress. With respect to the detailed ways in which the identity of the "hate crime victim" has been framed, mobilized, and institutionalized, the work of Jenness, Broad, and Grattet offer a comprehensive sociological analysis of the political processes that enabled it to become a meaningful category of condition and identity.

Other notable hate crime scholars, namely James Jacobs, Kimberly Potter, and Jessica Henry, have also stressed the importance of identity in the politicization of hate-motivated crime.[45] Taking a markedly different point of view from Jenness, Broad, and Grattet, they too claim that hate crimes are a socially and politically constructed phenomenon driven by the interests and social mobilization of particular identity groups. However, for Jacobs, Potter, and Henry, hate crime is a social construct, fabricated from self-serving identity politics, media hyperbole, and dubious statistics. "Before the mid-1980s, the term 'hate crime' did not exist," they remark, "'hate crime' as a term and as a legal category of crime is a product of increased race, gender, and sexual orientation consciousness in contemporary American society."[46] Claiming that there is nothing new or special about violence directed at minorities, they retort that there should not be a socio-legal response to it beyond what there has traditionally been.

According to Jacobs and Potter, the creation of hate crime laws is a response to the organized pressures of identity groups who see an epidemic of violence and national crisis where there is none. The politicization of hate crime, they argue, is an effect of catering to alarmist special interests and ultimately results in the creation of societal divisions where there were none: "This pessimistic and alarmist portrayal of a fractured warring community is likely to exacerbate societal divisions and contribute to a self-fulfilling prophesy. It distorts the discourse about crime in America, turning a social problem that used to unite Americans into one that divides us."[47] Theirs is a powerful statement distorted by an ideological notion of a homogeneous and mythic "America," one that does not bear the scrutiny of history or political analysis. Responding to this criticism of hate crime's status as a socially constructed phenomenon as fictive, artificial, and driven by political divisive interests, Jenness and Grattet note the following: "Recognizing that policy domains are rooted in social constructions does not, however, mean that the social conditions they address are not real or, by extension, that the social facts and attendant suffering underlying the problem are only illusory."[48]

In response to the scholarship and the social mobilization of the "good" victim as the "legitimate" victim comes an important critique coming from queer studies. Addressing the homophobic construction of "dangerous gayness" that is well positioned within classic victimological discourse and the constitution of gay men who engage in public sex as a "self at risk," Elizabeth Stanko and Paul Curry warn of the effects of self-regulation of victimization as a "strategy of governance."[49] Wary of criminological knowledge produced by victimization surveys that both document and constitute the queer subject as being "at risk at all times," they note that this condition category of ontological insecurity, to cite Anthony Giddens,[50] locates homophobic violence within a responsibilization paradigm.[51] As such, they remark that such knowledges contribute to the generation of "the expectation that 'good citizens avoid crime.'"[52]

As theorized by David Garland, responsibilization is "a new mode of governing crime" whereby the neo-liberal state "alone is not, and cannot effectively be, responsible for preventing and controlling crime."[53] The work, and responsibility, of citizens (and of citizenship) is that of partnerships, networks, and joint initiatives with public, private, and quasi-private agencies and organizations for the effective management of safety and security. Accordingly, "the morally responsible individual or self is a key provider of safety and security in this new order of crime control."[54] Speaking to this neo-liberal configuration of citizenship and security, Nikolas Rose writes that "as far as individuals are concerned, one sees a revitalization of the demand that each person should be obliged to be prudent, responsible for their own destinies, actively calculating about their futures and providing for their own security and that of their families."[55] As partners in prudence, individuals are "also to secure themselves against crime risks and to take care not to make themselves victims of crime."[56]

Failure to satisfy this requirement of private and individual responsibility for safety and security, warn Moran and his colleagues, "may impact on a person's status as a good [read 'responsibly prudent'] victim and citizen."[57] Their wary prognostication, interestingly, situates gay and lesbian prudence uneasily within the responsibilization of safety and security, whereby citizenship may come at the cost of policing and managing dissident sexuality. Crime prevention and the self-disciplinary techniques that it proffers "foist ... the problem of crime onto the shoulders of would-be victims."[58] For queers, this kind of management of risk through self-disciplinary techniques often involves a policing of the "queer" self, or what Gail Mason calls "body-mapping," "a cartographic matrix of practices for surveying, screening and supervising the times, places and ways in which one is manifest as homosexual."[59]

For Stanko and Curry, the self-policing and surveillance of sexual identity and unconventional gender expression is a strategy of governance that has "neatly and efficiently transform[ed] coercive control into self-control" – the queer who is always at risk of victimization must always be on guard for the homophobe, policing and regulating his or her identity and desire at all times in order to fulfil the obligation of private prudentialism.[60] Problematically, "the wider political regulation of self-identities [that is a condition of responsibilized citizenship]," they note, "acts to resist the positive work of queer activism against violence."[61]

A number of scholars have noted that the American hate crime movement is an odd conflation of seemingly antithetical social movements. Tracing how the hate crime movement is a product of "strange bedfellows," Jenness, Broad, and Grattet claim that the civil rights movement, the contemporary women's movement, the gay and lesbian movement, and the crime victim's movement have converged, in part, producing the hate crimes movement in the United States and abroad.[62] According to Jenness and Broad, "the discursive themes emanating from the 'rights' movements of the 1960s and 1970s formed the sociopolitical terrain that inspired and continues to fuel the contemporary movement to recognize, respond to, and criminalize violence motivated by bigotry in the United States."[63] The product of this ideological and political mobilization "overlap" converged around the issue of rights and harm.[64] They note that groups on the left and the right of the American ideological spectrum surprisingly united around the issue of violence as a criminal issue that terrorizes communities – for the hate crime movement, these communities are minority groups – and that such violence was in need of a socio-legal response.

Interestingly, this merging of strange bedfellows with respect to competing identity claims and politicized rights is not correspondent of the Canadian example in which alliances have been made across rights-seeking groups and not explicitly with victim rights groups. As illustrated by an examination of expert committee witnesses who appeared before the various government houses with respect to the advocation of hate crime laws, major stakeholders have predominantly been the Jewish community, as represented by B'nai Brith's League of Human Rights, and the lesbian, gay, bisexual, and transgender (LGBT) community, as represented by Equality for Gays and Lesbians Everywhere (EGALE). The oddity of conglomeration, in fact, seems to be where the resistance gathers, with extreme conservative political and religious groups advocating resistance alongside respected free speech advocates and scholars.

Canadian legal scholar, Kent Roach, offers a uniquely Canadian examination of hate crime identity politics north of the US border. Examining the Canadian phenomenon of victims' rights and due process, he notes that all victims' rights advocates do not march under the same banner. Instead, those on the right traditionally side with state and police interests, and those on the left seek equality for disadvantaged and marginalized groups.[65] Positioning gays and lesbians on the side of equality-seeking politicization, a claim backed up by other political scientists and socio-legal scholars like Miriam Smith, he writes that the demands for equal protection under criminal law produced a number of troubling outcomes.[66] One result was the "pit[ting] of the accused's due-process claims against the equality claims of disadvantaged groups."[67] In this contest of claims, the criminalized, who are most often marginalized, and the marginalized, who are disproportionality criminalized, compete against each other for protections and recognition under the law. Moreover, like many who debate the remedial effects of criminalization and enhanced punishment, he challenges the notion that the use of the criminal law actually remedies, deters, or controls crime.[68]

Another vexing concern is the use of criminal sanction in the name of minority rights. Other Canadian legal notables, specifically Walter Tarnopolsky and Richard Moon, have also questioned the use of criminal law as an advancement of legal equality and equal protection to groups historically ignored or targeted by law. Internationally, of course, this issue is equally pressing. Trans legal scholar and prison abolitionist, Dean Spade, is troubled by the politicization of hate crime and the desire of marginalized subjects to align with state interests: "By desiring recognition within this system's terms, we are enticed to fight for criminalizing legislation that in no way will reduce our experiences of marginalization and violence."[69] He warns of aligning queer and trans politics with "corporate-sponsored white gay and lesbian rights organizations" and calls for the rethinking of the use of criminal law as an advancement of legal equality and equal protection for marginalized communities.[70]

In "Wounded Attachments," Wendy Brown questions the potentiality of an emancipatory project located in identity-based claims, whereby the conditions of identity production is subject to a late modern liberal, capitalist, and disciplinary bureaucratic social order. She asks: "What are the particular constituents ... of identity's desire for recognition that seem as often to breed a politics of recrimination and rancor, of culturally dispersed paralysis and suffering, a tendency to reproach power rather than to aspire to it, to disdain freedom rather than practice it?"[71] Warning of the affective attachments to political and social exclusion, pain, and suffering, her observation is pointed with respect to the call for punishment by rights-seeking groups.

With respect to the Canadian criminalization of hate crime politics, Roach notes the government responded to the mobilizing efforts of interest groups like B'nai Brith and EGALE by codifying a sentencing doctrine already in Canadian case law. The enhanced sentencing provision, he remarks, was largely a symbolic gesture lacking in any substantive movement towards equality. *Debating Hate Crime* regards this observation and offers a close reading of the objections to the creation of the enhanced sentencing provision and the particular resistance to the inclusion of sexual orientation to the bill. Although it may not have had any substantive effect upon equality, as Roach suggests, the resistance to it, and especially to the inclusion of sexual orientation to the list of protected categories, deserves a thorough analysis. Furthering his critique of the legal provision, Roach queries its very efficacy. Insofar as the enhanced sentencing provision was a punitive response that required enhanced punishment for bias motivation in criminal offences, he notes that "the fact that Parliament did not create a separate offence" potentially frustrated the prosecution of hate crimes.[72]

Lastly, his critique questions the creation of this legal provision within the larger sentencing restructuring that Canada underwent in the mid-1990s. To the degree that hate bias was now seen under Bill C-41 as an aggravating factor at sentencing, he argues that the codification of Canadian sentencing principles – such as proportionality – under the same bill "may dilute the symbolic and educational value" of the enhanced sentencing provision.[73] Mark Carter, challenging the value of the enhanced sentencing provision as an "anti-discrimination" strategy, warns that such principles may have detrimental and unforeseen effects on other non-retributive sentencing principles under Canadian criminal law.[74] Insofar as *Debating Hate Crime* does not look at legal judgments or judicial discourse, these observations merit investigation and would stand as an interesting future project.

Popularly coined in the media and in governmental debates as "Canada's hate crime law," the *Criminal Code*'s enhanced sentencing provision has refocused the issue of hate, criminality, and punishment by recommending that judges account for hate motivation in their sentencing calculus as an aggravating factor. As these debates have revealed, parliamentary opinion for the necessity of this provision reflects broad and disparate perspectives. Insofar as advocates have cited the need for such a provision as a deterrent response to a growing threat of violence and intolerance towards minority citizens, particularly gay men and lesbians, opponents have characterized it not only as an unnecessary measure but also as an index of political pandering to minority group interests and a "homosexualist" subversive agenda that seeks to undermine Canada's very moral fabric. From statements such as these, it is eerily apparent that within Canada's political constitution of the hate crime victim deemed worthy of state recourse and protection, the opposing models of social construction held by Jenness and Jacobs and their various colleagues are firmly rooted in the affective undercurrents of the political constituency of the Canadian hate crime victim.

A Canadian Context of Hate

Insofar as hate propaganda has had a criminal presence under Canadian law since 1970, hate itself has regrettably had a ubiquitous presence throughout Canadian history. At an institutional level, a racist ideology of white supremacy and Anglo-Saxon superiority has manifested at various historical points as national projects of indigenous colonization and forced assimilation, slavery, restricted immigration, head taxing, and wartime internment. Individual and group acts of hate, including that of organized hate groups, have included bombings of synagogues, racist assaults, cross-burnings, neo-fascist rallies, anti-Semitic propaganda, white supremacist campus recruitment, "nipper tipping," the desecration of Sikh temples and Muslim mosques, queer bashings, and racist, anti-Semitic, and homophobic murders.[75] Although hate as a legal concern is a relatively new phenomenon under Canadian law, falling within anti-discrimination and criminal law, the presence of hate itself has had a long and ignoble history.

A number of factors have resulted in the issue of hate being addressed by federal law. Two distinct, but related, clusters of social phenomena mark the constitution of hate crime law in Canada. Occurring in the 1960s and then in the late 1970s, the first cluster of social phenomena was comprised of a marked rise in extreme right-wing activity, a growing national consciousness around issues of discrimination and human rights, an organized lobbying effort against anti-Semitism, and a cautious awareness of the power of technology and media. The dynamic confluence of these events, acts, and states of political and social consciousness ultimately culminated in the creation of Canada's hate propaganda statutes in 1970 and, later, the *CHRA*, which included section 13, a provision making it a prohibited discriminatory practice to use the telephone to communicate hatred against a protected group.[76]

The second cluster of social phenomena resulted in the creation of the enhanced sentencing provision in 1996. Largely, the political push to bring in enhanced sentencing as a way to address and redress hate-motivated offences came from concerned and affected parties who traditionally bore the weight of prejudicial violence: Jews, racialized minorities, and gays and lesbians. The politicized efforts of the Jewish community, best exemplified by the anti-hate crime advocacy and data collection of B'nai Brith, stood as a model of political lobbying for other minority groups, particularly the gay and lesbian community. Marking a shift from the more radical liberation movement strategies of the 1970s and the AIDS activism of the 1980s, the Canadian gay and lesbian community in the 1990s was invigorated and politicized mainly by two socio-legal concerns: equality rights, with a strong emphasis on same-sex marriage, and homophobic violence, which experienced a spike in occurrence early in the AIDS crisis.

Significantly, it was the organized advocacy and institutional recognition of social movements – in particular, rights movements that incorporated an emphasis on civil rights and protections for racialized communities, on the rights of crime victims, and on the equality rights of sexualized citizens – that led the government to study, examine, and legislatively respond to the issue of hate-motivated victimization.

Interestingly, the repeal of section 13 of the *CHRA* found currency in a renewed engagement with the issues of freedom expression. Although freedom of expression had been the subject of controversy for some time, the momentum was initially a result of a growing disquiet by the Christian Right to human rights rulings involving, for the most part, speech that discriminated against gay men and lesbians, exposing them to hatred and contempt. However, the real impetus for repeal came about as a result of two human rights complaints, one against an online article written by Mark Steyn and the other against republished cartoons depicting the prophet

Mohammed.[77] Both complaints stated that the materials had anti-Islamic content and that they discriminated against Muslims, subjecting them to hatred and contempt. As published authors and well-connected media personalities, both Steyn and Ezra Levant, against whom the second of the two complaints was launched, were incredibly media savvy. Herein began a growing political campaign to repeal section 13 in which strange bedfellows made curious allegiances in order to dismantle discriminatory speech restrictions under Canada's federal human rights regime.

There was an outlier to federal hate legislation, an offence regarding hate motivation and mischief to religious property, created immediately after the terrorist attacks of 9-11. Roughly a month after the events of 9-11, the government introduced an omnibus bill that was designed "to enhance the federal government's capacity to protect Canada from terrorist threats as well as contribute more effectively to international efforts aimed at combating global terrorism."[78] Within the 175-page bill was a short clause calling for the amendment of section 430 of the *Criminal Code* that would add a new provision making hate-motivated mischief relating to religious property a criminal offence. To a large extent, the provision was a response by the government to a rash of criminal offences, including assault and damage to religious property and community facilities, against Canadian Muslims and those perceived to be part of this ethnic group. Similar to the hate-motivated attacks in the United States following the terrorist attacks of 9-11, perpetrators rationalized their attacks on those individuals perceived to be Muslim, Arab, and South Asian as justifiable "retaliation."

The Toronto Police Service's hate crime report for that year documents a significant jump in violence and vandalism against Muslim, Arab, South Asian, and Sikh communities. Interestingly, the report highlights a correspondent increase in anti-Semitic violence and vandalism. The overview notes: "The 66% increase in reported hate crimes was largely a result of the September 11th, 2001 terrorist attack on the United States. Throughout history crimes of hate have generated imitation, repetition and retaliation. This is clearly evident from the events that followed September 11th."[79] Speaking to Parliament, Liberal Member of Parliament Sarmite Bulte stated: "More unfortunately, here in Canada some Canadians of Muslim faith have been made the targets of the anger Canadians are feeling against those whom they feel are responsible."[80]

Despite then Minister of Justice Anne McLellan's assurance that the bill was "the most rigorously scrutinized piece of legislation" of her political career, Bill C-36 moved through the House of Commons in an expedited fashion, achieving royal assent in two months.[81] Immediately upon introduction of the bill, legal scholars and political scientists stressed the need for enhanced democratic deliberation, expressed concern over the extent and breadth of new federal and policing powers, and argued for the inclusion of sunset clauses on the most controversial powers contained in the *Anti-Terrorism Act* (*ATA*).[82] While the *ATA* itself attracted immediate academic response and significant media scrutiny, the provision to amend the criminal offence of "mischief" received little to no attention.[83] Within parliamentary debates, much of the debate circulated around issues of terrorist financing, expanded policing powers, finite emergency measures, and Canada's commitment to democracy, multiculturalism, and national security. The parliamentary secretary to the minister of Canadian heritage was one of the few who addressed this new hate crime provision, stating that "such mischief would create fear among worshippers of a specific religion and divert them from the practise of their religion."[84] Since this clause received essentially unremarkable legislative engagement, there was limited data upon which to draw a close discursive engagement. For this reason, I felt that there was not enough material to include it as a chapter within the book.

With respect to Canadian scholarship on hate, the majority of Canadian hate crime scholarship has tended to focus on legal cases – *Keegstra* and *Citron v Zundel*, for example – and on Supreme Court of Canada decisions.[85] *Debating Hate Crime*'s object is not law or judicial decisions but, rather, legislative debate. Other Canadian scholarship has tended to concentrate on the philosophical concern of free speech and freedom of expression.[86] Legal philosophers, Richard Moon and Wayne Sumner, have argued persuasively against hate speech laws stressing the dangers of such censorship in a democratic liberal nation such as Canada.[87] This scholarship has offered a particularly distinctive Canadian perspective on freedom of expression, adding immense value to international debates and concerns over hate speech and its regulation.

With respect to historical research on hate and discrimination, much of Canadian scholarship has centred on the history of legal discrimination[88] and on the historical social movement of organized hate groups.[89]

Constance Backhouse's *Colour-Coded* offers a fascinating historical view into Canada's legal engagement with discrimination and racial hatred. Two of the book's chapters, for example, concentrate respectively on the infamous labour rights case of Yee Clun and on the Ku Klux Klan's terrorism of a mixed race couple in 1920 Oakville, Ontario.[90] Warren Kinsella's national bestseller, *Web of Hate: Inside Canada's Far Right Network*, provides a detailed and comprehensive view of some of Canada's extreme right organized hate groups, particularly those active during the 1980s and 1990s.[91] *Debating Hate Crime* is indebted to these and other scholarly engagements with the subject of hate, prejudice, and vilification, to the philosophical debates with respect to the principle of the freedom of expression and its censorship, and to the legal analysis of judicial decision making in seminal Canadian hate crime and hate speech cases. It endeavours to add to these engagements using a different lens, employing a close reading of legislative debates and committee testimony in order to probe the affective undercurrents of the debates on hate, hate crime, and hate speech laws.

Structure of the Book

Primarily, the book is laid out historically in terms of its organization, beginning with the first of Canada's hate crime laws – the hate propaganda statutes of 1970 – and ending with two somewhat conjoined chapters that respectively examine the prorogued debates of Bill C-279, an act that sought to amend the *Criminal Code*'s hate propaganda and enhanced sentencing provisions and the *CHRA* to include the terms "gender identity" and "gender expression," and the concurrent debates of Bill C-304 regarding the repeal of section 13 of the *CHRA*. I remark that it is "primarily" structured in this way to indicate that Chapter 5 deviates somewhat from this form. Chapter 5 spans two distinct historical periods involving section 13 of the *CHRA*: its inception in 1977 and its repeal in 2013. Other than this slight anomaly to a chronological structure, the book moves progressively through the major legislative debates that dealt with the creation of, and amendments to, three areas of federal hate law: the hate propaganda statutes, the enhanced sentencing provision, and section 13 of the *CHRA*.

The substantive analysis of the hate debate begins with Chapter 1. Examining the governmental debates and the policy report of the committee led by Maxwell Cohen, which led to the creation of Canada's first hate propaganda statutes in 1970, this chapter analyzes the language and the argumentation of the need for new criminal law and an expansion of governmental censorship. Running concurrently or, more accurately, just beneath these arguments of the necessity for such restrictive legislation were signs that threats to Canadian society did not simply come in the form of anti-Semites, racists, and government censors. Counterpoint to the way in which necessity for the law was presented as a rationally based assessment that could be measured quantifiably or evaluated by social and psychological sciences of the day, the impassioned figurative language of politicians and lobbyists evoked elements of disease, pathology, ill heath, and irrationality. To the proponents of hate speech laws, the modern era and its technology of mass persuasion could corrupt humanist rationality and produce a sick nation prone to mass hysteria and racist scapegoating. To the opponents of laws censoring free speech, the lobbying efforts calling for the necessity of such laws indexed an alarmist and hysterical response, one intimately connected to pseudo-scientific racist beliefs of the early twentieth century labelling Jewish people as degenerate and susceptible to "female" pathological afflictions. With this in mind, the work of the chapter is twofold. On the one hand, it documents the seminal political debates of Canada's hate propaganda laws and the social context of those debates, and, on the other hand, it explores the underlying tenor of these debates, remarking that the perceived threat to Canadian values and identity – to its very body politic – is configured around the notion of pathology and irrationality, figuring most interestingly and problematically in the anti-Semitic stereotype of the "pathological Jew."

In Chapter 2, I perform a close discursive analysis of the debates surrounding the inclusion of the words "sexual orientation" to the enhanced sentencing provision of Bill C-41, an omnibus bill on sentencing reform that was passed in 1996. The chapter traces the logic of four resistant positions held by opponents to the inclusion of sexual orientation. These four positions, while distinct, inevitably attempted to weave together a coherent logic of exclusion. These positions were, in no particular order, to remove the enhanced sentencing provision completely from the bill; to remove mention of all enumerated groups; to remove the phrase "sexual orientation" from the list; and to set definitional limits to the term "sexual orientation." Competing epistemologies of victimhood, as argued in the House of Commons and given as testimony before the Commons' Standing Committee of Justice and Legal Affairs, positioned gays and lesbians, on the one hand, as "innocent law-abiding Canadians who are sadly victimized by violent attacks" and, on the other hand, as a special interest group driven by the "homosexualist" agenda whose very claim to victimhood was rebuffed, deemed illegitimate, and defined as dangerous to the nation. These debates mark the struggle of the inclusion of "sexual orientation" to the discourse of criminal victimization and Canadian national identity.

Chapter 3 returns the debate about hate to the hate propaganda provisions of the *Criminal Code*. At the heart of the debates of Bill C-250, an amendment to add "sexual orientation" to the list of identifiable groups in the hate propaganda statutes, was the issue of freedom of religious expression. These debates stressed, on the one hand, the right of sexual minorities to be protected from publicly incited vilification and, on the other hand, the religious right to preach scriptural literalism in its condemnation of homosexuality. Seeking to distinguish itself from the previous chapter, which mapped the opposition to Bill C-41 in the House of Commons debates, this chapter shifts its focus from the House to the Senate and examines, not the Senators' opposition to Bill C-250, but, rather, the arguments presented by the Senate committee witnesses who voiced opposition to the bill.

The witness opposition framed its concern, predictably, around the issue of speech censorship and the harms that would stem from such censorship – a chilled climate on legitimate debate and rightful dissent. Less predictable, to a certain extent, was the way in which witnesses from the Christian Right, who were the majority of the oppositional witnesses, framed harm as a harm to their right of religious expression and religious speech. In addition to classic libertarian arguments against the amendment and against the hate propaganda statutes all together, the arguments of the Christian Right displayed what could be characterized as a "fantastical" apprehension of religious persecution by the state. A critical analysis of these particular debates on Bill C-250 exposes vividly imagined scenarios of religious persecution and of "catastrophic effects" involving dire and degenerative social outcomes if the amendment were to become law.

Chapter 4 notes the ways in which the debate over hate crime and hate speech law has shifted from debates that focused on democratic liberty and on legal protections for Jewish Canadians and racial minorities to debates that pitted protections for sexual and gender minorities against conservative values and religious rights. In particular, the chapter closely examines the debates surrounding the opposition to the amendment that sought to include "gender identity" and "gender expression" to the existing list of identifiable groups in the hate propaganda statutes. At the heart of the debates was the notion of humanness and abjection. Insofar as proponents of the legislation argued for the material and moral necessity of a bill that would position trans Canadians within human rights law and under *Criminal Code* hate crime protections, opponents used two distinct, but related, strategies in order to reframe the issue of rights and legal protections so as to position humanness outside of the transgendered experience. Taking what appeared to be a wholly legitimate stance against the proposed legislation, critics and opponents claimed that the proposed bill was unnecessary and redundant and that the language of the proposed legislation, particularly with respect to the term "gender expression," was overly broad and undefined and thus subject to legal ambiguity. The second main argument against the bill played on irrational fears of sexual threat and reconfigured the issue of legal protection in such a way as to recast the transgendered as "something" abject from which to be protected. Opponents raised bizarre scenarios of rape in public washrooms by men disguised in women's clothing and the need for government to withstand the amendment in order to protect women's sexual security. Looking closely at the ways in which humanness and ambiguity are the driving tropes of the debates, the chapter emphasizes the way in which the liminal citizen and the radically excluded other are products of these tropes.

Chapter 5 examines the debates and committee testimony surrounding the controversy of section 13 of the *CHRA*. The impugned section, which is a human rights mechanism that made it a discriminatory practice for anyone to repeatedly communicate by telephone, by a telecommunication undertaking, or by a computer-based communication, including the Internet, any matter that is likely to expose anyone to hatred or contempt by reason of the fact that he or she is a member of a particular identifiable group, found itself the subject of a private member's bill that sought its repeal. At the heart of the debate on Bill C-304 was the issue of free speech, discriminatory and hateful expression, and major shifts in the lobbying efforts of agenda-driven groups. Framed in classically libertarian terms, arguments for the bill stressed a number of key factors. First, freedom of expression is the "bedrock" upon which all other democratic freedoms are built. The impugned section, claimed the bill's mover, ate away at this fundamental freedom. Second, the human rights mechanism is a broken, tyrannical, and bureaucratic process that is ill-suited to investigate and adjudicate issues of hateful discriminatory telephonic messages, often catching legitimate expression in its stifling democratic public debate. Third, the section is unconstitutional and, by its continued presence under law, threatens a nation built on the protection of fundamental freedoms and rights. Against these arguments, those who opposed the bill and sought to keep section 13 in the *CHRA* attempted valiantly to reclaim democratic freedoms and the protection of rights.

They also attempted to clarify and set the record straight on a number of claims and issues surrounding the support of the section's repeal, including rebutting the claim that the courts had ruled the section to be unconstitutional and identifying the motive of the bill as part of the government's political agenda. These attempts to defeat the bill proved ultimately unsuccessful, perhaps due to the persuasive and misleading arguments of bureaucratic abuses and political witch hunts and to the belief that the legitimate concerns regarding the problematic aspects to the section could not be amended and fixed. In some ways, it is fitting that this is the book's final substantive chapter since it draws attention to a growing backlash and resistance to hate speech regulation and to a partial dismantlement of human rights protections for minorities at the level of the federal government.

1

Hate Propaganda and the Spectre of the Holocaust

No piece of legislation brought before Parliament has been discussed
as fully, or debated as strenuously in as many parliamentary committees and in both houses, nor has a bill been under consideration for
as long a time as has the present bill.

– Senator David Croll, Senate, 30 April 1970,
as quoted in Martin, *Politics and Rhetoric*

Hate propaganda, like prejudice of all kinds, is destructive. It is
destructive of the majority because it corrupts the majority, and it is
destructive of minorities because it can place minorities in a position
where they are made to feel unworthy.

– Mark MacGuigan, House of Commons, 7 April 1970,
as quoted in Martin, *Politics and Rhetoric*

It would be twenty years before the term "hate crime" would enter popular
discourse through politics and law. It was the unnoticed nascence of the
Internet, whose popular development would not be realized until the mid-
1980s. It was a time of social upheaval, political activism, and a changing
national consciousness. The 1960s, writes Bryan Palmer, would be "truly
unsettling ... in terms of destabilizing notions of Canadian national identity."[1] One of the destabilizing elements to an emerging postwar Canadian
identity was the growing presence of anti-Semitic activity. Organized rallies
and marches, public speeches, and the mass mailings of anti-Semitic materials by neo-fascist groups did not align with the ideological notions of

Canada as a progressive and peaceful society. The organized dissemination of anti-Semitic vitriolic at a time when Canada was attempting to establish itself as a progressive political world player and a beacon for human rights eroded confidence in this particular vision of a modern Canada.

In January 1965, the then minister of justice, the Honourable Guy Favreau, appointed a Special Committee on Hate Propaganda headed by Maxwell Cohen, dean of McGill University's Law School "to study and report upon the problems related to the dissemination of varieties of 'hate propaganda' in Canada."[2] Advisory in scope, the Cohen Committee, as it became known, recommended that changes to Canadian law were necessary, particularly changes to the *Criminal Code*.[3] Noting the inadequacy of Canadian law regarding group defamation, it recommended the creation of three new criminal offences with respect to the advocation or promotion of genocide against an identifiable group, the public incitement of hatred against an identifiable group that would likely lead to a breach of the peace, and the wilful promotion of hatred against an identifiable group.[4] As Cohen himself reflected, "few pieces of legislation in recent years have evoked or provoked such strong divisions of opinion."[5]

At the centre of the division of opinion was the issue of freedom of speech and the safeguarding of democratic values in a free society. While much of the debate on the issue of hate propaganda and its addition to the offences listed under the *Criminal Code* circulated around the issues of criminal censorship and the balancing of democratic rights, the underlying tenor of debate focused on the necessity of such laws at that particular time in Canadian history. On the one hand, advocates for the amendments stressed the dangers inherent in the psychological and technological impact of hate literature on those who might be easily persuaded and seduced by its message of vilification and intolerance. On the other hand, opponents to the proposed laws remarked that there was no such crisis of moral integrity and the true danger was to democratic rights and their necessary preservation.

With a backdrop of recent anti-Semitic incidents, including a neo-Nazi rally in a Toronto public park,[6] human rights advances provincially, nationally, and internationally,[7] and cultural shifts in the understanding of mass communication brought on by the Marshall McLuhan revolution,[8] the issue of the necessity for laws that would curtail speech and expression appealed to both those who sought such legislation and those who opposed it. Debates in both the House of Commons and the Senate, as well as witness testimony in two Senate committees, returned again and again to the issue of the necessity of raising it alongside the more philosophical debate of democratic freedoms.

For those advocating the necessity of these laws, they argued that recent anti-Semitic events and the quality of the disseminated hate speech constituted, to borrow from American jurisprudence, a "clear and present danger" to minority communities. Moreover, the potentially unconstrained broadcasting of such vilified speech, made possible by technological advances in mass communication in the twentieth century, reoriented the impact of such speech from a crowd of listeners to a global village. Opponents of the legislation perceived no real threat in the level and quantity of racist and anti-Semitic hate speech since they felt the nation had a burgeoning moral development, reflected in Canada's international commitment to human rights and the addition of anti-discrimination clauses in the provincial human rights codes. To them, the expression of some vile and hateful speech was a necessary evil in a diverse and polyvocal democratic society.

Running concurrently or, more accurately, just beneath these arguments of necessity were signs that threats to Canadian society did not simply come in the form of anti-Semites, racists, and censors. As noted in these debates, discussions, and witness testimonies, the threat revealed itself most powerfully by way of trope, anxiety, and stereotype. Insofar as necessity was presented as a rationally based assessment that could be measured quantifiably or evaluated by the social and psychological sciences of the day, elements of disease, pathology, ill health, and irrationality littered the language and arguments of law-makers and political lobbyists. With this in mind, the work of this chapter is twofold. On the one hand, it documents the seminal political debates of Canada's hate propaganda laws and the social context of these debates and, on the other hand, it explores the underlying tenor of these debates, remarking that the perceived threat to Canadian values and identity – to its very body politic – configured around the notion of pathology and irrationality, which figured most interestingly and problematically in the anti-Semitic stereotype of the "pathological Jew."

More generally, the chapter notes that peppered among arguments for and against hate speech laws were deeper concerns about rationality and the health of the modern Canadian body politic. Rational arguments and concerns on both sides gave sway to anxieties about the corrupting presence of the irrational and the psychologically pathological. To proponents of hate speech laws, the modern era and its technology of mass persuasion could corrupt humanist rationality and produce a sick nation prone to mass hysteria and racist scapegoating. To the opponents of laws censoring free speech, the lobbying efforts calling for the necessity of such laws indexed an alarmist and hysterical response, one intimately connected to pseudo-scientific racist beliefs of the early twentieth century, which labelled Jewish people as degenerate and susceptible to "female" pathological afflictions.

Canadian Anti-Semitism

In the early 1960s, a small band of neo-Nazis in Toronto, having ideological and organizational links to racists in Birmingham, Alabama, and other neo-Nazis in Montreal, undertook a campaign to widely distribute leaflets and pamphlets that primarily included anti-Semitic and racist diatribes on Holocaust denial, Hitler's "final solution," and racist conspiracy theories.[9] Anti-Semitic and racist materials were also stuffed into mailboxes in Jewish neighbourhoods,[10] dropped from the Maple Leaf Gardens' rooftop, and distributed on the University of Toronto campus. By 1965, under the leadership of John Beattie, the group had organized several outdoor rallies flaunting a recently amended bylaw stating that "no person shall publicly preach, lecture, declaim, recite, harangue or engage in any other form of public speaking in a City park except at a time and place approved by permit."[11]

Beattie announced that he planned a rally in Allan Gardens on 30 April 1965 and that fifty supporters would be present with swastika armbands.[12] The Canadian Jewish Congress (CJC) issued a statement remarking that the threat of such a demonstration was "insulting and provocative ... and pose[d] a threat to peace and good order."[13] While different records and media differ on the number of protestors who responded to Beattie's provocation, there were around 1,500 to 500 people who showed up to protest the neo-Nazi speech.[14] What ensued was a spontaneous clash between those protesting the rally and those at the park in attendance. Dubbed the Allan Gardens Riot, it would mark the second time in Toronto history when anti-Semitic provocation would lead to riotous behaviour.

A climate of anti-Semitism in Canada existed well before 1965. Historian Gerald Tulchinsky and others have documented discrimination against Canadian Jews since the early twentieth century with respect to housing, employment, insurance, education, and access to public services.[15] In some instances, these policies and practices of discrimination accompanied overt acts of violence, including those of intimidation, assault, and the destruction of property. Insofar as this climate of anti-Semitism produced material harms, the thwarting and limiting of opportunity, civil rights, engaged citizenship, and security were also symbolic means through which Jews were excluded from the narratives of Canadian nationhood, narratives structured upon the myth of a white, Christian settler society. Like other disenfranchised and racially excluded groups, including other non-Christians and racialized groups such as Blacks, Asians, and South Asians, Jews were constituted by racist national narratives as alien, as other, and as a threat to the nation. Hate speech and anti-Semitic propaganda played a particular role in the exclusion of Jews from Canadian society and a Canadian national imaginary by appealing to a myriad of racialized stereotypes, irrational fears, and scapegoating rationalities, including the invocation of medieval Christian myths of Jewish sacrificial satanic blood rituals, modernist anxieties over revolutionary Communism and uncontrolled capitalism, and degeneracy theories of racialized pathology.

In the early twentieth century, for example, Quebec Jews suffered through decades of anti-Semitic propaganda by leading French-Canadian nationalists and public intellectuals, including popular journalists and Catholic clergy.[16] As documented by Joshua MacFadyen, local priests would urge their congregations not to sell land to Jewish immigrants and were instructed "to drive the Jew politely far out of Canada and particularly from Quebec."[17] In *La Libre Parole* (*Free Speech*), a newspaper published by Association Canadienne de la Jeunesse Catholique (ACJC), an association of French-Canadian youth dedicated to nationalist and religious action, Jews were described as "parasites and filthy vermin, as the forces behind every villainy and scandal, and as 'seducing' girls into buying things they don't need."[18] In 1910, Quebec City notary Joseph Edouard Plamondon was invited by the ACJC to give one of three major lectures on "The Jew."[19] Plamondon drummed up anti-Semitic sentiment by invoking Jewish ritual murder, a medieval Christian anti-Semitic myth that claimed that Jews sacrificed Christians, particularly children, in a blood-letting ritual to Satan in order to garner his favour.[20] Describing Jews as "a menace to the country," Plamondon argued that "Jews should not be given the same rights as other citizens."[21] These inflammatory anti-Semitic opinions, including those that accused Jews of "subverting the established order," lead to riotous and criminal actions against the Quebec City Jewish community.[22] Responding to the threat of violence and civil unrest, the Jewish community established the Jewish Legislative Committee to defend their civil rights and sued Plamondon for libel.[23] Despite the action being lost on the technicality that the law of libel did not cover group defamation, MacFadyen notes that "the Plamondon affair was an important step in Canada's journey towards hate propaganda legislation [as it was] among the first recorded words in Canadian Jewish history questioning the legal ability to defend an identifiable group against hate propaganda."[24]

By the early 1930s, the anti-Semitic fascism that infected Europe had spread throughout Canada. Manifesting somewhat differently than the scourge that plagued Europe, Canadian fascism ranged from beliefs of an "international Jewish financial conspiracy," which was held by the Alberta Social Credit Party,[25] to the published stories about Jewish ritual murder in the *Winnipeg Canadian Nationalist*, to marches and punch-ups by fascist military-styled groups "emulating Hitler's brownshirts and Britain's blackshirts" in Quebec and Ontario.[26] As Tulchinsky notes, the editorialization of perceived Jewish subversion included that of rank, exploitative capitalism, and financial conspiracy as well as Communism, which was described as a "lie ... to brutalize the working class and worsen [global] economic illnesses."[27] Anti-Semitic weeklies, like *Le Goglu* and *Le Miroir*, published articles that supported the beliefs of its editor, Adrien Arcand, leader of the fascist National Social Christian Party. These articles propagated his belief that "Jewry, because of its very essence, because of its destructive instincts, because of its eternal legacy of corruption, because of its exclusively materialistic sense – this is the great danger."[28] In response to Arcand's anti-Semitic weeklies, Peter Bercovitch and Joseph Cohen, two Quebec members of the provincial parliament, introduced a group defamation bill in the Quebec Legislative Assembly. "Although the bill offered protection to all groups," MacFadyen observed that "*Le Devoir* and other papers argued that it was nothing more than an attempt by the Jews to gain 'special privileges.'"[29]

In Ontario, discriminatory practices in the insurance industry and in anti-Semitic signage, which included signs stating "no dogs or Jews allowed," came under the scrutiny of the provincial government and the CJC, eventually culminating in the legislation of several anti-discrimination acts.[30] Leading up to the Second World War, incidents of fascism flared up across Canada. In 1933, Toronto was engulfed by a series of provocative fascist displays, including the formation of a group in the Beaches area calling themselves the Swastika Club who paraded up and down the boardwalk attempting to intimidate local residents.[31] Moreover, tensions rose dramatically that summer with the unfurling of a large swastika at a local community baseball game at Christie Pits by anti-Semitic and fascist agitators. This bold display ignited a riot, the second largest in Canadian history at that time, between Jewish spectators and their allies and fascist provocateurs.

This ugly history of anti-Semitism would clash with the shifting moral consciousness of a postwar, post-Holocaust modern nation. In the postwar period, with the rise of human rights conventions and an acute consciousness of the effects of propaganda on mass populations, a number of anti-discrimination policies had been provincially legislated across Canada. In Ontario, for example, the provincial legislature passed two bills in the early 1950s, the Fair Employment Practices Act and the Fair Accommodations Practices Acts.[32] The former act declared the province's "allegiance to the principles of the *United Nations Charter* and the *Universal Declaration of Human Rights* and rendered illegal any discrimination on the grounds of race, colour or creed in hiring or promotion in any employment in the province."[33] The latter act outlawed discrimination in public accommodation, services, and facilities to which the public was customarily admitted. Despite these advances in social policy, ideologies of a Jewish threat, difference, and corruption continued to manifest in public pronunciations.

The CJC and Its Lobbying Efforts

Having experienced a long and sustained history of discrimination, prejudice, and hate, the Jewish community, primarily represented politically by the CJC, worked for decades to combat anti-Semitism and discrimination through the courts, legislative reforms, anti-defamation work, and goodwill educational campaigns.[34] With respect to the issue of hate propaganda and a legal response, the CJC had appeared in as early as March 1953 before a joint committee of the House of Commons and Senate on the revision of the *Criminal Code* requesting that a formerly held definition of sedition involving incitement to violence against different classes of British subjects be restored in criminal law.[35] Having reviewed a number of *Criminal Code* provisions, including sedition, public mischief, mailing obscene or scurrilous material, defamatory libel, intimidation, and spreading false news, the CJC came to the conclusion that there was "no legal basis to fight hate propaganda in the criminal courts" and that the law of tort "offered little prospect for success should a group defamation action be filed."[36] Over the next decade, its Joint Community Relations Committee (JCRC), partnered with B'nai Brith, continued their lobbying and backroom diplomacy, raising the issue of hate propaganda regularly with its annual *démarches* to the ministers of justice.[37]

A change in this manner of discreet lobbying and backroom diplomacy came about in 1963 when a surge in neo-Nazi activity, primarily anti-Semitism, flooded Toronto and, to a lesser extent, Montreal and other Canadian cities in British Columbia, Alberta, Saskatchewan, Manitoba, New Brunswick, and Nova Scotia.[38] As outlined in Cohen's report, the distribution of hate propaganda materials in the form of leaflets, pamphlets, handbills, postcards, and magazines were disseminated through the postal service, hand-delivered, and dropped from buildings.[39] Typically, the vitriolic of neo-Nazi and white supremacist hate propaganda named Jews as "a criminal race," demanded that Communist Jews be executed and that all others be forcibly sterilized, and identified Communism as a Jewish conspiracy bent on "Jewish control, national decline [and] racial ruin."[40] The end of the so-called "quarantine treatment," whereby the CJC had privately and quietly attempted to voice opposition to hate propagandists, was in part a concerted effort and a "calculated risk" to expose publicly the neo-Nazis and their vituperative literature.[41] The risk, as Ben Kayfetz notes, was in the expansion of the forum for this literature. Would the public be contaminated by such knowledge or react to it with civil outrage? Speaking to Congress about the *sha shtil* (do not rock the boat) policy of quarantine, Sydney Harris, co-chair of the JCRC, remarked: "It is no longer a time for us to be silent ... if unchecked by the barriers of public disavowal, disfavour and illegality, [the hatemonger's message] may spread to inundate our society before we recognize the disaster."[42]

Abandoning the quarantine treatment, the CJC engaged in a public campaign for legislation that sought support beyond the Jewish community and went beyond face-to-face consultations with Cabinet ministers. As a result of their campaign, unsolicited support in the form of demands for government redress and legal reform came from across the country from church leaders, the Manitoba Bar Association, the Canadian Federation of University Women, the National Convention of the Royal Canadian Legion, and several municipal newspapers, including the *Toronto Star*.[43] In a speech to a Montreal audience in April 1964, Opposition leader and "father" of the *Canadian Bill of Rights*, John Diefenbaker called for curbs on hate literature, stating the "distribution of anti-Jewish and anti-Negro literature is of an outrageous and offensive nature that cannot be justified as an exercise of freedom of speech,"[44] a position he would later abandon at the time of legislative debate.[45]

As a direct result of the CJC's public campaign, the first of a series of private members' bills were presented and had first reading in the House of Commons in 1964 and 1965.[46] Bill C-21, an Act Respecting Genocide, which was introduced by Montreal Member of Parliament (MP) Milton Klein, prescribed, as drily noted by William Kaplan, "the death penalty for anyone who, with genocide in mind, killed a member of a group" as well as a mandatory ten-year prison sentence for anyone who, with genocide in mind, caused bodily or mental harm to a member of a group or deliberately inflicted on a group, or a member of a group, conditions of life calculated to bring about the physical destruction of the group.[47] More modest in scope, MP David Orlikow's bill, Bill C-43, an Act to amend the Post Office Act, sought to make it an offence to use the mail to distribute hate propaganda against those distinguished by race, national origin, colour, or religion. As Kaplan notes, "at the suggestion of the government, both bills were sent to the House External Affairs Committee for study, indicating a growing parliamentary interest in the subject [particularly of genocide, a matter ruled by international convention] and reflecting the growing public interest."[48]

Alongside these efforts by private members, the CJC continued its mission for major legislative reform to the *Criminal Code*. As revealed by Maxwell Cohen's private papers, which are archived in the National Archives of Canada, he was "active behind the scenes," working with the CJC and meeting with the minister of justice, the Honourable Guy Favreau on 17 October 1964.[49] This little known fact, unearthed by Kaplan, reveals that it was Cohen and the CJC who initially "proposed the establishment of a small working committee to 'study in depth the problem of possible effective legislation to control or eliminate the publication and distribution of hate materials.'"[50] Framed to the minister as a balancing of "the need to suppress the malice and poison of such publications with the need to keep open all proper lines of free expression in a democratic society," Cohen's suggestion was well received by Favreau, and in early January 1965, the Cohen Committee was fully established with the blue ribbon appointments of Dr. James Corry, principal of Queen's University; Father Gérard Dion, professor of industrial relations at Université Laval; Saul Hayes, the executive vice-president of the CJC; Dr. Mark MacGuigan, professor of law at the University of Toronto; Shane MacKay, executive editor of the *Winnipeg Free Press*; and Pierre Elliott Trudeau of the Faculty of Law of the Université de Montréal. It is worthy to note that, despite the pedigree of the members, critics have cited that none of the members had expertise in criminal law.[51]

Cohen Committee and Its Conclusions

The committee was initially split about its scope and mandate. Issues of sociological and scientific research were raised with some members, who believed that such research was unnecessary and would overburden the committee. Ultimately, in the "interests of effective operation," the Cohen Committee agreed that no public hearings would be held or briefs solicited.[52] However, they did meet with several bureaucrats including the postmaster-general, several Department of Justice policy analysts, the chairman of the Board of Broadcast Governors, and an officer from the Intelligence Branch of the Royal Canadian Mounted Police.[53] Submissions and files with the minister of justice, along with records of the CJC, would be made available to the committee. Stressing the need for research, MacGuigan remarked: "A sound factual basis for our work is absolutely essential. We can only do this if we fully understand the weight of the interests being balanced. Without a factual basis our report might be sophisticated but not expert and informed."[54] In part, the committee felt that a sound factual basis was critical to their study in order to circumvent any charge of bias or interest. As Dion noted, "we must have a factual survey. The CJC asserts that there is a great problem but we cannot simply take the contention of one of the interested parties as conclusive without further investigation of the facts."[55] With this in mind, MacGuigan prepared one of two authorized studies that provided an extensive historical–analytical survey of sedition and related offences in the common law world.

The second study, which drew on socio-scientific evidence by eminent sociologists, psychiatrists, and psychologists of the day, was authored by Harry Kaufmann, associate professor of psychology at the University of Toronto, who submitted a survey of the "recent research and bibliography in the field of hate propaganda and group conflict as that literature and research ... evolved over the past generation, particularly since the end of World War II."[56] This research and evidence stressed several issues with regard to prejudice, hate propaganda, and group dynamics. First, prejudice was identified as a culturally learned condition in which education is not necessarily an antidote. Second, the theory of general persuadability claimed that "given the right technique and circumstances, human beings can be persuaded to believe almost anything."[57] The research noted that persons with low self-esteem or with a feeling of social inadequacy are more easily influenced by the propagandist. With respect to the hate propagandist, he typically will create a facade that exhibits several specific personality characteristics: likeability or attractiveness, an alleged high social standing or rank, supposed altruistic motivations, a sense of powerfulness, and a claim to insightfulness or clairvoyance. He will resort to "pseudo-logic and 'Alice in Wonderland' syllogisms."[58] He will identify with his targeted audience as typically "God-fearing, decent, patriotic citizens of a great country that is being run by traitors and dupes."[59] His appeal is emotional, and his message is highly repeated, vague, and one-sided.

Third, the "most tragic social and psychological consequences" lie with the target group.[60] The effect is a devaluation of self in which the target group can respond in three ways: by aggression, by avoidance, or by acceptance. Citing the Allan Gardens Riot of 1965, which in part prompted the creation of the Cohen Committee, the study noted the way in which the targeted group responded with aggression.[61] The second response – avoidance – might take the form of "passing," name changing, or self-ghettoization. The response of acceptance produces an inner tension, either consciously or unconsciously, which may take the form of demoralization, apathy, or resignation. Fourth, social pressure against the propagandist, disapproval, and discreditation may work to ameliorate the negative effects of hate propaganda. Lastly, "the establishment of a law [censoring hate propaganda will] create a public consciousness or 'a standard for excepted behaviour' that will help to check overt prejudice."[62]

In summary, the committee came to four principle conclusions unanimously. The first stressed that the distribution of hate propaganda, particularly in Ontario, was a serious problem. They noted that the neo-Nazi and white supremacist tracts targeted racial, religious, and ethnic groups and were particularly provocative with respect to the Jewish community in Canada. Materials that came through the post and that were distributed through mass pamphleting, for example, raged about "Jewish conspiracies" and "Jewish control, national decline, racial ruin." The propaganda materials, they judged, "could not in any sense be classed as sincere, honest discussion contributing to legitimate debate, in good faith, about public issues in Canada."[63] Despite the committee's acknowledgement that the amount of hate propaganda being distributed, and its measurable effects were "not sufficient to justify a description of the problem as one of crisis or near crisis proportions," they deemed that "the problem is a serious one."[64] Drawing on the socio-psychological survey of Kaufmann, the committee forewarned of a time of emotional and financial crisis under which the public might fall susceptible to such ideas. The social and psychological damage towards a desensitized majority and sensitive minority target groups, they cautioned, would be "incalculable."[65]

Second, the report stressed the inadequacy of the legal remedies in dealing with the acts of intimidation, group defamation, and threatening groups with violence. Seeing the twentieth century as an age marked by a "growing sense of social inter-dependence," the legal rationale for excluding groups under defamation law appeared increasingly anachronistic and beholden to a "more individualistic age."[66] Third, noting the seemingly evident distinction between "legitimate" and "illegitimate" public discussion, the report noted that freedom of expression is not, nor ever was, an absolute right. As a "qualified right," public expression must strike a balance between social interests in the "full and frank discussion necessary to a free society" and "the social interests in public order and individual and group reputation."[67] Fourth, the Cohen Committee affirmed the democratic safeguard in which "preference must always be given to freedom of expression rather than to legal prohibitions directed at abuses of it."[68]

For the members of the Cohen Committee, the stain of the twentieth-century's past had forever tainted the belief that human beings had the ability to distinguish truth from falsehood and good from evil. "In a number of ways," they wrote, "we are less confident in the 20th century that the critical faculties of individuals will be brought to bear on the speech and writing which is directed at them."[69] Differentiating between the historical rise of democratic philosophy and liberalism of the eighteenth and nineteenth centuries and the modernist age of technological revolution, they questioned the rationality of man when confronted with the allure of modern communication and media. The arguments of early liberalism – namely that the confrontation and exchange of ideas elicited man's faculty of reason and produced more enlightened ways of thinking and being in the world – were inadequate and unrealistic expectations for the modern age. "The successes of modern advertising, the triumph of impudent propaganda such as Hitler's," they noted, "have qualified sharply our belief in the rationality of man."[70]

Particularly disturbing to the committee were the seductive elements of modern technological media – colour, music, and spectacle. This concern echoed the historically contemporaneous popular media theory of Marshall McLuhan that claimed "the medium is the message."[71] In *Understanding Media*, McLuhan argued that modern "electric" technologies of the early to mid-twentieth century – radio, film, and television – had effects upon audiences beyond their apparent content (the texts, narratives, stories).[72] Attributing "rationality" to the Western cultural mindset of textuality and literacy – that is, the medium of the "uniform and continuous and sequential" – McLuhan wrote that "we have confused reason with literacy, and rationalism with a single technology. Thus in the electric age man seems to the conventional West to become irrational."[73] The Cohen Committee feared that when matched with speech that played to human emotion, particularly to anxiety, fear, and frustration, these new forms of alluring communication – radio, television, motion pictures, mimeographic print, and telephone – would reach mass audiences and have a mass effect. Under the effects of the technological spectacle, the committee warned, "the individual is swayed and even swept away by hysterical, emotional appeals."[74]

The notion of the individual being "swept away" into the sphere of the mob also signifies conventional mass psychology of the twentieth century. Critiquing early seminal works in psychology, Lisa Blackman and Valerie Walkerdine note that the notion of the crowd or collective stood in opposition to the "sane and rational, the civilized [and governable] bourgeois individual."[75] They note that mass media was problematized in the early twentieth century as a means to influence the masses who were viewed as being overly suggestible and irrational. Moreover, in an additional nod to McLuhan, the Cohen Committee remarked that modern society was now complex, globalized, and heterogeneous, no longer simple and familiar: "Nowadays, the mobility of populations expose most of us to the unfamiliar, inviting us to react adversely to the unfamiliar in times of stress."[76] It would be these particular observations and warnings that would inspire the arguments for the creation of hate propaganda law in Canada.

Legislative History

> No piece of legislation brought before Parliament has been discussed as fully, or debated as strenuously in as many parliamentary committees and in both houses, nor has a bill been under consideration for as long a time as has the present bill.
>
> – Senator David Croll, Senate, 30 April 1970

On the recommendation of the Cohen Committee that "action by Government is necessary," legislation patterned by the report was introduced in the Senate by the government in November 1966 as Bill S-49, although it never reached the committee stage.[77] Kayfetz notes that the reason why the bill was initiated in the Senate "rather than taking the more usual step of first placing it in the House of Commons was that the Senate had more leisure" to give it full consideration.[78] Reintroduced the following year as Bill S-5, it died in the midst of Senate Committee hearings due to the proroguing of an unstable Parliament. After a majority Liberal victory under Pierre Trudeau in 1968, the bill was once again reintroduced in Senate. Now Bill S-21, the proposed legislation was put before the Senate Standing Committee on Legal and Constitutional Affairs in February 1969. After extensive witness testimony both by those favouring the brief including the CJC, the Manitoba Human Rights Association, the Canadian Labour Congress, the Canadian Council of Christians and Jews, and the Association of Survivors of Nazi Oppression, among others, and by those opposing it including the Canadian Civil Liberties Association, Frank Scott, a former dean of the McGill Law School, and Harry Arthurs, an associate dean of Osgoode Law School, the bill passed the Senate but died subsequently with the adjournment of Parliament in 1969.

In its last and final incarnation as Bill C-3, the proposed legislation was given second reading and referred to the House Committee on Legal Affairs in the autumn of 1969 where John Turner, the then minister of justice, advocated for its adoption. On third reading, the vote was eighty-nine (pro) to forty-five (contra), with 127 members conspicuously not voting or absent from the House. After the Senate continued to debate whether to press the Supreme Court of Canada to rule on its constitutionality under the *Canadian Bill of Rights*, the bill ultimately passed the Senate and received royal assent on 11 June 1970.

Locating Danger

In the Cohen Committee's conclusion on hate materials in Canada, it stated that "the actual and potential danger caused by present hate activities in Canada cannot be measured by statistics alone."[79] This stress upon the unquantifiable – that is, upon the qualitative effects of hate propaganda – supported the rational basis argument that there was no necessity for the law, particularly at that point in Canadian history. Senator Daniel Lang, speaking in regard to Bill C-3, remarked that he was aware of "only seven objectionable pamphlets" and that the "three known mental incompetents in Canada who from time to time engaged in trying to incite hatred ... have now disappeared."[80] Objectors took notice of the report's apologetic characterization of the threat as "a clear and present danger," despite the limited number of individuals engaged in the dissemination of hate literature.[81] Seizing on a statistical basis to determine the necessity of such legislation, the Progressive Conservative member for Peace River, Gerald W. Baldwin, stated that "no particular, sudden emergency has arisen which calls into being the need for this legislation ... There is no clear and present danger."[82] Graham Park, vice-president of the Canadian Civil Liberties Association, distinguished the present time, being 1969, from the early 1960s, the point at which the CJC raised the alarm about hate propaganda: "Our feeling now is that the situation is more in hand ... There is no situation of crisis."[83]

This notion of alarmist sensibilities also found its way into the debates in the characterization of the proposed legislation as "panic legislation."[84] Warning against over-reacting to a few seemingly isolated incidents of hate speech, MP René Matte called for cooler heads: "We should not panic to the extent of opposing one of the most sacred and inviolable of rights, the right of speech, the right of the individual to express his opinion."[85] Rash and ill-thought out legislation, opponents argued, had the likely potential for dangerous legislation that would curb individual rights to speech and expression. Responding to such fears, proponents of the legislation noted that the introduction of laws at a time of crisis or panic inevitably risked them being misapplied, abused, and misinterpreted. New Democratic Party member David Lewis remarked: "You hear the most sensible discussion of a law like this in times like these precisely because the danger is not so great as to make people too anxious, too obstinate and too inflexible ... it is much wiser, much safer to introduce this kind of law when there is no crisis, when there is no present and immediate danger, than when there is a crisis."[86]

The issue of fabricated crisis, irrational panic, imagined threat, and special interests peppered the proposed legislation's long history. In questioning Louis Herman of the JCRC, Senator Lionel Choquette took issue with the JCRC's argument that the neo-Nazi materials it was presenting as evidence to the Special Committee on the Criminal Code in 1968 constituted a threat serious enough for criminal legislation. Drawing a comparison between the reaction to anti-Semitic neo-Nazi propaganda and virulent literature targeting French Canadians, Choquette stated: "You do not find French Canadians who will try to shove this type of legislation down people's throats."[87] A year later, Senator David Walker questioned the constituent support for the bill, remarking: "We are all against hate discrimination, but with respect to the actual bill itself, has anybody, other than the Jewish Congress, supported the bill which is before the Senate today?"[88] Citing the "wide support ... by Canadians in all walks of life," Saul Hayes of the CJC responded: "While we must be special pleaders ... the legislation that we have in mind ... is legislation that we believe is for the benefit of the entire community."[89] The belief in the issue of wide support seemed troubling particularly to Choquette who asked Gérard Rancourt of the Canadian Labour Congress if his advocacy for the legislation was inspired by his group affiliation:

> SENATOR CHOQUETTE: I will ask you point blank ... Are you a French Jew?
> MR. RANCOURT: No, I am not a Jew. I am a French Canadian.
> SENATOR CHOQUETTE: Oh, I thought you were. You are certainly taking quite an attitude.[90]

The resistance on the part of some senators to the idea that the Jewish community had legitimate and sound reasons for advocating for the proposed legislation demonstrated a suspicion whether the material was real and warranted any broad political concern. Suggestions that the danger was only felt by a few self-interested Canadians added to the belief that there was no necessity for the new laws since the threat was negligible and perhaps even an imaginary product of a hyper-sensitive minority group.

A Discrete Instance of Racialized Pathology

On 19 May 1970, in a brief address to the Senate, Senator Josie Quart entered the debate regarding the necessity for legislation. Speaking from a free speech position, she contended that such legislation was not rationally necessary. Assuring her listeners that her rise in the Senate would "not to contribute a few emotion-packed words to the riot of rhetoric to which we have been exposed," she stated the following:

> The peddlers of hate in our midst are a minuscule group of social misfits, more to be pitied than arrested. Their minds are positively ill. But, it may be that on the other side there is a group of alarmists and sympathy-seekers who seem to derive pleasure from constantly flailing [sic] themselves with the thought that they are hated and that their lives are in

danger from someone who is actively seeking their annihilation. In my opinion, this is simply not true in Canada, and to pass legislation such as this will merely serve to lend credence to the delusions of those who feel a need for protection from a non-existent danger.[91]

This statement is rhetorically and metaphorically rich, particularly Quart's choice of words regarding those who actively sought the bill's enactment. In her oppositional opinion, the danger posed by hate propaganda to minority groups in Canada was "non-existent" and merely a product of "a group of alarmists and sympathy-seekers." In characterizing these "alarmists and sympathy-seekers," she suggests that they "derive pleasure from constantly flailing [sic] themselves with the thought that they are hated and that their lives are in danger." To her, succumbing to these apprehensions, which she names "delusions," would only lend credence to the mistaken belief that the anti-Semitic propaganda being distributed by neo-fascist groups posed a threat to Jewish citizens and Canadians at large.

First, her choice of words signals an irrational apprehension to a non-existent threat. Second, she states that there is "pleasure" derived from thoughts of persecution and threat. Furthermore, the expression of this pleasurable persecutory complex is by way of "alarm" and "flailing." Insofar as these signifiers denote heightened sensitivity to imaginary danger, incongruous affective response, and erratic behaviour, Quart's pronouncement might suggest that the call for legislation is pathological in its appeal. Following Roland Barthes's praxis of deconstruction and revelation of the process of ideological signification, I turn to nineteenth-century theories of pathological degeneracy and "Jewishness" in order to demonstrate the way in which pronouncements can be seen to reify anti-Semitic sentiments.[92]

Nineteenth-century theories of race and degeneracy, espoused by Social Darwinists, shifted the theological paradigm of "dangerous Jewishness" that was evinced by the medieval theological myths, which essentially held that Jews were children of Satan conspiring to destroy Christendom, to one of pseudo-science.[93] As Sander Gilman notes, "the discourse concerning the Jew moves from a theological to a pseudoscientific paradigm during the course of the nineteenth century" in which the dangerousness of the Jew resided not in his will to destroy Christendom but, rather, in his inherent biological "type" as psychopathological.[94] According to Gilman, theories of Jewish degeneracy were broadly held by leading scientists of the day and reified by social science discourse and political tracts, claiming Jews were "not simply ill, not simply mentally ill, but specifically hysterical and neurasthenic."[95] As Gilman notes of nineteenth-century sexological theories, such as Richard von Krafft-Ebing's theory of Jewish neurasthenia, Jews manifested "abnormally intensified sensuality and sexual excitement."[96]

One particular view of nineteenth-century Jewish psychopathology that took hold was that of hysteria. For example, the nineteenth-century neurologist, Jean-Martin Charcot, whose work pioneered the study of hysteria before that of Sigmund Freud, "stressed the 'especially marked predisposition of the Jewish race for hysteria.'"[97] A type of nervous disorder that never shook its uterine and feminized connotations, hysteria's symptoms were extensive and vague but, nevertheless, were thought to be excessive corporeal manifestations or symptoms of a hidden aetiology of a psychopathology. Phillippe Pinel, an eighteenth-century French physician, described hysteria as "great physical and moral sensitivity, abuse of pleasures, vivid and recurrent emotions, voluptuous conversation and reading."[98] Other manifestations, noted by Charcot, included odd somatic behaviours, like "flailing," performative malingering, and spontaneous vocalizations.

If we read "flailing" as a close homonym of "flaying" (the mistake made may be just a Hansard transcription error), the "alarmists and sympathy-seekers" take on a different pathology beyond that of hysteria and are characterized as whipping themselves up in a delusional frenzy of imagined and perversely pleasurable persecution. This notion of frenzied and imagined persecution maps quite closely with the figure of Charcot's performative malingerer and of Pinel's abuser of pleasures. The "sympathy-seekers" are thus doubly deviant and doubly psychosexually pathological since hysteria and paranoia are now united with sado-masochism and self-flagellation. As "delusional alarmists," those individuals pushing for the legislation are further characterized as suffering from a paranoid ideation of persecution, a notion very much linked to anti-Semitic rhetoric. Holocaust denial, for example, is structured upon the belief that millions did not die at the hands of the Nazis and that the genocide of the Holocaust is a fabricated hoax or a fantastical delusion of persecution. Moreover, since it was the CJC who were the original lobbyists of the proposed bill and one of its central advocates, it is troubling that there is a rhetorical paradigmatic link to those characterized as "delusional" and "alarmist" and the CJC.

Insofar as Quart never actually identifies the "alarmists and sympathy-seekers," her words have a particular resounding quality that is vexing. But her words – flowery, metaphoric, theatric – are also oddly vague and unspecified. Unlike the words of Plamondon or the Toronto Beaches Swastika Club of "Hail Hitler," however, her words are devoid of explicit anti-Semitic context. They simply call attention to "delusional alarmists and sympathy-seekers" who "derive pleasure from constantly flailing [sic] themselves with the thought that they are hated and that their lives are in danger." In themselves, the words appear to bear no relation to anti-Semitism and racial animus. In fact, any mention of a people, an ethnic or racial group, or a religious community is notably absent. However, an absent signifier is not a sign that a thing is not present; the thing – in this case, anti-Semitic sentiment – may exist by way of paradigmatic associations that mask its true relation. It is historical record that those who brought the issue of hate propaganda to the government and spoke about hate and a growing apprehension about intolerance were primarily leaders of the CJC. In this context, then, Quart's pronouncement can be read to be historically and discursively linked to ideological notions of "Jewishness" as a degenerate type, which sought pathological pleasure in raising the alarm of imminent danger and in producing a perpetual and paranoid status of victimhood.

Potential Dangers

Other concerns about the dangerousness of the proposed legislation centred on arguments of government censorship and the abuse of police powers. Civil libertarians viewed the various incarnations of the proposed legislation as "dangerous" to Canadian rights and freedoms. The notion of state censorship on expression was thought to be an egregious violation of inviolable rights. Specifically, as originally drafted, the section on wilful promotion of hatred had no protections regarding what Harry Arthurs, former associate dean at Osgoode Hall Law School, referred to as "limitation as to the time, place, or circumstance of the communications which are forbidden."[99] Tory member Melvin McQuaid, citing Arthurs, warned of the section's breadth as a serious infringement to his free expression and states: "My interpretation of this provision its terms were wide enough to prohibit me as a private citizen, within the confines of my own home, from inciting even the members of my immediate family to hatred or contempt of any kind."[100]

Several members took note of the apparent irony of the position of the Trudeau government on this particular issue of private interference. Referencing the recent amendments to the *Criminal Code* that decriminalized homosexual acts between two consenting adults in private, opponents to the proposed legislation noted the seeming contradiction: "This is a rather peculiar move for a government which has taken the state out of the bedrooms, that it would now put the state into the den and family room."[101] Such serious and legitimate concern for the issue of state interference led to the inclusion of "other than in private conversation" to the proposed section.

Another area of deep concern revolved around the power of the police to determine or discern a breach in law around hate expression. As an attempt to restrict police powers, changes were made to the proposed sections on genocide and wilful promotion that required the consent of the provincial attorney general to move forward criminally. Such a requirement did not apply to the incitement section so that police still had to respond immediately upon the likelihood that the incitement would lead to a breach of peace. Despite the framing of this requirement as a safeguard to expression, critics saw such powers as being susceptible to political influence. Wrongly attributing this political influence to federal party powers, Robert Thompson remarked: "That changes it from law to political discretion. It would apply not to all citizens. It would apply only to the citizens Mr. Turner [the minister of justice] wanted it to apply to."[102]

The arguments warning of using law, particularly criminal law, as a punitive tool for social control and moral regulation were met by opposing arguments that advocated the law as being educative and protective. In defence of the legislation and in response to arguments of it being a form punitive control, Justice Minister John Turner echoed sentiments expressed in the House of Commons and in various Senate committees by like-minded members and witnesses respectively: "The criminal law is not merely a sanction or control process. It is reflective and declaratory of the moral sense of a community and the total integrity of a community. It seeks not merely to proscribe, but to educate. It seeks to set forth a threshold of tolerance and standards of minimum order and decency."[103] Asserting the normative value affirmed by such legislation, MP Andrew Brewin argued: "It has been said that you cannot legislate to make men good and that you cannot strike down attitudes of mind. I suggest that is not entirely a sound statement. Legislation is clearly an educative factor ... Legislation will not make us perfect, but it can help to mould public morality."[104] Similarly, speaking on behalf of the JCRC and evoking the place of Jewish historical memory, committee witness Fred Catzman claimed: "Our experience has demonstrated that it is always useful and educational for the Government to declare as a matter of policy what the social conscience of the population subscribes to."[105]

On the side of morality, both camps claimed as their own Canada's burgeoning human rights record – both domestically in terms of the *Canadian Bill of Rights*, various provincial human rights codes, and anti-discrimination legislation and internationally with respect to the United Nation's *Universal Declaration on Human Rights*.[106] Strategically deployed by both sides of the debate, opponents to the legislation argued that the adoption of such laws would sully[107] and pervert[108] Canada's international reputation as a just society. Its enactment, they argued, would transgress human rights in Canada. Citing the Ontario Human Rights Commission and the growing application of human rights law provincially, MP Eldon Woolliams noted that Canada had "a new method of approaching this problem [of racism]." Questioning the value of criminal law for issues of racism and group defamation, he continued, "in my opinion we do not need more criminal law. Why involve the police, and why have trials?"[109]

In response, advocates argued that the bill reflected a human rights ethos, particularly with respect to the proposed section on genocide. "This bill discharges Canada's obligation to the United Nations convention on the crime of genocide," noted MP Stanley Haidasz.[110] Beyond serving as a domestic commitment to international human rights obligations, advocates claimed it was a "necessary protection."[111] Highly symbolic, the debated legislation was pulled this way and that by its advocates and critics, each side citing it as a measure of Canada's human rights standard.

Most potently, the spectre of Nazism, the Second World War, and the Holocaust figured in the legislative debates on hate propaganda. Insofar as the Cohen Committee's report made direct, instrumental links between the effects of the Nazi propaganda machine and the Holocaust, and the CJC and the JCRC forewarned of a crisis to Canadian social harmony that paralleled that of 1930s Germany, the trope of Nazism was also used ambiguously by those in legislative contest. On the one hand, proponents argued that a peaceful and secure nation such as Canada could one day fall victim to powerful and corrupting political ideologies and, under such influence, be reduced to a hellish state of fascist tyranny and gross human indignities. On the other hand, opponents vehemently objected to such a characterization of Canada, fighting the image that the nation could be corrupted so easily by virulent literature: "Any comparisons between these two countries, if intended to conjure up the spectacle of a Canadian Third Reich, must be dismissed out of hand."[112] As Senator George White asked his peers:

> Are the citizens of Canada being put on a par with the Germany of Hitler and his gang of storm troopers and SS guards, and on a par with the people of certain other countries from which there are reports from time to time of acts of genocide? What type of breed are we Canadians in 1969 that we need such a bill? I think it was Shakespeare who used the phrase, "the happy breed," which definition may well be applied to we Canadians.[113]

White's image of the "happy Canadian" stood in marked juxtaposition to Hitler's "gang of storm troopers and SS guards."[114] Such rhetoric, despite its naive-sounding construction, reflected accurately the government's positive constitution of the 1960s Canadian. Caught up in an era of political and civil unrest and liberation, Canada nevertheless remained naively innocent and on the side of moral good, at least according to the amendment's opponents. Speaking before the Standing Senate Committee on Legal and Constitutional Affairs, Harry Arthurs, arguing against the need for such legislation stated: "Far from infecting the Canadian public with the virus of hate, this brief racist episode appears to have generated some degree of resistance in the Canadian body politic."[115] To those who held a deep belief in the moral resilience of Canada, it was a nation "happy" and "healthy" that could withstand the "virus of hate."

Not everyone believed that hate was a virus that the Canadian body politic could withstand. Proponents emphasized the urgency of the bill forewarning of hate's potential to spread and corrupt if not checked. Committee witness Michael Rubenstein of the Jewish Labour Committee of Canada stated: "In failing to legislate against the dissemination of literature which preaches hate and often the elimination of whole ethnic groups ... is opening the door to abuses which can quickly spread and threaten the institution of democratic government itself."[116] Emphasizing the power of modern technology to disseminate information more quickly than ever before and highlighting technology's seductive allure of its message, Paul Goldstein, national president of the Association of Survivors of Nazi Oppression stated that the country was "dealing here with the greatest and most lethal communicable disease of the century" – that of race hatred.[117] Insofar as race hatred was characterized as a lethal communicable disease, the thinking was that it would attack and weaken vulnerable populations, bringing inevitable civic death to the once vibrant Canadian body politic.

Conclusion

After decades of being subjected to discrimination and hateful propaganda, the Canadian Jewish community discarded their private strategy of quiet backroom diplomacy with legislators. Responding to a surge of hateful, racist, and anti-Semitic materials, the CJC and other concerned citizen groups petitioned government to amend the Canadian *Criminal Code* with the addition of three new offences that addressed hate propaganda. After several years, one committee report, several committee hearings, and numerous debates in both seats of government, hate propaganda legislation received royal assent. A colourful response to these concerted efforts and prolonged debates was voiced by MP Philip Givens who stated: "I must say I have never listened to so much balderdash and tommyrot in my life as I have heard on this particular subject."[118]

While much of the debate on the issue of hate propaganda and its addition to the offences listed under the *Criminal Code* circulated around the libertarian and liberal concerns for free speech and the balancing of democratic rights, the underlying tenor of debate focused on the necessity of such laws at that particular time in Canadian history. On the one hand, advocates for the amendments stressed the dangers inherent in the psychological and technological impact of hate literature on those who might be easily persuaded and seduced by its message of vilification and intolerance. On the other hand, opponents to the proposed laws remarked that there was no such crisis of moral integrity of the nation and that the true danger was to democratic rights and their necessary preservation. The rhetoric of the debates was rich in its description of Canadian society and the threats that it faced with respect to hateful expression.

Decades later, another group of marginalized Canadians would mobilize, legally challenge, and politically lobby for legal rights and protections. With the seismic legal shift that took place with the entrenchment of a constitutional bill of rights in 1982 – the *Canadian Charter of Rights and Freedoms* – the Canadian gay and lesbian liberation adapted, for the most part, into a politically organized rights-seeking movement.[119] While much has been written about gay and lesbian liberation and gay and lesbian rights-seeking mobilization, particularly around the issue of same-sex marriage,[120] little has been written about the political lobbying for and against the inclusion of sexual orientation as a protected group under Canada's *Criminal Code*. With the politicization and mainstreaming of the gay and lesbian movement came a much broader awareness about inequality faced by sexual minorities. This recognition would have multiple effects. On the one hand, as Miriam Smith remarks, "the legalized networks of lesbian and gay activism were successful in pushing the courts toward the recognition of rights claims."[121] However, on the other hand, a growing resistance seemed to be mobilizing as well.

While there is no published evidence of a direct correlation between the demands for, and the advancement of, rights for gays and lesbians and an increase in homophobic violence in the 1990s, my sense is that there certainly was such a correlation. A growing concern and rising anxiety about violence directed at sexual minorities, in part, can be demonstrated by the government's policy interest in such violence.[122] Similarly, the emergence of police hate crime victimization reports and data gathering, and an emerging academic interest in violence against sexual minorities, illustrates an awareness and engagement with this social phenomenon.[123]

Matched with this policy engagement with the issue of homophobic violence was an increasingly politicized conservative and Christian Right who led an organized campaign to challenge gay and lesbian legal recognition. The following chapter closely examines these mobilizations by discursively mapping and deconstructing arguments for and against the inclusion of "sexual orientation" to Canada's enhanced sentencing provision.

2

Legislating Victims of Hate

"Before the mid-1980s, the term 'hate crime' did not exist."[1] Canadian hate crime scholars, Julian Roberts, Cynthia Petersen, Martha Shaffer, and Marie-France Major have all noted that the mid-1990s in Canada were characterized as a period of hate crime "crisis" and "epidemic" against which law was summoned to respond.[2] Following the hate crime movement in the United States, Canadian minorities, including gay men and lesbians, mobilized to frame the victimization of the last twenty-five years as a social condition deserving of social empathy and institutional and legislative response. The framing of gays and lesbians as legitimate victims of hate-motivated violence – that is, as innocently injured people who have been harmed by forces beyond their control and thus deserving of legal protection and redress, became a central political demand of the gay and lesbian community in the 1990s. Alongside marriage equality claims and other equality-seeking legal and political challenges, gays and lesbians mobilized around hate crime victimization, actively demanding status as legally protected citizens. It would be a political battle with a newly emerging and vigorous foe – the Christian Right – who found political support in such parties as the Reform party of Canada.

In this chapter, I perform a close analysis of the contested terrain of competing knowledges of gay and lesbian victimhood as played out in the House of Commons debates and committee testimony of Bill C-41, the sentencing reform bill. In particular, my focus is on the enhanced sentencing provision and its inclusion of the term "sexual orientation." I trace the logic of four resistant positions held by opponents to the inclusion of sexual orientation. These four positions, while distinct, inevitably attempted to weave together a coherent logic of exclusion. These positions were, in no particular order: remove section 718.2(a)(i) completely from the bill; remove mention of all enumerated groups; remove the phrase "sexual orientation" from the list; and set definitional limits to the term "sexual orientation."

The place of sexual orientation under and before the law of Canada made its first statutory appearance in Bill C-41.[3] In September 1994, Justice Minister Allan Rock introduced Bill C-41, the sentencing reform bill.[4] A product of nearly two decades of inquiries, commissions, reports, and research, this omnibus bill proposed, as one of its provisions, a subsection that would allow a judge to take into consideration at the time of sentencing "evidence that the offence was motivated by bias, prejudice, or hate based on race, national or ethnic origin, language, colour, religion, sex, age, mental or physical disability, sexual orientation or any other similar factor" as an aggravating circumstance.[5] A relatively short provision in a bill some sixty-three pages long, section 718.2(a)(i) contained two words – "sexual orientation" – that would be at the centre of a prolonged and divisive debate in the House of Commons.[6]

Major sentencing reform provisions were "dwarfed" by a phrase for which there was intractable resistance to define.[7] A product of the Liberal election campaign promises of 1993, the explicit inclusion of sexual orientation to the enumerated list of "vulnerable groups who are typically the victims of hate motivated violence" would ignite a national debate, not only about special interest groups and the so-called privileging of one crime over another but also about the very "truth" of the victimization of gays and lesbians and their claim to legitimate victimhood.[8] Competing epistemologies of victimhood, as argued in the House of Commons and given as testimony before the Commons' Standing Committee of Justice and Legal Affairs (Justice and Legal Committee), positioned gays and lesbians, on the one hand, as "innocent law-abiding Canadians who are sadly victimized by violent attacks" and, on the other hand, as a special interest group driven by the "homosexualist" agenda whose very claim to victimhood was rebuffed and deemed illegitimate.[9] These disparate positions configured the legislative terrain of the gay and lesbian subject of hate violence. Taken together, they provide further insight into the constituted identity of the sexual and gendered minority victim of "hate crime" and socio-legal narratives of anti-lesbian, gay, bisexual, and transexual violence in Canada.

Liberal Promises

Leading up to the 1993 federal election, the Liberal party published *Creating Opportunity*, a "red book" of political promises and liberal philosophy.[10] While the book mainly centred on economic policy, it touted a broadly applied philosophy of "reciprocal obligation" that could be applied to social and legal policy as well. "We believe," stated the red book, "that if Canada is to work as a country, Canadians have to see themselves as belonging not to a society composed of isolated individuals or of competing interest groups, but to a society of reciprocal obligation, in which each of us is responsible for the well-being of the other."[11] In this particular framing of responsibility, the Liberal party's emphasis on what it termed "reciprocal obligation" allowed it to enter into the mired controversy of "sexual orientation" as an advocate of human rights, while simultaneously preserving an arms-length distance from the issues of non-normative sexuality. Thus, the Liberal commitment to gay rights was magnanimously framed as responsibility to the other.

Insofar as *Creating Opportunity* was an election campaign product, its promises were framed vaguely and in highly rhetorical terms. For example, with respect to the direct issue of hate crime and sexual orientation, the book addressed the issue briefly in two sites: personal security and equality. With an ever so brief mention to gender, race, religion, age, and sexual orientation, it expressed commitment to protecting the rights of citizens from violent crime. In a similarly rhetorical way, the book spoke of the "core values of Canadian society [as] a strong belief in the equality of our citizens."[12] Noting that "gay communities have ... become targets" of crimes motivated by hatred, the Liberal party promised that it would "take measures to combat hate propaganda" and enhance programs promoting tolerance and mutual understanding.[13]

Another promise of *Creating Opportunity* was "a comprehensive, integrated, and progressive reform of our sentencing system." This took expression in the government's sweeping omnibus bill on sentencing reform, Bill C-41. In Parliament, much of the government's rationale for the bill was framed around the government's "Trudeau-esque" commitment to a "just, peaceful and safe society."[14] Secretary of State Sheila Finestone remarked that Bill C-41 reflected the Liberal government's "commitment to protecting the fundamental right of all Canadians to live without being afraid, to live in peace and security, and to live as equals."[15] This combined sentiment of equal rights and right to security shaped much of the government's stand not only with respect to Bill C-41 more broadly but also to the inclusion of the term "sexual orientation" to the enhanced sentencing provision specifically. As one Liberal member noted, "a vote for this bill is a vote against discrimination and hate towards individuals and groups."[16]

In Parliament, the government challenged claims by the Reform party that the bill was supported only by elites, arguing that it had received wide popular support. Citing the endorsement of the United Church of Canada, B'nai Brith Canada, the Canadian Jewish Congress, the Federation of Canadian Municipalities, the chief of the Ottawa police force, the chair of the Ottawa-Carleton Regional Police Services Board, the Centre for Research Action on Race Relations, the Urban Alliance on Race Relations, the chief of the metropolitan Toronto police force, the Canadian Association of Chiefs of Police, and the mayor of the city of Toronto, the government argued that the enhanced sentencing provision reflected values, not only of a Liberal philosophy but also of a Canadian value system of which the *Canadian Charter of Rights and Freedoms* was one shining achievement of Liberal provenance.[17]

The Logic of Exclusion

Resistance to including "sexual orientation" in the list of enumerated groups under the proposed provision came predictably from the Reform party, which was at the time Canada's western-based, self-identified populist party that represented "a neoconservative mixture of free enterprise economics and morally conservative social policy" and dissident Liberals who opposed any political recognition for gay rights.[18] Their arguments took four positions that, while distinct, inevitably wove together to produce a more coherent logic of exclusion. These positions were, in no particular order: remove section 718.2(a)(i) completely from the bill; remove mention of all enumerated groups; remove the phrase "sexual orientation" from the list; and set definitional limits to the term "sexual orientation." These arguments of exclusion did not form a neatly orchestrated narrative. Rather, they were raised at various points in the debate, at times contradicting, and, at other times, informing, their mutual rationalities. Marked against these arguments of exclusion were the voices of inclusion, including the New Democratic Party's Svend Robinson and the Bloc Quebecois's Réal Ménard, two "out" members of parliament (MP), and numerous supportive Liberals, most notably the Honorary Allan Rock, then minister of justice and attorney general, Hedy Fry, then parliamentary secretary to the minister of health, Bill Graham, Stan Dromisky, and backbencher Sue Barnes.[19]

In an effort to remove section 718.2(a)(i) from Bill C-41, its opponents argued that its inclusion was unnecessary and highly redundant. This argument of redundancy followed two tracks. The first, as argued by Liberal dissident, Roseanne Skoke, in committee, was that the *Criminal Code* had a "hate crimes section already ... which means an individual can be charged for a hate crime."[20] Erroneously meshing existing hate propaganda law, which did not include sexual orientation as a protected identifiable group, with the proposed enhanced sentencing provision, Skoke formed an imaginary hybrid of legal protection for gays and lesbians.

The second track of the redundancy argument restricted itself correctly to the judicial practice of sentencing whereby legal knowledge of "texts, illustrations and periodicals and case law" informed judge-made law in the adjudication of hate-motivated offences.[21] Insofar as judges had been recognizing ad hoc hate motivation against racial, religious, and sexual minorities as an aggravating factor in sentencing from as early as 1977, the redundancy argument could not be easily dismissed by those attempting explicit inclusion.[22] Nevertheless, the defenders of the provision attacked the accuracy of Myron Thompson's unmeasured claim that the judiciary had been applying this sentencing principle "very effectively."[23] Testifying before the Justice and Legal Committee as an expert witness, Mark Sandler, senior counsel to B'nai Brith's League for Human Rights, advocated the statutory importance of section 718.2(a)(i): "What I have seen as counsel dealing with these cases across Canada is an uneven application of the judge-made law by various judges."[24] This issue of the eyewitness account by a well-respected lawyer of the "uneven application" of the provision substantially weakened the redundancy claim, so much so that the Reform party and its Liberal allies reoriented their redundancy strategy.

"An assault," voiced Reform's Dick Harris, "is an assault is an assault."[25] In a rather "Thatcherite" response to crime, Harris reduced all assaults to a state of equivalency whereby differences among assaults were rendered without significance, particularly without symbolic or political significance.[26] Here, redundancy was used as a sign of transparency. By this, I mean that the referent – "an assault" – was both paradigmatically and syntagmatically organized into a meaning system of hyper-equivalence. Much like Gertrude Stein's famous modernist declaration, "a rose is a rose is a rose, is a rose," the statement "an assault is an assault is an assault" is seemingly unambiguous, transparent, and dully tautological.[27] However, one possible function of such a tautology would be to reduce something to such a state of equivalence that its meaning becomes commonsensical.

This notion of common sense, as espoused by the Reform party and its supporters, draws on the evangelical and fundamentalist belief in a literal reading of the Bible, whereby literalism, according to Peter Gomes, "liberates [the reader] and the text from obscurantism and secret knowledge not readily accessible to any believer, by the use of common sense."[28] Derived from Reformationist and Enlightenment philosophical traditions, literalism holds that the meaning's significance is to be found at the literal level "fixed and discernable by the application of the faculties of reason and common sense."[29] Thus, crimes motivated by hate are rendered indistinct from those not motivated by hate, and the symbolic message of the attack and the symbolism of its judicial response – the enhanced sentence – are rendered insignificant and without true meaning. Oddly enough, this common-sense argument of equivalency was repeated, almost mantra-like, throughout the House of Commons' debates and the Justice and Legal Committee's hearings by the proponents of exclusion, whereby phrases like "a victim is a victim is a victim," which was uttered by REAL Women's national vice-president, reduced hate crime and victimization to a system of hyper-equivalence.[30]

It was not a big leap for the Reform party to position this literalist argument as an argument of equality. "Reformers believe in true equality," claimed Reform member Garry Breitkreuz, "and that all Canadians are equal before the law. Every time the government divides us into different categories it creates the politics of envy, which divide us rather than unite us."[31] This "politics of envy" argument finds common links with James Jacobs and Kimberly Potter's warning that "by redefining crime as a facet of intergroup conflict, hate crime laws encourage citizens to think of themselves as members of identity groups and encourage identity groups to think of themselves as victimized and besieged, thereby hardening each group's sense of resentment. This in turn contributes to the balkanization of American society, not to its unification."[32] This imaginary vision of America the melting pot as a cohesive and egalitarian society brought to "balkanization" by special interests and identity politics can be read as scapegoating minority concerns and historic victimization.[33] According to Reform members, the "politics of envy" is fraught with risk, including the creation of "elites" and the generation of "rational" resentment towards minorities, which in turn may be translated into a "justifiable" hatred and bias.[34] Reform MP Jack Ramsay, warning of this "rational" causation, alerted Parliament to the risks of hate crime law: "After all was said and done we all stood equal before the law and that is what is being destroyed. At least the sense of that is being destroyed; that the government is introducing legislation creating special rights for special status for some citizens." "That is what will create bias," stated Ramsey, "if one grants special rights and special privileges to individuals, one will see other individuals resenting that. They will see the bias and the prejudice occur ... It is aiding and abetting those feelings ... we will see the anger, the frustration and the hate.[35]

Not only is the creation of hate crime law constructed as a predictor of civil strife and violence, but it is also viewed as its causal agent. Here, the enhanced sentencing provision is constituted as precipitatory to the very violence it legislatively seeks to target. Circular reasoning and common-sense rationality relocates violence against minorities as understandable, reasonable, and teleological. Insofar as the Reform party members were positioning themselves as proponents of "true equality," they were also positioning themselves and their constituents as the discriminated, the disadvantaged, and the violated as well as part of a larger, silent Canadian majority – "not hyphenated Canadians, not divided Canadians" – whom the government dismissed in favour of minority special interests.[36]

Acting out their warning of a politics of envy, Reform members openly expressed their dissatisfaction with the provision and its protection of minority status. Taking a strident tone, Ian McClelland asserted: "I am absolutely fed up with being discriminated against. It is really starting to get to me. After studying the legislation, I see no mention of white, middle aged, sort of Catholic males."[37] Insofar as the legislative provision named race, age, religion, and gender as protected statuses, McClelland's understanding of its protections indexes a highly defensive posture in which someone with social privilege represents himself or herself as a marginalized subject who is outside of the law. This identificatory posture of defence is also apparent in Myron Thompson's criticism of the list of enumerated groups. Citing his social difficulties as an overweight child, he questions why obese people were not explicitly mentioned in the legislation.[38] That is, why was his particular "identity" as being overweight not given consideration and protection in the proposed legislation? These parliamentary expressions of a politics of envy were met with outrage from the other side of the House of Commons. Liberal Hedy Fry, responding as a visible minority to one such claim, stated: "What does that member who spoke so glibly know about hate and prejudice? The member is one person of a majority group in the House. He has status. He does not ever have to know what it is like to be vilified or discriminated against. I know what it is like."[39]

In some instances, the Reform party's expressions of a politics of envy and resentment were transformed into visions of minorities gone criminally mad and held unaccountable by the proposed hate crime provision for their depraved violence. Rank anecdotes of "Vietnamese gangs … pillaging and terrorizing [white] neighbourhoods" deteriorated into allegories of castrating, man-hating feminists with blood-dripping hunting knives and crazed smiles.[40] For example, referencing an anti-feminist cartoon from Carleton University's student newspaper that depicted these caricatured homicidal, man-hating women, Reform member Diane Ablonczy petitioned Parliament:

> In a recent issue of the student newspaper in Ottawa's Carleton University there was a cartoon depicting a smiling female carrying a large hunting knife and asking women whether their lives would be helped by the total elimination of penises. Another cartoon showed her holding a dripping axe over the heading "No guilt," I would like to ask my colleague why

she can support a bill that would consider hatred against some groups more serious than hatred against others. The group that was the object of these cartoons is not listed in Bill C-41.[41]

In another instance, after commending the Christian brethren for their committee testimony, which included citations from Leviticus and Deuteronomy, that expressed "compassion for members of the homosexual community," MP Morris Bodnar then offered personal knowledge of anti-heterosexual, hate-motivated violence into the record.[42] According to his "understanding," vigilante gays were beating up heterosexual families in their homes, and so he endorsed the provision since it would protect him and his family from such violence: "I think of myself, my wife, my son and two daughters at home. I consider that section [section 718.2(a)(i)] protects them and me in the event of a heterosexual – and I put myself in that category – being beaten up in any way by a group of gays because of sexual orientation. *It's my understanding that is starting to occur.*"[43] These visions of madness and disorder blatantly betray a populist anxiety of a nation not only filled with "Vietnamese gangs," castrating feminists, and groups of home-invading gays but also turned upside down and inside out, where power relations of racial, gender, and sexual privilege are terrifyingly inverted and where the law is protecting the lawless.

The response to such conservative anxiety and outrageous predictions was swift and varied. For every claim made by the Reform party and its supporters about the risks of enumerating groups in the legislation, the government had to counter it with, as Allan Rock phrased it, "the rigour of logic [and] the evidence in front of us."[44] Stan Dromisky, defending the government's position and echoing his fellow Liberals, argued that Bill C-41 did not give special rights to anyone: "It protects all Canadians. Every Canadian has a nationality, a race, an age, a gender, a sexual orientation, and a religious belief."[45] This simple argument of inclusion, and others like it, attempted to disarm the volatile issue of special rights, to counter predictions of a backlash against such protection for minorities, and to rebuff stories of minorities as lawless vigilantes.[46]

Insofar as the government was generally able to position such anxieties as unfounded and to derail the opposition to the explicit listing of protected statuses, it encountered a much more vehement and intractable position against the inclusion of "sexual orientation." Unlike the negative reactions and opposition to the enumeration of a general list of protected categories, the opposition to the inclusion of "sexual orientation" generated a uniquely different set of arguments. First, it was argued that the inclusion of "sexual orientation" to section 718.2(a)(i) was part of a larger political agenda that was attempting to "slip sexual orientation into the *Charter* through the backdoor."[47] Second, opponents to the provision argued that gay men were not a discriminated against minority but, rather, a well-organized, wealthy, and highly educated lobby. Third, they claimed that stories of gay and lesbian victimization were unsubstantiated and, thus, unbelievable. Lastly, if gays were subject to violence, the detractors' logic contended, then it was necessarily contingent upon their risky sexual behaviours and often self-inflicted. Combined, these arguments for the exclusion of "sexual orientation" from the provision attempted to produce an illegitimate and undeserving recipient of governmental protection. What follows is a close analysis of the contested terrain of competing knowledges of gay and lesbian victimhood as played out in the debates and committee testimony of Bill C-41.

"Backdoor" Legislation

The fear I hear is that the motivation of the government is not honest, is not up front, and what they are trying to do is slip sexual orientation into the *Charter* of Rights through the backdoor.

– Val Meredith, Surrey-White Rock-South Langley, Reform

One objection to the inclusion of sexual orientation to the list of protected groups was that the government was attempting to advance gay and lesbian rights by pushing "sexual orientation" through a piece of (criminal) legislation in the hope that it would be amended to human rights legislation with little public notice. This so-called backdoor approach to human rights legislation met with great resistance from the Reform party and its allies.[48] "It is not an innocuous thing," argued Jay Hill, "it is not an inconsequential thing. It actually is the first step in a logical legal sequence for that undefined term to be included in the *Charter of Rights and Freedoms*."[49] Such apprehensions, whether judged to be insightful, repressively alarmist, or both, garnered force from other volatile political issues of the time, particularly the Liberal government's own commitment to gay and lesbian rights. In its "red book" of 1993 election promises, the Liberals, under the leadership of Jean Chrétien, pledged a commitment to amend the *Canadian Human Rights Act* (*CHRA*), although as political scientist David Rayside notes, they did so "without specifying sexual orientation."[50]

The issue of amending "sexual orientation" to the *CHRA* had a sustained and unsuccessful history of almost two decades following the passage of the act in 1976. Rayside notes that since its inception, the Human Rights Commission (HRC) had "inaugurated an annual ritual of recommending the addition of sexual orientation to the act."[51] This annual recommendation of the HRC, coupled with Quebec's inclusion of sexual orientation to their *Human Rights Code* in 1977 and the equality guarantees of the *Charter* that came into effect in 1985, essentially opened the door to gay and lesbian equality-seeking activists.[52] As argued by Tom Warner, by 1985 "the [gay liberationist] advocacy focus shifted overwhelmingly towards pursuit of legislated equality rights."[53]

Some of the effects of this social, legal, and political tour de force that met with the displeasure from the Reform party and its social conservative allies during the debates around Bill C-41 were the addition of "sexual orientation" to seven provincial human rights codes,[54] the unfulfilled, but articulated, promises made in 1992 by then Justice Minister Kim Campbell and her Conservative government to include sexual orientation to the *CHRA*,[55] and the Ontario Court of Appeal's reading of "sexual orientation" as an analogous ground in the federal human rights code on the basis of the *Charter's* section 15(1).[56] It was this history of rights politics and litigation, together with a socially conservative ideology, that fuelled the staunch resistance by the Reform party and others to the inclusion of "sexual orientation" to the provision.

Resistance conjoined with a discourse of risk. Criticized as being part of a thinly veiled Liberal agenda of "social engineering," the effects of this inclusion to Bill C-41 were shaped by its adversaries as an attack upon democracy, the family, and the church.[57] More extreme opinions suggested that "if we in the House pass the bill we will propel ourselves down the slippery slope of governmental redefinition of the family, of governmental sanction of unhealthy relationships."[58] Such a forewarning of downward social spiralling located this risk squarely in the inclusion of "sexual orientation." Here, the spectre of "unhealth" and national morbidity is located in the homosexual union and can be read as a criticism of the supposed dysfunctional, degenerative, and potentially lethal "nature" of gay and lesbian relationships.[59] Described as a potential "avalanche" sweeping away the traditional family unit, detractors argued that the inclusion of sexual orientation to the provision would "inevitably lead ... to new limits for the majority of people who do nothing more than go to work, go to church, pay their taxes, raise their kids and ask nothing more than to be left untouched as much as possible by the long arm of the Liberal state apparatus."[60] Such statements, which were frequent and common both in the House of Commons and in the Justice and Legal Committee, located risk not in the marginal status of gays and lesbians but, rather, in the lives and rights of the "average person"[61] and "ordinary Canadians"[62] who in some way would be "limited" by the inclusion of the words "sexual orientation" to an enhanced sentencing provision.

Roseanne Skoke, Liberal member for Central Nova, exploited this polarizing belief. Arguing that "the specific inclusion of the words sexual orientation gives legal recognition and legal status to a faction in society which is undermining and destroying Canadian values and Judeo-Christian morality," she matched the "inherent and inviolable rights of family and the rights of the church" against the individual rights claims of "special interest groups" and pitched natural law against man-made, politically driven positive law.[63] Her urgent warning against the "homosexualist agenda" whipped up a petition-writing campaign of staggering numbers.[64] In the House of Commons, she announced that as of 6 June 1995 the House had received "over 83,000 signatures on petitions directly related to the wording of sexual orientation [and that her] office had received over 10,000 letters, faxes and telephone calls confirming the views, values, principles and morality of Canadian people."[65]

According to other House members whose constituents had received information from church groups or other conservative groups, like Focus on the Family, the content of these alerts and calls for action were profoundly misleading, often remarking that the inclusion of sexual orientation to the provision would fundamentally alter the constitution of the Canadian family and limit religious freedom of expression. Liberal member Carolyn Parrish, responding to the agitation felt by her constituents, ended up speaking to a local church group in order to correct some of the misconceptions produced by such an anti-gay/lesbian campaign. Bringing the matter before the House of Commons, she remarked: "I have had church groups in my area send me profoundly disgusting pieces of literature because members of Parliament have sent them letters stirring them all up with false information."[66] Indicative of this campaign of Skoke and others was a battle for the public's belief in, and support of, specific so-called "truths" about gays and lesbians.

According to its critics, if inclusion were a "backdoor" means of getting sexual orientation into other sites of rights-based law, it would be impossible to contain once it was in place. Warnings from the Reform party and its allies stressed that the government was "leaving itself wide open" and subject unilaterally to the whims and interests of "an active movement for paedophilia" and activist courts to define the term.[67] Warning of the need for civic prudence, Dennis Mills stressed that the inclusion of sexual orientation to the enumerated list would lead "to legitimizing other forms of sexual orientation we would not want to approve."[68] Urging others about the need to contain the term by an explicit definition, Paul E. Forseth drew upon the "expert" testimony of committee witnesses: "Witnesses had come before the justice committee and stated that sexual orientation could mean anything, including transsexuality and even pedophilia[69] ... to my mind, the term 'sexual orientation' is pretty broad. It could involve all kinds of repugnant possibilities, even those that are illegal."[70] When asked by committee member, Tom Wappel, whether in his opinion "sexual orientation" did have a legal definition, Robert Wakefield, director of the Ontario Criminal Lawyers Association, remarked: "I don't think there's a legal definition of it. It's a psychiatric term [that includes] deviant behaviours."[71] Similarly, John Conroy, chair of the Committee on Imprisonment and Release, opined that "it could be any kind of sexual orientation, and it could be something that, as you say, is illegal."[72] Stressing both the non-legal nature of the term and the term's apparently uncontainable meaning, committee members appealed to select expert and common-sense knowledges about the definition of sexual orientation. This appeal to seemingly objective, skilled, and transparent knowledges, I note, stands in stark contrast to the Reform party's other characterization of committee witnesses – that is, to witnesses who were in favour of sexual orientation's inclusion as a select group of special interest seekers.[73]

In an attempt to guide his fellow parliamentarians' knowledge of the term sexual orientation, Tom Wappel, one of the vocal Liberal opponents to the inclusion, submitted a discussion paper to the House of Commons entitled *Sexual Orientation: Issues to Consider*.[74] Citing a number of "scientific" authorities including Dr. Greenberg and Dr. Paul Cameron of the Family Research Institute and author of *The High Cost of Sodomy*, Wappel framed sexual orientation in the broadest of terms by syntagmatically linking the words "sexual orientation," "homosexuality," and "pedophilia" in a number of places.[75] He made his case against inclusion using a range of expert knowledge, including "authorities" on homosexuality such as Focus on the Family, a radically conservative, Christian family-rights organization, the *Alberta Report*, a neo-conservative magazine, and scriptures from Christian and Muslim religious texts.

Against the alarmist notion that paedophilia and other paraphilias would be legitimately protected under Canadian law, Justice Minister Allan Rock stated:

> It has now been some 17 years since the first of the provincial human rights acts was amended to add sex orientation as a ground upon which discrimination is prohibited. In all of that time the consistent use of that provision and interpretation of that provision have been that sexual orientation encompasses homosexuality, heterosexuality, and bisexuality. There has been no confusion on that point. It has not been the subject of controversy or difficulty in the tribunals or courts ... The authority for that proposition is most recently – and I use this as an example – the judgement of the Federal Court of Appeal in *Egan v. Canada*, where Mr. Justice Robertson, I believe it was, made plain that the term "sexual orientation" encompasses homosexuality, heterosexuality, and bisexuality.[76]

Notwithstanding this clear reference to the legal interpretation of sexual orientation as being limited and definable to three named sexual orientations, social conservatives nevertheless resisted such authority, preferring instead their expert witnesses and their own discovery. Accordingly, Jim Slater, vice-president of Public Policy for Focus on the Family, argued that sexual orientation had no legal standing: "I know that Mr. Rock has said differently. I just do not happen to believe what he has said. For instance, in any of the court cases where we've been present as interveners, I don't find any judgements that have, as Mr. Rock has claimed, defined what sexual orientation is."[77]

Fuelling this resistance to the inclusion of "sexual orientation" to section 718.2(a)(i) was the socially conservative argument that gays and lesbians – in particular, gay men – were not a discriminated against minority but, rather, a well-organized, wealthy, and highly educated lobby. Representing REAL Women of Canada at the Justice and Legal Committee hearings, Gwendolyn Landolt stated that "the homosexual activists pushing for special recognition or protection are a powerful interest group, which is using its considerable wealth and political clout to piggyback on the legitimate claims of genuinely discriminated people."[78] Responding to such claims, John Fisher of Equality for Gays and Lesbians Everywhere (EGALE) remarked: "I wish I knew who all these wealthy homosexuals are, and I wish we had more of them in EGALE. I'm familiar with the study that identifies lesbians and gays as a fabulously wealthy, privileged class. Again, it's based upon very poor research methodology and a bunch of stereotypes and misconceptions."[79]

The study to which Fisher referred was a 1988 American marketing study by the Simmons Market Research Bureau that surveyed readers of several gay magazines. These findings appeared in a 1991 *Wall Street Journal* article about marketing strategies geared towards the gay community.[80] Broadly criticized for its weak methodology, this survey claimed that gay American households earned an average of $55,430 per year compared to a national average of $32,144 and averages of $12,166 and $17,939 for black and hispanic households respectively.[81] As Didi Herman observed, the Christian Right deployed this data as part of an anti-gay/lesbian strategy designed to prove that gays and lesbians were not a disadvantaged group (and thus were undeserving of civil rights) and to create a political wedge between the gay and lesbian community and other minority communities, particularly the Afro-American and Hispanic communities.[82]

Interestingly, in Justice and Legal Committee testimony, the issue of minority status and whether gays and lesbians had a legitimate claim to it was reduced to a numbers game built on this economic data. On the one hand, opponents of the inclusion of sexual orientation to the provision argued that gays and lesbians did not make up a demographic of 10 percent of the adult population as Alfred Kinsey's[83] classic studies concluded but, rather, that their numbers were much smaller. According to this argument, although small in numbers, this minority nevertheless suffered no discrimination or political disadvantage as a class.[84] In essence, the numbers game reduced gays and lesbians to an insignificant population while simultaneously offering that their economic privilege unfairly advantaged them socially and politically. As Jim Slater of Focus on the Family argued, "the homosexual community is known by many people across the country to be a powerful lobby at various levels of government and in society. They are, however, only some 2% of our social unit here in our nation. Yet they have achieved positions from which they can speak with some power and authority."[85] The construction of gays and lesbians as being disproportionately influential, both economically and politically, negated any minority status that may have been accorded to them strictly by their numbers.

Landolt's claim, that "the homosexual activists pushing for special recognition or protection are a powerful interest group, which is using its considerable wealth and political clout to piggyback on the legitimate claims of genuinely discriminated people; race and gender are listed in the human rights legislation of the provinces and also in section 718.2," deserves additional attention. In this particular understanding of gay and lesbian activism, a seemingly illegitimate group – "homosexuals" – was attempting to profit from the struggles and rights claims of "legitimate" groups, which were distinguished, as she noted directly after this declaration, by race and gender.[86] The "piggybacking" trope suggests that gays are attempting a free ride, in essence, by being carried on the backs of "genuinely discriminated people." Her use of the "piggybacking" trope, to my mind, echoes a similar concern raised earlier about "backdoor" activism whereby gays and lesbians were attempting to "slip" sexual orientation into the *Charter*. Taken together, these sodomitical tropes represent gays and lesbians as dangerous and deceptive[87] freeloaders devoid of an ethical politics.[88]

Illegitimate Victims

To the extent that gays and lesbians were constituted by their detractors as a deceptive, privileged, and powerful group, their very victimization by acts of hateful violence was questioned by those who opposed the inclusion of "sexual orientation" to the provision. The question of believability, though, was reformulated in this context of victimization as a question about knowledge. That is to say, the question – are gays and lesbians believable in their claims of victimization – was restated by those who sought to exclude "sexual orientation" from the provision as how do we know about their victimization? This epistemological shift was critical for the provision's opponents for it seemingly established "truth." Moreover, the reframing of the question about victimization in this way shifted a more apparent socially conservative argument about the "homosexual" subject, with his or her so-called "activist agenda" and "perverse lifestyle" practices, to seemingly impersonal, objective knowledges of the scientific method. That is to say, such a question about the knowledge of victimization relocated the truth of victimization from the evidentiary body of the queer subject – the assaulted body, the traumatized psyche, the first-person narrative – to a body of evidence that was amassed by apparent hard data and impersonal statistics. For example, John Nunziata, a Liberal opponent to the inclusion of sexual orientation, framed this question when he argued:

> As far as I know, and I have asked several members of the [Justice and Legal Affairs] committee, there was no study presented to the committee and there was no evidence other than anecdotal evidence ... The member for Burnaby-Kingsway [Svend Robinson] and others can talk about a particular hate motivated crime that happened in Vancouver, Toronto, or Halifax.[89] We know these crimes take place. But how often do they take place? Does the government have that evidence? Does the minister have a study that indicates that 1,000, 1,500, 2,000 or 10,000 so-called hate motivated crimes are taking place?[90]

For Nunziata, the veracity of anti-gay and lesbian hate-motivated victimization could only be realized in terms of statistical evidence.

Before addressing how the contestation over the knowledge of victimization was enacted in the House of Commons, the issue of statistical evidence of gay and lesbian victimization and the claim that there was "no study presented to the committee and there was no evidence other than anecdotal evidence" needs to be contextualized. EGALE did submit a brief to the Justice and Legal Committee in December 1994.[91] In this brief, it was noted that "there is no Canadian equivalent of the American *Hate Crimes Statistics Act* to measure the incidence of homophobic violence."[92] Rightly, EGALE's notation drew attention to the fact that Parliament had not responded to a private member's bill, Bill C-455, which called for hate and bias crime statistics to be collected by the federal government similar to the US *Hate Crimes Statistics Act* and the data collected by the United Kingdom on racially motivated bias crime.[93]

Nevertheless, EGALE's submission cited a number of studies conducted by various gay and lesbian groups both in Canada and the United States. The Canadian studies included a 1990 New Brunswick study on discrimination against lesbians, gays, and bisexuals, a 1994 public interest research study on homophobic abuse and discrimination in Nova Scotia, and a 1994 preliminary finding of anti-gay/lesbian violence in Vancouver.[94] Deferring to the Quebec Human Rights Commission in its 1993 report on public violence and discrimination against gays and lesbians, EGALE stated that "the Commission accepted the American figures of the National Gay and Lesbian Task Force (NGLTF) that one-fifth of gay men and one-tenth of lesbians have been physically assaulted."[95] Thus, Nunziata's complaint that there was no statistical evidence to support anecdotal claims of victimization was inaccurate.

Whether an oversight or a blatant disregard for EGALE's submission, Nunziata's claim illuminated the very problematic resistance to statistical evidence produced by advocacy that was positive towards lesbian, gay, bisexual, and transgender (LGBT) issues, such as the evidence brought forward by EGALE in the Justice and Legal Committee. Moreover, what might be considered as "neutral" empirical data produced through police statistical reports on bias crime also met with resistance. Liberal members Rock and Barnes respectively noted in the House of Commons that bias crime statistical reports from the Ottawa-Carleton and Toronto police forces concluded that hate crimes motivated by sexual orientation represented the third largest category of hate-related offences.[96] In committee, Reform MP Thompson approached these reports according to the actual numbers of incidents versus the percentage of incidents in order to diminish the ranking of bias crimes motivated by sexual orientation. Citing the 1993 Metropolitan Toronto police report, he remarked:

> I see that in 1993 there were 155 offences under this category [of general bias], and 16 of them were based on sexual orientation, just barely 10%. Some 50% were on race; that is the high part ... I'm trying to figure out what's the motivation, what's the reason for adding sexual orientation to the list, when obviously we're doing a pretty good job of it now, and obviously from the numbers from a city of 3.5 million people it is not an outrageous amount of crime.[97]

Thompson's observation that hate crimes committed against gay men and lesbians does not add up to "an outrageous amount of crime" fails to acknowledge the harmful impact of bias crime, whether it is understood in terms of its often excessive display of violence,[98] its prolonged negative effects post-trauma,[99] or its ontological injury.[100] As Roberts observed, "it would be a mistake to measure the importance of hate crimes simply by the number of incidents reported to police ... These statistics fail to convey a sense of the true harm inflicted upon the individuals or groups that are the target of hate crimes."[101]

In addition, the appeal to statistical evidence as the exclusive source of authentication and veracity of anti-gay and anti-lesbian hate-motivated victimization is in need of contextualization. First, as noted by criminologist Julian Roberts in the Justice and Legal Committee, hate crimes are "one of the most under-reported crimes of all, if not the most under-reported crime."[102] Specifically, the under-reporting rate of hate crime victimization motivated by sexual orientation is "particularly high when compared to other groups who are often the victims of hate-motivated offences."[103] In part, the issue of under-reporting anti-LGBT bias crime is connected to the risk of public disclosure by non-out gay men and lesbians as well as to a reluctance to report to police complex issues of historical victimization by, and the institutionalized homophobia of, police.[104] With respect to police data collection in the 1990s, Roberts noted that Canada had no federal collection of hate crime data and that across police jurisdictions hate crime statistics suffered from a lack of definitional uniformity, differences in collection protocols, and an absence of dedicated police bias units or expertise.[105]

Despite the multiple sources that authenticated and verified anti-gay/ lesbian violence and victimization brought before the House of Commons and the Justice and Legal Committee, the dominant narrative voiced by the opponents to the inclusion of sexual orientation kept attempting to constitute the queer subject as inauthentic, illegitimate, and incredible and, thus, undeserving of socio-legal protections. The final argument that I bring to light in these legislative debates involves testimony and evidence given before the Justice and Legal Committee that attempts to discredit the queer subject as a legitimate and authentic victim of violence. "What if I were to tell you," stated Reform MP Thompson, "that most of the crimes committed against, say, homosexuals are committed by homosexuals?"[106] This suggestion of self-victimization undermines the constitution of gay men and lesbians as targets of homophobia and heteronormativity and reproduces them as targets of their own self-directed violence. This is seen quite clearly in the dialogue between Reform party member Paul Forseth and Justice and Legal Committee witness, Gwendolyn Landolt, national vice-president of REAL Women of Canada:

Paul Forseth: "The information I'm getting is that a fair amount of assaults on gays, especially in public areas like a park, are perpetrated by gays. *It's gays against gays* because of the types of relationships they have – the jealousies and whatnot. Do you have any information on that?"[107]

Landolt's response: "I think that's a very valid point. The incidence of violence between lesbians and between homosexuals is extremely much higher. There are studies on that and if you want me to provide them, I can. They bash each other. Don't think it's necessarily these terrible heterosexuals doing terrible things to homosexuals.[108]

This exchange raises several notions about violence, self-victimization, and homosexuality, all of which need examination and a critical response.

This notion of self-victimization – "gays against gays" – needs historical contextualization. The notion of the self-victimizing homosexual has its origin in the classical victimology of Hans von Hentig[109] and his followers, embedded in which are neo-Freudian ideas about self-loathing and self-hatred as a defensive posture against an irrepressible and dreaded desire – homosexuality. These theories[110] were dominant in the United States in the 1940s and 1950s when social stigmatization, clinical pathologization, and political oppression of gay men and lesbians was the reality. It was in this milieu that von Hentig developed his theory of the deviant victim as being vulnerable to predators insofar as he or she lacked social protections and the benefits of the law, including police protection and civil rights. However, mixed with his theory are two neo-Freudian psychiatric notions. The first is that the subject is psychically terrorized by his own irrepressible same-sex desire due to a failed Oedipal resolution, which is defensively turned into hatred for other gay men whom the subject will victimize.[111] Under this aspect of the theory, the homosexual is a predator, and it is his own group whom he victimizes. Forseth's comment about gay men attacking other gay men in parks mimics this theory of self-victimization.

The second notion of classic victimology *qua* neo-Freudian theory is that the homosexual is in some way precipitatory to his victimization. Within this aspect of the theory, such precipitation usually takes the form of psychological weakness or a masochistic tendency. It was believed that the supposed psychological weakness of the homosexual constituted him as a vulnerable risk taker whose poor judgments lead him into situations with a high risk of victimization – like seeking an anonymous sexual partner in a park at night. Here, the assessment of risk and pleasure is structured around poor judgment and psychological instability rather than a calculated assessment of risk and pleasure. In addition, neo-Freudian theory problematically argues that the homosexual is both effeminate (hence, the psychoanalytic linkages to masochism[112]) and self-loathing.[113] Thus, according to this theory, the homosexual, in lacking supposed masculine qualities of strength and self-assurance, seeks out or perhaps stumbles upon the sadistic, dominant personality of the victimizer and falls victim to that dynamic. Of course, if the homosexual is masochistic, weak, and vulnerable, how is it that he is also psychically characterized as a sadistic predator?

Despite these inconsistencies, such theories were quite popular with the studies of gay men as victims in the 1970s and 1980s. With this as their intellectual pedigree, Jess Maghan and Edward Sagarin argue that homosexuals, as they term gay men, are found to be both victims and victimizers. "Much but not all victimization of homosexuals takes place in the hands of heterosexual society and of various people who make a complete heterosexual identification," they argue, "it seems clear that some of the homosexual victimization is at the hands of homosexual offenders."[114] Describing a "rage against society," they argue that the self-loathing and ostracized homosexual targets out of opportunity, finding "a ready target in his own backyard, neighbourhood, or bedroom. So it is with homosexuality."[115]

Such work was later challenged, if not discredited, by others in the fields of victimology and psychology. Perhaps the earliest shift in the neo-Freudian notion of the pathological homosexual finds resonance in the work of George Weinberg. In his seminal work, *Society and the Healthy Homosexual*, Weinberg coins the term "homophobia" and stresses that societal fear of the homosexual is both irrational and inculcated to youth at a very young age.[116] This phobia manifests in an irrational prejudice against homosexuals and, for the homosexual himself, this prejudice may manifest in self-loathing, which for the most part does not lead to violent victimization of his own group. Mostly, Weinberg notes that this self-loathing was self-directed and manifested in depressive and suicidal tendencies. His critical argument is that the irrational fear and hatred of gay men is structurally reproduced and sanctioned by societal institutions, which was taken up by the gay liberation movement in the 1970s, which rejected the pathologization of gays and lesbians and, in this liberation from the pathological model, refocused on societal and structural oppression and the stigmatization of gays and lesbians.

As Louie Crew and Rictor Norton remark, "negative self-concepts [are] entirely the result of unjustified guilt [and shame] that has been internalized by the constant pressures of homophobic society."[117] Contemporary gay/lesbian and queer scholarship speaks of heteronormativity and the social regulation of bodies and desires.[118] The refusal to acquiesce to heteronormative gender codes by queers, for example, produces societal backlash and potential violence.[119] As Elizabeth Stanko and Paul Curry observe, "in short, homophobic violence is a form of governance of sexual differences which poses direct and actual danger to its individual recipients for 'just' being or being perceived to be 'not straight.'"[120] In this model, homophobic violence is not directed at the group or the self but, rather, is an external violence that attempts to oppress and regulate sexual and gender difference.

Thompson's references to "their types of relationships" and "jealousies and whatnot" are veiled codes that infer that gay and lesbian intimate relationships are fraught with instability and destructive emotionalism. This notion of "gay jealousy" has deep roots, one of which is a "moralistic" article by J.C. Rupp.[121] Brian Miller and Laud Humphreys in their article on gay male victims of assault and murder directly refute the 1970 claim by Rupp that jealousy between gay lovers is "a major causative factor in the murder of homosexual men."[122] Of their own research, they write: "No case in our sample could be classified as resulting from a dispute between present lovers or members of a love triangle."[123] Rather than gay relationships constituting a lethal threat, they note that "the gay world not only offers a variety of social, affectional, and cultural opportunities but also tends to protect members from those who may victimize them."[124]

Despite such contemporary research, Landolt responds to Forseth's problematic characterizations with her own veiled claim of same-sex domestic violence: "The incidence of violence between lesbians and between homosexuals is extremely much higher." Thus, she enters into the committee's record this alarmist claim as witness, but with no tangible evidence or any direct comparison to another group. Is this supposed violence higher than rates of domestic violence for opposite-sex couples? To this question, I make note of the following conclusion of studies on same-sex domestic abuse: same-sex and opposite sex intimate relationships experience comparable levels and rates of violence.[125] Insofar as some lesbians and gay men may experience domestic abuse, it is not at a higher rate than heterosexual domestic abuse, nor does it account for the majority of violence experienced by lesbians and gay men.

The length to which the political opponents to the inclusion of sexual orientation to the provision attempted to reproduce gay men and lesbians as illegitimate and inauthentic victims of violence is staggering. Despite such overwhelming and convoluted argumentation, Bill C-41, the omnibus bill on sentencing reform, was proclaimed in force on 3 September 1996, and the term "sexual orientation" was included as an enumerated category to the enhanced sentencing provision. The bill passed by a vote of 168 to 51. Although the debates were dominated by the opposition to the words "sexual orientation," in terms of actual numbers, the opposition was small. The government, enforcing strict party discipline, did not allow a free vote and threatened disciplinary action for dissent. Ultimately, only four Liberals voted against the bill: Roseanne Skoke, Tom Wappel, Dan McTeague, and Paul Steckle. In November 1994, McTeague was quoted in the press as stating that forty-six Liberals expressed concern about the inclusion of the term "sexual orientation," a claim on which he later backtracked.[126]

These parliamentary debates and Justice and Legal Committee testimony reveal the extent to which the legislative provision respecting hate motivation and the legitimacy of the status of gay men and lesbians as legitimate and authentic victims deserving of a legislative response were hotly contested. Competing epistemologies of victimhood, as argued in the House of Commons and given as testimony before the Justice and Legal Committee, positioned gays and lesbians, on the one hand – by supporters of the legislation – as "innocent law-abiding Canadians who are sadly victimized by violent attacks" and, on the other hand – by opponents – as a special interest group driven by the "homosexualist" agenda whose very claim to victimhood was rebuffed and deemed illegitimate.[127] Ultimately, these disparate positions configured the legislative terrain of the gay and lesbian subject of hate violence as unstable, positioned legally within the nomination of "legitimate hate crime victim" but straddled ideologically between legitimate and illegitimate victimization.

3

Bill C-250: A Censoring of Religious Freedom or a Protection against Hate?

It [Bill C-250] will swiftly impose a hate-crimes "chill" on those who object to the gay agenda. Before too long, those who speak out in opposition to government – or court-imposed gay rights – may find themselves pulling their punches out of fear of prosecution for their beliefs ... It is hardly fantastical to worry that an activist judge, armed with the hon. member for Burnaby–Douglas' law, could rule at the national level that all opinions troubling to gays are hateful, and none are protected, no matter what the *Criminal Code* says.

–Tom Wappel, House of Commons Debates, 6 June 2003

A lasting undercurrent present in the debates about anti-hate laws, particularly those involving the regulation or censorship of expression, has been a worry, legitimately so, about the erosion of free speech in Canada. The anxiety about a curtailment of rights and the effect that this could have on Canadian democracy and on the very nature of our body politic circulates within a political discourse of rights and national identity. Using a microcosm of this affective economy, this chapter identifies and analyzes Senate Standing Committee on Legal and Constitutional Affairs (Legal and Constitutional Affairs Committee) witness opposition to Bill C-250, the amendment to the hate propaganda statutes that sought to include "sexual orientation" to the list of identifiable groups protected under the legislation.[1] The witness opposition framed its concern, predictably, around the issue of speech censorship and the harms that would stem from such censorship. The Christian Right, who formed the majority of the oppositional witnesses, framed harm as a harm to their right of religious expression and religious speech. In addition to classic libertarian arguments against the amendment, and against the hate propaganda statutes all together, the arguments of the Christian Right displayed what could be characterized as a "fantastical" apprehension of religious persecution by the state.

This chapter distinguishes itself from the previous chapter on Bill C-41 and its analysis of the logic of exclusion that sought to keep the term "sexual orientation" from the provision. Although both chapters analyze the arguments and the rhetoric of opposition to these two pieces of legislation, these pieces of legislation are not comparable. Bill C-41 was an omnibus sentencing reform bill of which one aspect called for judges to consider the motivation of bias, hate, and prejudice as aggravating factors at the time of sentencing. Bill C-250 was an amendment to the existing hate propaganda law, which sought to include "sexual orientation" under the term "identifiable group." As well, these two bills were handled approximately eight years apart. If there appears to be commonality and redundancy, I note that this is significant. Why is it that nearly eight years after the passage of Bill C-250 were social conservatives and their political allies once again before governmental committees voicing opposition to another piece of hate crime legislation that had as its focus the term "sexual orientation"? To dismiss an analysis of this particular bill as redundant cedes legitimate inquiry and analysis of right-wing rhetoric to a different socio-legal issue – the inclusion of "sexual orientation" as a protected group under Canada's hate propaganda laws.

The Spectre of the "Gay Agenda"

The spectre of the "gay agenda," "activist judges," and the suppression of speech by an oppressive government regime littered both the parliamentary and Senate debates and committee hearings on Bill C-250, a private members' bill seeking, by amendment to the hate propaganda statutes, the expansion of "identifiable group" to include "sexual orientation" under sections 318 and 319 of the *Criminal Code*.[2] This chapter identifies and analyzes opposition to this amendment by way of witness testimony presented to the Legal and Constitutional Affairs Committee.[3] Seeking to distinguish itself from the previous chapter that mapped the opposition to Bill C-41 in the House of Commons debates, this chapter shifts its focus from the House to the Senate and examines, not the Senators' opposition to Bill C-250 but, rather, the arguments presented by the committee witnesses who voiced opposition to the bill. The witness opposition framed its concern, predictably, around the issue of speech censorship and the harms that would stem from such censorship – a chilled climate on legitimate debate and rightful dissent. Less predictable, to a certain extent, was the way in which witnesses from the Christian Right, who were the majority of the oppositional witnesses,[4] framed harm as a harm to their right of religious expression and religious speech. In addition to classic libertarian arguments against the amendment, and against the hate propaganda statutes all together, the arguments of the Christian Right displayed what could be characterized as a fantastical apprehension of religious persecution by the state.[5]

Resistance to the amendment had a long history in failed bills.[6] Originally tabled as Bill C-326 in 1990, the private member's bill brought forward by Svend Robinson sought to amend the hate propaganda statutes with the addition of "sex" and "sexual orientation" as identifiable groups.[7] In the House of Commons, Robinson argued for the need to criminalize hate literature directed at women, lesbians, and gay men, claiming Parliament must "send out a clear message" to the Canadian people that hate literature "will not be tolerated in Canada."[8] A year later, Robinson reintroduced the proposed amendment as Bill C-247; this too died in the House of Commons.[9] Seven years later, in 1999, as Bill C-263, Robinson tried again to expand the list by limiting his proposed amendment to "sexual orientation." It is interesting to note that despite the wording of the amendment to include only the term "sexual orientation," he stated that the purpose of the bill was to expand the hate propaganda protections to include "gay, lesbian, bisexual and transgender people."[10] This bill also died quickly in the House, yet re-emerged in late 2001 as Bill C-415. Noting the timing of the bill – a week after the homicide of Aaron Webster in Stanley Park by a group of gay-bashers – Robinson spoke passionately about the need to protect lesbian, gay, bisexual, and transgender (LGBT) people against the public incitement of hatred. He remarked that the Canadian government, by its continued exclusion of "sexual orientation" from the list of identifiable groups, delivered the message that gay men and lesbians were "in fact second class citizens in [their] own country."[11]

Since Parliament was prorogued prior to Bill C-415 receiving royal assent, Robinson sought to reintroduce his bill in October 2002, now as Bill C-250, pursuant to Standing Order 86.1, a special provision that allowed for the reinstatement of private members' bills at the same stage they had reached in the previous session without requiring a motion.[12] Thus, when the third session of the thirty-seventh Parliament convened, the bill had already passed by the House of Commons at second reading and was referred to the justice committee.[13] "My bill," he stated, "seeks only to extend that same level of protection to those who are targeted on the basis of their sexual orientation. It is important to note that this bill in no way limits or threatens the freedom of religious expression or religious texts."[14]

The perception of threat to religious expression and expression more generally permeated the Legal and Constitutional Affairs Committee's testimony from Christian and social conservatives who spoke about the various ways in which adding "sexual orientation" to the list under "identifiable groups" would bring about a legal atmosphere of censorious oppression to those who spoke out against homosexuality. Stating that the bill would have "catastrophic" effects, the president of the Canada Christian College gave evidence that "if the bill were passed, people could be convicted under this and sent to prison."[15] In an even more fantastical vision of the effects of the amendment, Gwendolyn Landolt, national vice-president of REAL Women of Canada, claimed that not only would the bill "prohibit thought," but it would "require us to think certain thoughts."[16] While not clearly articulated to the committee, this notion of mind control and loss of individual liberty of conscience and religious belief is one element in a more elaborate, and fantastic, vision of a "homosexual agenda," an activist liberal court, and a persecuted Christian and social conservative minority.[17]

Another witness, Janet Epp Buckingham, director of law and public policy and general legal counsel of the Evangelical Fellowship of Canada, foretold that the Bible would be labelled as "hate literature."[18] The exaggerated claims, inflamed rhetoric, and illogical conclusions drawn by the witnesses who opposed the bill seem fantastical in light of the jurisprudential history of hate propaganda under Canadian law and the numerous protections built into sections 318 and 319 against zealous prosecution and frivolous or malevolent concern for the fundamental rights of freedom of religion and freedom of expression contained in the *Canadian Charter of Rights and Freedoms*, including that of religious expression.[19] Responding to a comment made by one of the witnesses, Senator David Smith remarked: "Sometimes I have the feeling that the evangelical community – which I know well because that is my background – sense conspiracies that are not really there."[20]

Fantastical Apprehensions

"Anyone who may object to the homosexual agenda will be regarded as hateful," stated the representative from REAL Women of Canada to the Legal and Constitutional Affairs Committee, "anything could happen to anyone."[21] The hyperbolic expansiveness of such a claim – anything could happen to anyone – reveals the extent to which the Christian Right and social conservatives feared the impact of the inclusion of "sexual orientation" to the identifiable groups listed under the hate propaganda statutes. At the heart of their apprehensions was the belief that, with the addition of "sexual orientation" to the groups protected under sections 318 and 319 of the *Criminal Code*, any public speech, particularly religious speech, expressing an objection to homosexuality would be met with criminal sanction. Their arguments can be summarized as taking four basic tenets: (1) the amendment would censor religious opinion on the subject of homosexuality, thus producing a chilling effect on public speech in Canada; (2) the terms constituting the propaganda laws were vaguely defined and thus subject to prosecutorial abuse; (3) there were no legal protections offered to the right of legitimate expression; and (4) the state would be increasingly zealous in their prosecution of those expressing an opinion on homosexuality that did not support, as social conservatives termed it, "the homosexual agenda."

Of great concern to the detractors of the bill was the meaning of the term "sexual orientation." They argued that the term was too vague and lacked definition under sections 318 and 319. Drawing on psychological definitions of the term, they expressed vexation that the term "could include all sorts of deviations from heterosexual sex," noting that pedophilia had been defined as an "orientation" under that behavioural science.[22] Reverend Richard Parkyn, appearing without organizational affiliation, stated that in his opinion "adding 'sexual orientation' to this section opens the door to the protection of the pedophile, the predator, and the polygamist."[23] Echoing similar arguments made against the inclusion of "sexual orientation" to the enhanced sentencing provision in 1994, these apprehensions towards the vagueness of the term were dismissed as being without justification. As Svend Robinson noted in the committee, "the words 'sexual orientation' are not new to Canadian jurisprudence. They have been in Canadian law since 1977 [under the Quebec *Charter of Human Rights and Freedoms*]."[24] Senator Serge Joyal reiterated this point by stressing that every provincial human rights code enumerated "sexual orientation" as a protected group and that it was read into section 15 of the *Charter* by the Supreme Court of Canada's majority opinion in *Vriend v Alberta* in 1998: "It is not a concept we invented for the purpose of this bill ... Section 15 of the *Charter*, which we cherish as Canadians, has been interpreted as including sexual orientation by the Supreme Court of Canada repeatedly. In other words, it is not another vague concept."[25]

Another site of anxiety focused on the notion of hate itself: "What is hate? No one knows."[26] Suggesting that in the existing statute this term was both vague and unknowable, Landolt attempted to validate her perception by citing then Justice Beverley McLachlin's dissenting opinion in *R. v Keegstra*.[27] Quoting McLachlin, Landolt read into testimony:

> The first difficulty lies in the different interpretations which may be placed on the word "hatred." The *Shorter Oxford English Dictionary* defines "hatred" as: "The condition or states of relations in which one person hates another; the emotion of hate; active dislike, detestation; enmity, ill-will, malevolence." The wide range of diverse emotions which the word "hatred" is capable of denoting is evident from this definition. Those who defend its use in s. 319(2) of the *Criminal Code* emphasize one end of this range – hatred, they say, indicates the most powerful of virulent emotions lying beyond the bounds of human decency and limiting s. 319(2) to extreme materials. Those who object to its use point to the other end of the range, insisting that "active dislike" is not an emotion for the promotion of which a person should be convicted as a criminal.

To state the arguments is to make the case; "hatred" is a broad term capable of catching a wide variety of emotion.[28]

Any assurances by then Chief Justice Brian Dickson's clarification in the majority opinion that "hatred" under section 319(2) meant "a most extreme emotion that belies reason; an emotion that, if exercised against members of an identifiable group, implies that those individuals are to be despised, scorned, denied respect and made subject to ill-treatment on the basis of group affiliation" offered little comfort to Landolt. Further, it appears that she took no solace in his direction that "a dictionary definition may be of limited aid to such an exercise" in that "by its nature a dictionary seeks to offer a panoply of possible usages, rather than the correct meaning of a word as contemplated by Parliament."[29] Despite Landolt's anxiety that the law was vague and overly broad, those issues had been settled constitutionally under *Keegstra* some fourteen years earlier. As the case reflected, the term "hatred" under section 319(2) was limited to the most extreme expression and not merely to distasteful, disliked, or offensive expression.

A further source of apprehension for the bill's detractors was the fear that, with the addition of "sexual orientation" to the meaning of an identifiable group, there would be increased and vexatious prosecutions for those who voiced opposition to homosexuality. "I have a concern that the day will come that the word 'genocide' will be applied to a person simply objecting to a certain sexual orientation on moral, religious or simply personal convictions," argued Parkyn.[30] As an attempt to allay this worry, witnesses in the Legal and Constitutional Affairs Committee arguing for the bill responded by citing the number of times the various sections of the hate propaganda laws had been used. Speaking for Equality for Gays and Lesbians Everywhere (EGALE), Trevor Fenton gave testimony stating that there had been only one prosecution under the genocide section and that there had "not been a single case involving a prosecution" under 319(1).[31] Both Fenton and Robinson gave testimony noting that only five cases had been prosecuted under section 319(2), four successfully.[32]

Despite the limited number of prosecutions under section 319(2), the representative from the Evangelical Fellowship of Canada held that "while there have not been many prosecutions under this section, up to this point it has not included sexual orientation, and there is a huge public debate about sexual orientation and same-sex marriage in our society." She went on to say that "we are concerned that this section will actually be used much more than it has been previously."[33] Janet Buckingham's apprehension, while acknowledging the limited historical use of the hate propaganda laws, has proven to be unfounded. To date, there have been no charges under any of the hate propaganda laws involving "sexual orientation." As Robinson noted in the committee, "this bill is largely symbolic; I would be the first person to concede that. There will not be a lot of prosecutions under this legislation. Yet the symbolism is enormously important because it says to gay and lesbian people that our lives and our safety and our security are just as important."[34]

With respect to the various checks and balances built into the propaganda laws, including the requirement of the consent of the attorney general in order for a charge to be laid under sections 318 and 319(2) and four defences structured principally around truth and good faith arguments, the objectors to the amendment argued that these protections were insufficient and offered a false sense of civil security against the power of the state. Speaking to the requirement of the consent of the attorney general prior to any charge being laid, Landolt claimed that this provision was merely political smoke and mirrors: "We know that attorneys general are simply political officials. They are part of a political party and are simply doing what is politically correct. They are not upholding the law; they are promoting party policy. We have no guarantee that the attorneys general will protect us."[35] In a much less conspiratorial tone, the president of the Canada Christian College correctly noted that section 319(1) did not provide any attorney general protection.[36] However, insofar as the intention behind securing the attorney general's consent is the avoidance of frivolous prosecution and a high likelihood of conviction, the fact that section 319(1) has never been used should have offered some solace to those who questioned the absent requirement of the attorney general's consent.[37]

With respect to the built-in defences under the then-current statute, section 319(3)(b) stated the following: "No person shall be convicted of an offence under subsection(2) – if, in good faith, he expressed or attempted to establish by argument an opinion on a religious subject." By the time Bill C-250 had reached the Legal and Constitutional Affairs Committee in March 2004, after much debate in the House of Commons, the bill was expanded by way of an additional clause that added to the defence "or an opinion based on a belief in a religious text." As Fenton noted of section 319(3)(b), this particular defence "unequivocally tells the courts that the Bible and other scriptures are not hate literature and are off-limits to prosecutors."[38] Despite this addition to the then-current defence of religious belief, Derek Rogusky of Focus on the Family argued that "Bill C-250 poses a real risk to the religious freedom and freedom of expression that Canadians enjoy. The defences against prosecution and/or conviction are rather limited."[39]

As proof of this belief of ineffective defences and as an index of what would follow if Bill C-250 became law, Buckingham, legal counsel for the Evangelical Fellowship of Canada, cited a case in which the Ontario Court of Appeal ruled on section 319(3).[40] This case involved the publication and distribution of pamphlets and the communication of telephone messages by a Christian pastor who claimed that all Canadian Muslims are part of a worldwide terrorist conspiracy that poses a threat to the security and well-being of Canadians.[41] The trial judge opined that "although Mr. Harding denies having the intent to promote hatred when disseminating his message, he was at best wilfully blind," and he sentenced Harding to a concurrent three-month conditional sentence and two years probation.[42] Buckingham took issue with the phrase "wilful blindness" as the legal standard, which she claimed was much lower than "wilful promotion" as set out in the statute. However, addressing this very issue, Justice Karen Weiler of the Ontario Court of Appeal wrote:

> Wilful blindness is more than mere recklessness. Criminal law treats wilful blindness as equivalent to actual knowledge because the accused "knew or strongly suspected" that inquiry on his part respecting the consequences of his acts would fix him with the actual knowledge he wished to avoid. The appellant's submission that wilful blindness is insufficient to support the stringent *mens rea* requirement contained in s. 319(2) because it limits freedom of expression is not supported by the jurisprudence. Wilful blindness satisfies the stringent *mens rea* requirement for the offence of wilfully promoting hatred and does no violence to Dickson C.J.C.'s definition of the mental element for the offence in *Keegstra*, supra. The trial judge did not convict the appellant based on

an insufficient *mens rea* requirement and Dambrot J. did not err in upholding his conviction.[43]

Buckingham's defence and use of such a case – a religious vitriol against Muslim Canadians – as an example of sound religious expression and of an oppressive legal apparatus appears slightly misplaced.

With direct respect to the weary claim that legal protection of sexual orientation always comes at the cost of freedom of religious expression, Clair Schnupp, a psychologist speaking as an individual witness against the bill, stated:

> The courts have simply failed to protect religious freedom against claims based on sexual orientation ... I also have a concern that was expressed by the Evangelical Fellowship of Canada, that the Bible could easily – and I think will – be classified as hate literature, at least sections of it. Then what do we have for healing as Christians? ... You [the Evangelical Fellowship of Canada] warned that people of faith would be specifically targeted if Bill C-250 were to become law.[44]

The claim that the courts had failed to protect religious freedom in favour of sexual orientation was an oblique citation to three cases that were referenced by opponents to Bill C-250 during the Legal and Constitutional Affairs Committee hearings: *Vriend*, *Owens v Saskatchewan (Human Rights Commission)*, and another unnamed case, none of which was ill considered by the courts.[45]

In *Vriend*, for example, Delwin Vriend, a laboratory coordinator at a Christian college that held "strong religious views against homosexuality and homosexual practices," was fired from his job upon the discovery of his sexual orientation.[46] Vriend's complaint to the Alberta Human Rights Commission was rejected on the ground that "sexual orientation" was not a prohibited ground of discrimination under the listed objectives of the *Individual's Rights Protection Act* (*IRPA*) in Alberta.[47] He sought a declaration from the Alberta Court of Queen's Bench that the omission in the provincial human rights code breached section 15 of the *Charter*. The trial judge found that the omission of protection against discrimination on the basis of sexual orientation was an unjustified violation of section 15 and ordered that the words "sexual orientation" be read into the relevant sections of the *IRPA* as a prohibited ground of discrimination. This decision was overturned by the Alberta Court of Appeal. On appeal to the Supreme Court of Canada, the unanimous decision held that the legislative omission constituted a *Charter* violation that could not be saved under section 1 and ordered that the words "sexual orientation" be read into the prohibited grounds of discrimination in the appropriate provisions of the *IRPA*.[48] Thus, in this case, what was ruled on by the Supreme Court of Canada was not whether the act of firing Vriend from his job at a Christian college constituted discrimination but, rather, whether Vriend had recourse to the Alberta Human Rights Commission to lodge a complaint of discrimination against the college. That is to say, no ruling was made that trumped gay rights over religious rights.

The second case cited by religious conservative witnesses was *Owens*.[49] In *Owens*, three separate human rights complaints were made against Hugh Owens for publishing in a local newspaper an advertisement for a bumper sticker that displayed references to four Bible passages – Romans 1, Leviticus 18:22, Leviticus 20:13, and 1 Corinthians 6:9–10 – on the left side of the sticker. An equal sign (=) was situated in the middle of the sticker, with a symbol on the right side of the sticker. The symbol on the right side was comprised of two males holding hands with the universal symbol of a red circle with a diagonal bar superimposed over top.[50] A number of experts in human sexuality, various religions, and religious fundamentalism testified as to the message of the sticker and the impact of that message. Based on this testimony and the testimony of Owens himself, the Board of Injury found Owen's advertisement to have violated section 14(1)(b) of the Saskatchewan *Human Rights Code* in that the publication of this representation "exposed the complainants to hatred, ridicule and an affront to their dignity because of their sexual orientation" contrary to the code.[51]

Responding to this case, Buckingham stated:

> Our concern is, if there is a criminal provision, people will then face criminal action on it ... The decision [in *Owens*] simply talked about Biblical texts promoting hatred against gays and lesbians. That is the precedent stating that these Biblical texts promote hatred against gays

and lesbians. We then wonder what kind of protection we can have for the Bible now that such a precedent exists ... People said afterwards that the Bible had been labelled "hate literature."[52]

At the heart of this misapprehension by Buckingham was the confusion between human rights law and criminal law. As Richard Moon notes, under Canadian law there are two distinct mechanisms to deal with hate promotion: "the criminal prohibition against hate promotion considered in *Keegstra* 1990 and provincial and federal human rights code provisions against racist expression."[53] Thus, section 13(1) of the *Canadian Human Rights Act*, prior to its repeal in 2013, stated that it is a "discriminatory practice" contrary to the act for a person to "communicate telephonically ... repeatedly ... any manner that is likely to expose a person or persons to hatred or contempt by reason of the fact that that person or those persons are identifiable on the basis of a prohibited ground of discrimination."[54] In terms of provincial human rights codes, the BC *Human Rights Code*, for example, states under section 7(1):

> A person must not publish, issue or display, or cause to be published, issued or displayed, any statement, publication, notice, sign, symbol, emblem or other representation that (a) indicates discrimination or an intention to discriminate against a person or a group or class of persons, or (b) is likely to expose a person or a group or class of persons to hatred or contempt because of the race, colour, ancestry, place of origin, religion, marital status, family status, physical or mental disability, sex, sexual orientation or age of that person or that group or class of persons.[55]

Section 7(2) makes clear that the prohibition does not apply to private communication, a communication intended to be private, or a communication related to an activity otherwise permitted by this code.

Insofar as the law responds to hateful expression under both human rights and criminal law paradigms, the differences between human rights law and criminal law are significant. First, the aim of the human rights statutes is conciliatory, not punitive or carceral. As then Chief Justice Brian Dickson wrote for the majority in *Canada v Taylor*, the aim of human rights codes "is not to bring the full force of the state's power against a blameworthy individual for the purpose of imposing punishment."[56] Insofar as individual acts of discrimination are thought to be part of a systemic practice, for the most part, Richard Moon writes that the response of human rights law is conciliatory, educational, and remedial.[57] Where conciliation and resolution have failed, the human rights tribunal may make "a variety of orders, including a compensation order or an injunction against further wrongful acts."[58] As a last resort, criminal sanction may be imposed on the individual who refuses to obey the tribunal's order and who is found to be in contempt. That is to say, criminal punishment is not a result of hate speech but, rather, a result of disobeying a court order.

Second, as noted by EGALE's Trevor Fenton in the Legal and Constitutional Affairs Committee, in order to violate human rights law one must "merely expose an identifiable group to hatred or ridicule."[59] Whereas, under criminal law, the accused must have promoted hatred that under the *Criminal Code* indicates "active support or instigation." Third, violation of human rights law does not require a mental element; the effect of discrimination is what matters. On the other hand, the promotion of hatred under criminal law must be wilful, which under *Keegstra* means that it is both intentional and purposeful; wilful does not include recklessness. This wilfulness, like every other element of the offence in section 319, must be proved beyond a reasonable doubt by the Crown. Fourth, under human rights law, good faith as a defence is irrelevant, whereas, section 319(3) provides four defences, two of which are explicitly good faith and the other two are truth and public benefit defences. Responding to the Christian Right's use of the *Owens* case to infer that the citation to religious texts offered no defence of religious expression and that religious expression was in fact under attack by the state, and further that what transpired under human rights law could be mapped neatly onto criminal law, Fenton stated: "With respect, I submit that this case [*Owens*] is simply not relevant to the bill in front of you. Using a human rights case like *Owens* to discredit a *Criminal Code* provision betrays a considerable misunderstanding of our legal system.[60]

A number of senators, the chief exception being Senator Anne Cools, expressed incredulity at the claims and fears voiced by witness representatives of the Christian Right. Responding to the veiled argument by Charles McVety that anything expressed religiously about sexual orientation –

rather than religious condemnation specifically of homosexuality – could be caught by a vaguely worded bill, Senator David Smith asked: "You really think that if this bill passes, that anyone who preaches against fornication or adultery … will run the risk of being charged on this?"[61] Others countered with pointed discussion about limits under Canadian law. "Our freedoms," noted Senator Serge Joyal, "are not in any sense, in any area, absolute."[62] Citing a balance in civil society between pluralism, religion, and public policy, Joyal remarked that "freedom of belief does not trump the rule of law … There are limits to freedom of belief expressed publicly … If your religious belief endangers the right to physical integrity, then the law somewhere must place some limits on the expression of those beliefs publicly."[63]

The stress on "limits" may be read not only as a rebuke to outlandish claims and misguided beliefs expressed by some of the Legal and Constitutional Affairs Committee's witnesses but also as an attempt to shore up emotions and fears that were stirring up public controversy and agitation over the proposed bill.[64] "I want to address you on the issue of Bill C-250, which is of grave concern for hundreds of thousands, if not millions, of Canadians who are very much afraid of this bill," stated McVety, "we prayed that we would be defended against the attack that is waged through Bill C-250."[65]

And What of Paranoid Scenarios?

I think I am not paranoid, but I can see that … With the courts the way they are, you can expect anything nowadays, actually. I do not feel safe at all, I can tell you that.

– Dr. André Lafrance, Legal and Constitutional Affairs Committee

Fears of persecution took another peculiar form that was distinct from the fear of religious persecution. Two witnesses gave evidence to the Legal and Constitutional Affairs Committee arguing that their rights, differently constituted, would be at risk and their public beliefs about homosexuality would be subject to prosecution if Bill C-250 were to pass. In the case of one of them, a dermatologist representing the Canada Family Action Coalition, he was deeply distressed that his medical views on homosexuality would be subject to criminal sanction under the proposed amendment.

In the case of the other, a certified management accountant (CMA), her deep concern was the fear that this amendment would prohibit her right to speak out against "LGBT subcultures" and "sexually diverse family units."[66] For both witnesses, their free expression of homosexuality as a threat to a healthy society was under attack. To remove such a right, in their minds, would open Canadian society to both physical and moral decay. "Should Bill C-250 pass," stated the CMA, "I would not be able to oppose the many dangerous, risky and unhealthy homosexual sexual practices like sodomy, oral-anal sex and sadomasochism and others, and their social consequences for society."[67] What is particularly interesting are, not only the sustained expressions of anxiety and threat felt by these committee witnesses but also the descriptions, scenarios, and histories of homosexuality that each presented to the committee. The curious preoccupation with the figure of the "hyper-sexualized homosexual" as threat in the witness testimony of these two witnesses respectively beckons my attention, as does the affective matrix of the fear of persecution, love, and hate revealed by these two committee witnesses.

With respect to the CMA, her concerns about possible legal prosecution and censorship seemed unconnected to the purpose and effects of a bill that sought to add "sexual orientation" as a protected group under Canada's hate propaganda laws and seemed oddly misplaced focusing heavily on the sexual practices of her father, practices that were for her emblematic of gay sexuality. She argued: "Should Bill C-250 pass, I fear I could be prosecuted for speaking about the damaging repercussions and severe ramifications of homosexual sexual practices."[68] (Mis)interpreting the purpose, scope, and breadth of the bill, she remarked, "Bill C-250 will rule out any moral objections, bias and prejudice on the basis of sexual orientation. Under the guise of the undefined term 'sexual orientation,' this bill will protect persons who practise pansexuality from private and public criticism."[69]

Recalling her childhood, she spoke of a highly sexualized childhood environment in which her father's sexual practices with men affected her deeply:

I lived with my homosexual father in a highly sexualized environment. My mother and my two brothers and myself lived in this state. I was exposed to sexually inappropriate experiences from a young age, in-cluding pornography, drugs, alcohol and indecent sexual acts. I was exposed to under-age male recruitment, voyeurism, exhibitionism, sadomasochism, fetishism and group sex – for example, my father with 12 men ... I lived firsthand the secrecy, neglect, abandonment, manipu-lation, abuse and stress of growing up with a homosexual father whose sexual obsessions and imperative compulsions left my brothers and me unprotected.[70]

Within this environment of "secrecy, neglect, abandonment, manipulation, abuse and stress," she noted that "these experiences affected me deeply and robbed me of my innocence, my conscience, and the ability to exercise my voice. I could not express any opposition toward my homosexual father's lifestyle."[71]

With respect to this secreted and censored childhood, her opposition to Bill C-250 was framed thus: "Bill C-250 will remove my right as a child who grew up in this situation to the freedom of speech and freedom of expression to state opposition to particular forms of sexual behaviours, sexual diversity and family diversity ... I fear I could be prosecuted for speaking about the damaging repercussions and severe ramifications of homosexual sexual practices."[72] Framing her opposition to the legislation as an advocation for children's rights and children's voices, she argued that if the bill were to pass no one could speak out against what she perceived as inherently pathological LGBT familial units. "My concern," she stated, "is for this and future generations of children who are and will be exposed to GLBT sexual diversity and family diversity. All human beings are created equal, but not all sexual behaviours are equal. These kinds of sexual be-haviours and lifestyles do not create healthy, safe and secure home en-vironments for children."[73]

As expressed to the Legal and Constitutional Affairs Committee, her "fear" and "concern" was two-fold. On the one hand, her apprehension was that the proposed legislation would inhibit, by way of criminal sanction, her ability to speak out against "homosexual sexual practices." On the other hand, her inability to speak against these practices, to her mind, would create a dangerous and abusive situation for children being raised in LGBT households: "Bill C-250 will break down sexual barriers and foster sexually diverse family units that are not good for children."[74] If her account of her childhood is indeed accurate and true, her exposure to such an environment may well be constituted as traumatizing and abusive. However, despite this fact, her claim that such life was "typical of children in the GLBT subcultures" is a rash overgeneralized and offensive statement.[75] Her inability to distinguish this experience from other non-abusive familial experiences with LGBT parents is troubling. As someone who is speaking as a Legal and Constitutional Affairs Committee witness, her rhetorical collapse of her father's behaviour, the explicit sexual practices of men sexing men, and the issues of consent, age appropriateness, and coherent parent-child boundaries is unsettling.

Despite the graphic and morbid characterization of her father as an abusive parent and the troubling emblematic representation of gay sex more generally as exploitative, the witness claimed that she bore no malice towards the LGBT community at large nor to her father. "I have absolutely no hatred of any gay, lesbian, bisexual, transgendered or transsexual person," she claimed.[76] About her father, she stated: "I grew up in Toronto during the 1960s and 1970s with a homosexual father whom I deeply loved."[77] In the short testimony of this witness, the affective states of love and hate come together in the most intimate ways: by way of community, family, paternity, sexuality, and intimate knowledges. Both love and hate, notes Sara Ahmed, are forms of intimacy: "Where there is hate there is obviously an *excessive need* for the object. In other words, hate is opposed to indifference: in hate, the object makes a difference, but cannot satisfy the subject, whose need goes beyond it."[78] This mode of attachment realigns hate not as love's opposite but, rather, as something much closer and intimate. "Hate then cannot be opposed to love," writes Ahmed, "the subject becomes attached to the other through hatred, as an attachment that returns the subject to itself."[79] In the very presence of hate that forms the *raison d'être* of the Legal and Constitutional Affairs Committee hearings, it is curious to hear from an opponent of the bill that she harbours "no hatred" towards the very groups that are seeking protection from hate speech. Instead, for her, hate makes its appearance circulating within and among the LGBT community: "I was constantly exposed to the intolerant, derogatory, aggressive and hostile language so commonly used by GLBT people in their GLBT subcultures."[80]

Hate is classically displaced onto the subjects of hate, turning them into the haters. As Stefanowicz asks:

> What are you protecting? ... a gay person may speak a hateful word toward another gay person because he is a nudist or he is a bear; they do not get along. They have their own dress code: one group is very casual and has big bellies, and the other is into leather or whatever it is. They will not go to the same meeting places. They will be in disagreement with each other. There are many subcultures under the GLBT label. It is so diverse.[81]

In this somewhat incoherent account, hateful speech is a product of sub-cultural difference and diversity within the LGBT community. Love, too, circulates in peculiar ways alongside hate. The witness' love for her father comes into conflict with his sexualized "love" for a community of supposed haters. That is, inside this affective matrix, vitalized by displacements and intimate attachments, "hate" circulates alongside "love"; painful and abusive memories sit alongside love for the father; resistance to a bill supporting sexual minorities from hate speech is proffered as love and protection for children; vitriol and hate are identified as being endemic to the father's love objects. Little seems to be as it seems.

Quoting from an editorial printed in the *Ottawa Citizen* on 22 September 2003, a witness from the Canada Family Action Coalition stated: "Will a devout Christian or Jew be able to denounce homosexuality as a sin, but someone who employs a scientific hypothesis in objecting to homosexuality be charged with promoting hatred?"[82] At the heart of his testimony was his concern that "there is already a chill being felt by those who dare express views on homosexual behaviours that are based on non-religious considerations."[83] His assertion is an interesting one in that it shifts the debate about the dangerousness of the bill from an attack on faith-based belief systems to an attack on rational, measured, and verifiable systems of knowledge production. Thus, according to his apprehensions, it is the truth of science that potentially comes under attack with the suppression of medicalized speech.

With respect to the doctor's testimony, he cited two examples whereby a physician was called before a professional disciplinary board for making public statements about "the homosexual lifestyle."[84] The first reference was to Dr. Grant Hill, a former Reform party member of parliament, who, according to this committee witness, "in 1996, during the debate on what was then Bill C-33 ... simply stated that the homosexual lifestyle was unhealthy," and for this statement, he was summoned to appear before the College of Physicians and Surgeons of Alberta.[85] According to the committee witness, the college's verdict described Hill's comment as being "factually correct"; however, I have not been able to verify or explore the account of this verdict. Following this statement of vindication, this committee witness continued his praise of Dr. Hill noting: "Indeed, he was correct. Actually, Dr. Hill put it mildly because homosexual disease is very – and I want to insist on the word very – unhealthy."[86] Before proceeding to the second example, I would like to note that, three days after Dr. Hill's statement to the House of Commons, the Canadian Medical Association responded stating "there is no scientific evidence to back such a claim."[87] Moreover, I would like to suggest that the linguistic shift made by our committee witness from "homosexual lifestyle" to "homosexual disease" demonstrates an intensification of anti-gay rhetoric and produces a syntagmatic relationship between "homosexuality" and "disease."

His second example of undue scrutiny and disciplinary action was a personalized example. "A few weeks ago, a complaint was lodged against me to the College of Physicians of Ontario because I had a [self-authored] brochure in my office called, *The Deadly Con Game*, which deals with the silent epidemic of sexually transmitted diseases," stated this committee witness.[88] Without offering further explanation of the brochure and its arguments or the charge levelled against him, he continued, declaring: "It does not deal with HIV/AIDS; it deals with herpes and with genital warts, which are true epidemics."[89] The odd utterance, "it does not deal with HIV/ AIDS," works as a kind of pre-emptive retort or defence to a charge of homophobic inference or AIDS baiting. However, despite this veiled defence against AIDS baiting, he then cited his own research in another example of a "homosexual disease." The witness claimed: "In 1997, I wrote a study which showed that the risk for a homosexual male to become infected with the HIV virus – take my word – was 1,000 times – not 1,000 per cent but 1,000 times, which is 100,000 per cent – higher than for a heterosexual person. You can laugh ... These are not anecdotes; they are facts."[90]

Stressing his concern about "homosexual behaviour" and the importance of free speech, he argued, "pretending that the risk for a heterosexual man for getting HIV is the same as it is for a homosexual man is *a lie* that is conveyed by our own medical association and by the medical establishment. That is a lie, as I say, and I am willing *to defend* that publicly against anyone: the risk is a thousand times."[91] The witness's appeal to a discourse of scientific truths through the use of statistics and medical research – at times self-authored – was further supported by appeals to cultural media:

> Another detail even more *alarming*: I read in *Time* magazine recently that homosexual men have become big users of Viagra. I do not need to explain to you what Viagra does. Apparently, it permits homosexual men – who are notoriously promiscuous to start with – to have even more encounters in a given unit of time, with the result – guess what – a high incidence of tuberculosis and syphilis among homosexual men.[92]

The witness's claims did not go uncontested by the Legal and Constitutional Affairs Committee, despite Senator Anne Cools's invitation to speak further about "rimming" and sado-masochistic activities.[93] Responding to the doctor's statistical claims, Senator Raynell Andreychuk reminded the committee that "the overwhelming information is that HIV is not a homosexual concern. In Africa, it is more prevalent in women. It is a heterosexual concern, a children's concern, an orphan's concern, and a worldwide concern. We should attack it as a medical issue ... I would hope that we would be cautious with our facts when we put them out."[94] Similarly, Senator Tommy Banks responded to the witness's claim that "there is one group, and only one group [that being gay men], which is not allowed to give blood" by using himself as an outlier:[95]

> When one is advancing scientific opinions, one must be careful that they are correct. You said, among other things, that there is only one group of persons who are not permitted to give blood and that is not true. I am not permitted to give blood for reasons other than the ones that you have put. We must be careful when we are putting scientific arguments. I am not permitted to give blood because I take medication for high blood pressure and so they do not want my blood.[96]

Senator John Lynch-Staunton was particularly frustrated by the doctor's claims and continually questioned the relationship between these claims and the purpose of the bill: "What does that have to do with the bill?" and "my objection to his statistics was not on the validity of them; it was on what they had to do with this bill. I am sure I could throw out statistics on how heterosexual relationships lead to certain diseases, too, but what has that got to do with this?"[97] Drawing attention to the concentrated focus of the doctor's testimony on high-risk sexual behaviour as an index of homosexual sexual activity and health risk, Lynch-Staunton remarked:

> I do not know what the medical consequences of sexual behaviour have to do with this discussion. I resent *the attack* on anyone's sexual behaviour ... To have one group with a certain sexual behaviour or tendency condemned so adamantly, viciously and terribly as we have heard today is mean-spirited and distracts from the purpose of this bill, which is to give protection – if that protection is needed – in an amendment to the *Criminal Code*.[98]

Read literally, the doctor worries about the suppression of scientific and medical "facts" that point to a looming health crisis, one that exists particularly in the figure of the "hyper-sexed homosexual." Additionally, beyond suppression and professional censure, he anxiously fears criminal prosecution in the execution of his professional medical duty to alert the public if Bill C-250 is passed. "All I want to say," he concluded, "is that it will be a sad day if a law is passed which will make physicians who have a responsibility for the well-being of the public hesitant or reluctant to tell the facts as they are."[99] However, the adamancy and strength of the witness' claims prompted Senator Lynch-Staunton to make the following statement: "I am trying to put myself in your mind, with all due respect, and ask where the strong feeling comes from?"[100]

I will not speculate about the doctor or his need to defend himself from the "lies" conveyed by the medical establishment, nor on the doctor's worry over criminal prosecution for the free expression of his professional judgment under Bill C-250, nor on the doctor's "strong feelings" with respect to the diseased and perverse figure of the "promiscuous homosexual." However, I would like to summarize Sigmund Freud's theory of paranoia and note the way in which, according to Freud, persecutory paranoia appears to take the spectre of homosexuality as its object.

In "Psychoanalytic Notes on an Autobiographical Account of a Case of Paranoia," Freud theorizes paranoia as a psychic defence mechanism structured upon inversions of affect and syntactical displacements.[101] In this famous case of paranoia, Freud structures his theory upon the memoirs of Daniel Paul Schreber. In Freud's reading of Schreber's memoirs, he takes note of the grandiose, morbid, and emasculating qualities of Schreber's delusional beliefs. Schreber's persecutory delusions included the delusional belief that he was being poisoned by Geheimrat Flechsig, his doctor, that "his body was being handled in all kinds of revolting ways," contrary to the order of things, that his "body [was being] used like a strumpet" by God, that voices mocked his transformative sexual disgrace by calling him "'Miss Schreber,'" and that "he was dead and decomposing."[102] According to Freud, Schreber's intolerable wish of emasculation (*Entmannung*), as Freud describes it, is necessarily turned, by the masculine identified ego, into delusions of persecution, taking as its form the fear of sexual defilement, bodily and moral corruption, and death. Freud also remarks that Schreber remembers a dream in which he reveals that "it really must be very nice to be a woman submitting to the act of copulation."[103] Described by Freud in terms of the unbearable homosexual wish, this pleasurable revelation, which was revealed in a dream, is necessarily transformed by the force of repression into the mocking voices who call out "Miss Schreber" and jeer "this person who lets himself be f——d! [*sic*]."[104]

Speaking generally about the mechanism of paranoia, Freud writes: "What was characteristically paranoic about the illness was the fact that the patient, as a means of warding off a homosexual wishful phantasy, reacted precisely with delusions of persecution of this kind."[105] Noting an observational commonality of paranoiacs shared by his psychoanalytic contemporaries, Carl Jung and Sándor Ferenczi, he remarks: "We were astonished to find that in all these cases a defence against a homosexual wish was clearly recognizable at the very centre of the conflict which underlay the disease, and that it was in an attempt to master an unconsciously reinforced current of homosexuality that they had all of them come to grief."[106] "It is a remarkable fact that the familiar principal forms of paranoia," Freud states, "can all be represented as contradictions of the single proposition: 'I (a man) love him (a man).'"[107]

With respect to delusions of persecution, Freud writes that the contradictions "loudly assert: 'I do not love him – I hate him.'"[108] This is the unconscious formation that "cannot, however, become conscious to a paranoic in this form" and reveals itself by way on affective inversion: love turns into hate.[109] Moreover, Freud notes that "the mechanism of symptom-formation in paranoia requires the internal perceptions – feelings – shall be replaced by external perceptions. Consequently, the proposition 'I hate him' becomes transformed by projection into another one: 'He hates (persecutes) me, which will justify me in hating him.'"[110] Thus, Freud argues that the unconscious wish of the paranoiac – almost always a homosexual wish – is truly unbearable and can only seek expression in an inverted and negated form. This form takes expression in the complex syntactical displacement mapped out by Freud as "I do not love him – I hate him, because HE PERSECUTES ME."[111]

Whether the witnesses before the Legal and Constitutional Affairs Committee can be said to be truly paranoid in the Freudian sense or merely paranoid in a more vernacular sense – as a simple apprehension – it is significant that such an offensive was launched against Bill C-250. One cannot deny that this offensive took the position of being under attack and expressed itself through fear and anxiety: "We prayed that we would be defended against the attack that is waged through Bill C-250."[112] One also cannot deny that the concerns raised by the objectors appeared hyperbolic in the face of the evidence used to counter their fears: the built-in defences of the statute, the need for the consent of the attorney general in various sections of the law, the high threshold set by *Keegstra* in order to prove the elements of the case beyond a reasonable doubt, and so on. It is also interesting how the oppositional witness testimonies constituted themselves as victims of hate subject to harassment by gay and lesbian groups and to a legal violence deemed illegitimate.

Conclusion

This chapter illustrates the questionable positioning of Christian and social conservatives of victims of a repressive "hate crime" law that, according to them, protected the interests of an illegitimate, yet powerful, faction of civil society. In essence, this is one more example of the replication of the queer citizen as undeserving of the protection of law. In this case, the arguments voiced in opposition to Bill C-250 turn victimization on its head. In this topsy-turvy reality of radical conservatism, social conservatives are inversely transformed into victims of a hateful "gay agenda," "activist courts," and an oppressive government regime bent on their destruction.

The chapter notes the ways in which the debate over hate crime and hate speech law has shifted from debates that focused on democratic liberty and on legal protections for Jewish Canadians and racial minorities to debates that pitted protections for sexual and gender minorities against conservative values and religious rights. The following chapter will closely examine, in particular, the debates surrounding the opposition to the amendment that sought to include "gender identity and gender expression" to the existing list of identifiable groups in the hate propaganda statutes. These debates emphasize the trepidation and anxiety expressed by conservative groups over the inclusion of hate speech and federal human rights protections for transgendered Canadians. These oppositional concerns raised scenarios of rape in public washrooms by men guised in women's clothing and the need for government to withstand the amendment in order to protect women's sexual security.

4

The Trans "Bathroom Bill"

The bill does a small thing by adding trans rights to the *Canadian Human Rights Act* and by adding trans motivated hate to the hate crimes list. It is a small thing, but it is a magnificent thing.

– Megan Leslie, House of Commons debates, 7 March 2013

On 15 May 2009, New Democratic Party (NDP) Member of Parliament (MP) Bill Siksay introduced Bill C-389, *An Act to Amend the Canadian Human Rights Act (CHRA) and the Criminal Code* that sought to add the terms "gender identity" and "gender expression" to the *CHRA*'s prohibited grounds of discrimination and to the *Criminal Code*'s enumerated protected groups under the hate propaganda statutes and the enhanced sentencing provision.[1] The bill, the first to suggest these amendments jointly to the *CHRA* and the *Criminal Code*, married the issues of dignity and legal protection of transgendered Canadians to the issues of discrimination and hate-motivated violence and speech.[2] As with the political debates that grappled with the addition of "sexual orientation" to the enhanced sentencing provision and to the hate propaganda statutes, the opposition came primarily from conservative members of the House of Commons and Senate who took up both seemingly sound and bizarrely polemical arguments against the bill. Despite such opposition, this private member's bill would pass third reading in the House of Commons without amendment. However, it died on the order paper in the Senate when an election was called in 2011, abruptly ending what seemed a legislative "first." Revived a year later in the first session of the forty-first Parliament by NDP MP Randall Garrison as Bill C-279, it encountered similar resistance with opponents challenging the notion of the need for such legislation, objecting to what was characterized as the ambiguous and undefined language of the bill and raising scenarios of exploitation and abuse of the protections offered under the new law. As a matter of political expediency in the hope of shoring up a few more needed Conservative party votes,[3] Garrison removed the term "gender expression" from the draft and offered an internationally accepted legal definition to the term "gender identity." With these significant changes to the wording of the bill, it passed in the House of Commons, only to be interrupted at the third reading of the Senate for the summer recess of 2013.[4]

This chapter, in coming to a end of its analysis of the legislative debates and affective language of political argumentation surrounding key pieces of federal legislation on hate propaganda and hate-motivated violence, examines the legislative arguments for and against the addition of "gender identity" and "gender expression" to the *CHRA* and the *Criminal Code*'s hate provisions. The pairing of anti-hate speech and enhanced sentencing protections for transgendered Canadians with federal anti-discrimination law strategically aligned affective notions of hate and humanness with that of citizenship and legal community. It was a strategy that was actively used by supporters in order to frame the bill as fitting in with Canada's legal, political, and moral response to discrimination and violence directed at minority citizens. For example, in a rhetorical strategy designed to link Bill C-389 to other historical instances of minority political and legal struggle, Siksay noted that the introduction of the bill fell two days before the International Day against Homophobia and Transphobia and one day after the fortieth anniversary of the decriminalization of homosexuality.[5]

Similarly to the reading of Bill C-279 for the second time in the House of Commons, Liberal MP Irwin Cotler signalled the significance of the debate by meshing its occurrence with that of the thirtieth anniversary of the *Canadian Charter of Rights and Freedoms*.[6] The syntagmatic and temporal association of these historic events, that reshaped Canada's legal and moral terrain, to a piece of legislation that would, as Garrison characterized, "help complete … Canada's human rights project," had the symbolic effect of parceling trans rights and legal protections with that of international and national political struggles and human rights agendas.[7]

Insofar as proponents of the legislation actively spoke to the issue of human rights and human dignity and, more broadly, to the issue of humanness itself, framing these proposed inclusions as fundamental elements to the surety of Canada's progressively developing moral character, opponents used two distinct, but related, strategies in order to reframe the issue of rights and legal protections so as to position humanness outside of the transgendered experience. Betraying no affective reaction to the rights and dignity of transgendered Canadians, one rhetorical strategy appealed to the rigorous principles of good law-making. It was the responsibility of lawmakers, it was argued, to make sound and unambiguous legislation that would clearly represent the intention of Parliament and that could be read and understood plainly. Taking what appeared to be a wholly legitimate stance against the proposed legislation, critics and opponents claimed that the proposed bill was unnecessary and redundant and that the language of the proposed legislation, particularly with respect to the term "gender expression," was overly broad and undefined and thus subject to legal ambiguity.

The second main argument against the bill played on irrational fears of sexual threat and reconfigured the issue of legal protection in such a way as to recast the transgendered as "something" from which to be protected. Playing to the polemical and the hyperbolic, Conservative party members raised the spectre that such amendments would incur the criminal abuse of the law, allowing men dressed up as women to violate with impunity unsuspecting women and girls in public washrooms. Highly affective, this fantastic scenario of violation and sexual threat operated on multiple levels, invoking transgender expression as subterfuge and anxiety-provoking ambiguity and using the site of the public bathroom as an arena of in-between-ness where states of distinction – male/female, public/private, clean/dirty – were highlighted as precarious and easily violated. Despite the rhetorical differences of these strategies of opposition, this chapter reads them together in order to comprehend the subtle ways in which objectors used the trope of ambiguity as an affective index of otherness and the abject.

As in other chapters, the confluence and abuttedness of such diverse opinions index a point of entry into these debates that shift their analysis from one of strict legal interpretation and literal meaning to one of affective analysis. The contestation over legal protections and rights, the vexatious framing of ambiguity as threat, and the appeal to a "politics of trans dehumanization," as Kendall Thomas has coined it, demonstrate the ways in which the inclusion of "gender identity" and "gender expression" to the *CHRA* and the hate crime statutes of the *Criminal Code* signal the place of transgendered Canadians under law.[8]

Making (In)Human

Despite Bills C-389 and C-279 being acts that originally and jointly sought the addition of "gender identity" and "gender expression" to both the *CHRA* and the *Criminal Code*'s hate crime provisions, the parliamentary debate was overwhelmingly focused on the issues of anti-discrimination and human rights. Little discussion was given to the addition of these terms to the hate propaganda statutes and the enhanced sentencing provision. When raised, the issue of hate and hate-motivated violence operated as an outcome of discrimination and as evidence of the need for human rights protections. Insofar as the majority of the parliamentary debate was on the issues of anti-discrimination and human rights, this chapter reads this interest as the contestation of humanness itself for transgendered Canadians. To proponents, the legislative presence of these terms would have the effect of constitutively and symbolically writing in the transgendered as fully protected Canadian citizens. "Including trans people explicitly in human rights legislation can have a profound effect," observed Siksay, "a trans person makes the point this way, saying, 'How can I feel part of society if I cannot point to human rights legislation and say, there, I'm included'?"[9]

Since the effect of being written into law, which was a federal legislative first, was one of making human, of making citizen, the marked absence of such legal indelibleness had the effect of making inhuman. As Kendall Thomas notes of the human rights struggles faced by trans activists, "trans activists must contend with a social order and a legal regime of 'infrahumanity' under which transgendered people are viewed as 'non-persons, with no right to marry, to work, to use a public bathroom, or even to walk down the street in safety.'"[10] The place of transgendered citizens under Canadian human rights law – that is, their presence under law – was a critical issue of debate and one that would underscore the very issue of humanness of the transgendered.

To proponents, the acknowledgment of transgendered persons' absence under the protection of law was the first prong in a two-pronged strategy for inclusion: one prong indexing absence and the other strategic prong constituting presence. Noting the way in which he himself had to give voice to a silenced and most often invisible constituency, Siksay noted his authorship of the private member's bill as proxy by bringing to Parliament's attention that "at this time there [was] no openly trans member of Parliament."[11] Throughout the debates, covering the time span of nearly four years, the issue of absence, in terms of both invisibility and erasure, was used as a sign of the necessity for the legislation. MP Irwin Cotler, a passionate supporter of human rights, drew on an observation made by Justice Gérard La Forest who wrote that gender identity must be included as a protected ground in the *CHRA* because "to leave the law as it stands would fail to acknowledge the situation of transgendered individuals and allow the issues to remain invisible."[12]

As a witness before the Standing Senate Committee on Human Rights, Noa Mendelsohn Aviv, director of the Equality Program for the Canadian Civil Liberties Association, remarked that the issue of visibility is paramount to a deeper understanding around the necessity of the bill. Linking the legal absence of women, people of colour, and gays and lesbians to historical struggles of legal recognition, inclusion, and protection, she noted that these groups "were simply not seen as the people who received those fundamental rights of democracy or equality."[13] Similarly, Senate committee witness Robert Peterson of the Canadian Bar Association stated: "This is an opportunity for Parliament to make a very clear statement about the invisibility of transgender people. Having gender identity contained explicitly within this legislation allows for better access to justice; people can look at the legislation and understand clearly that these protections exist."[14] Without these explicit protections, as a textual and legal presence in both the *CHRA* and *Criminal Code*, advocates of the legislation argued that discrimination and violence allowed to continue without legal redress against the transgendered. As noted by trans legal theorist, Richard Juang, "despite its unquantifiability, [legal and civic] recognition's importance can be measured by the consequences of its absence: an unvalued person readily becomes a target or a scapegoat for the hatred of others and begins to see him or herself only through the lens of such hatred."[15]

To transgender theorists and activists, (in)visibility represents a conundrum of political and social ontology. Theorized as a double bind, the visibility of the transgendered body as a social, political, and ontological presence may bring with it recognition, validation, and acceptance: a kind of Levinasian knowledge of difference without the violence of radical alterity. However, with specular knowledge of difference comes the ethical response of the subject and if that is lacking, then the violence of a reading of radical alterity presents itself as a possibility. In her study of hate crime, Barbara Perry notes the way in which violence is triggered through the labelling of radical alterity.[16] She and other hate crime scholars write that to perpetrators of hate-motivated violence, boundaries of distinction, particularly those (artificially) constructed around race and gender, need to be maintained.[17] Transgression of these boundaries, often "discovered" by specularity, activates an affective response in the perpetrator that may lead to violence. Testifying before the House of Commons Standing Committee on Justice and Human Rights (Justice and Human Rights Committee), Hershel Russell, psychotherapist and trans activist and educator, recounted the anxiety that he felt during his transition: "Suddenly I'm this spectacle ... I faced a small but very real threat of physical and/or sexual assault ... we punish people who look gender ambiguous in this current society."[18]

Condemning the use of a transpanic provocation defence in the brutal homicide of Gwen Araujo, Kendall Thomas notes that the argument of provocation is similarly predicated upon the so-called "trauma triggered by [the perpetrators'] sudden discovery" that the victim, a transgender woman, was in fact biologically male.[19] With respect to the knowledge of radical alterity, Perry notes the way in which violence itself is a marker of distinction whereby the perpetrator asserts through the violent act that he is not the other.[20] The signifier of violence then both responds to the presence of difference – known through the eyes of the perpetrator as a threatening, radical alterity – and reinforces difference by distinguishing the hegemonic subject from the transgressive other. "Hate crime in particular," remarked Ryan Dyck, director of policy and public education for Equality for Gays and Lesbians Everywhere (EGALE), "is in part a result of us as a society believing, or not challenging, the notion that some people are less human than others."[21] Insofar as violence has been theorized as a response to the presence of difference, in some cases, as noted by Kevin Berrill and Gregory Herek and Herek, Roy Gillis, and Jeanine Cogan, excessive violence – to which trans people are most often subject – is an attempt to eradicate the transgressor, rendering him or her erased – that is, without presence and markedly absent.[22]

So if hatred, dehumanization, and violence are affects of noting radical alterity, the invisible transgender body escapes notice, bringing to the fore, once again, the double bind of (in)visibility. As noted, one experience of invisibility may be through the radical, often violent, erasure by the transphobic subject. In another experience of invisibility, the unnoticed flies under the radar of the anxiously surveillant. The unnoticed blends in, is not distinguished, and passes. Although this passing may be a means to escape scrutiny and violence, it nevertheless conforms to a "hegemonic cultural imaginary" in which gender identity and gender expression conform to prescribed parameters of "appropriate" behaviour, manner, speech, dress, and other signifiers of gender, race, class, and sexual orientation.[23] Thus, in itself, passing is a kind of erasure of difference. The erasure of "a wide, wide spectrum" of genders may be understood in itself as a kind of radical violence of the human condition.[24] Insofar as passing conforms to a hegemonic cultural imaginary, Elaine Ginsberg points out nonetheless that passing "forces reconsideration of the cultural logic that the physical body is the site of identic intelligibility."[25] Passing challenges, she notes, "the essentialism that is often the foundation of identity politics, a challenge that may be seen as either threatening or liberating but in either instance discloses the truth that identities are not singularly true or false but multiple and contingent."[26]

To many advocates of trans rights, transphobic violence represents an extreme, yet salient, sign of transgender invisibility, exclusion, and radical erasure. In his address to the Justice and Human Rights Committee,

Garrison led his discussion of the bill by noting that the date of the first day of witness testimony fell on the Trans Day of Remembrance, an internationally recognized day of memorializing and mourning transgendered and transsexual people who were homicide victims of transphobic violence.[27] Naming the discrimination and violence suffered by trans people as a "cycle of erasure," Greta Bauer, who was a witness before the Senate Standing Committee on Human Rights, gave evidence to the tragic causal effects of the lack of policy in employment and health care services, citing exceedingly high rates of unemployment and poverty and disproportionately high rates of depression and suicidality.[28]

Siksay similarly cited a number of studies, including EGALE's national school survey and the Trans PULSE study in Ontario, that documented high rates of violence and bullying in schools for trans youth, gross rates of workplace discrimination, inadequate and ineffective health care services for trans patients, and the most extreme acts of hate crime violence as evidence of profound social exclusion and the need for policy inclusion. Speaking to the outrage felt about the lack of protections and rights for trans Canadians, Liberal MP Mario Silva stated: "There is ample evidence, both statistically and anecdotal [sic], that confirms that transgender and transsexual Canadians experience disproportionate discrimination and even violence based on who they are and how they choose to live their lives. This is unacceptable."[29] Turning to the trope of visibility in her witness testimony, Bauer concluded that "greater visibility in this policy reinforces more knowledge about trans people, which will feed back into continued development, policy refinement, policy and greater protection. All of this supports the inclusion of trans people in employment, services and more broadly and more fully in Canadian society."[30]

Paired with the arguments, evidence, and testimony of invisibility, erasure and absence were powerful examples of the vital presence of trans people. In describing the need for Bill C-389, Siksay offered the House of Commons a narrative that highlighted the vitality and social and political engagement of trans people, including that of their seminal place in gay liberation struggles. Countering a sense of invisibility, Siksay noted that "trans people have always been part of our communities and are known across most cultures."[31] Most poignantly, it was the testimony of self-identified trans activists before the two committees who shifted the narrative of trans experience from one of loss, invisibility, discrimination, and violence to one of vitality, belonging, and fortitude. Sara Buechner and Hershel Russell offered their testimony based on their respective "lived experience."[32] Their personal and anecdotal stories of being a transgendered person in a world that subjected them to discrimination, humiliation, ridicule, and violence and that offered them little compassion, understanding, dignity, kindness, and equity were powerful reminders to committee members that discrimination and violence have attempted to eradicate the basic humanness from transgendered lives. "I'm happy to explain my own story to help people understand who trans people are," commented committee witness Sara Buencher, "we are just, as they say in music, the variations on the theme – the human theme."[33] Speaking to her transitioning, Buechner described a life before her transition in which she enjoyed the fruits of her talent and hard work as a classical pianist compared to a life of discrimination, loss, struggle, and survival after her transition, in which her world-class standing as a pianist was stripped from her, her ethical behaviour around students was questioned, she faced severe under-employment, and was subject to public harassment and sexual assault. She spoke of a childhood during which she was ridiculed and attacked for expressing gender variance in her choice of clothing and where no protections were given to her at school; rather, it was she who was reprimanded by the school for coming to school in girls' clothing.

Similarly, Russell, a psychotherapist specializing in transgender health, described his life as a transgendered man in which crossing international borders was a humiliating and often harrowing experience. "Once upon a time," Russell began, "I looked pretty convincingly like a woman. However, there was a period in between."[34] With that, Russell spoke of his transitioning and the discrimination and violence to which he was subject. Remarking on the way in which trans people are continuously subject to scrutiny, he recounted his worrisome and debasing experience on one occasion of crossing into the United States for a clinical conference and being subject to the body scanner multiple times by a tittering group of airport security officers. Anecdotally, he cited the Trans PULSE data on hate-motivated violence and on housing and employment discrimination and their corollary effects on mental health and suicidality, noting the "symbolic importance" of the government of Canada in voicing support for human rights for transgendered Canadians.[35]

Significantly, these stories of discrimination and suffering were matched beside stories – personal and anecdotal – of fortitude, self-realization, and successful contribution to the national community. For example, Buechner told the committees of her hiring at the University of British Columbia after failing to secure employment in her native United States and of her loving marriage to a Canadian man, and Russell indirectly spoke of his vital contribution not only to the trans community, but also to the larger community, as a prominent psychotherapist. In a statement that acknowledged the discrimination experienced by trans Canadians and the contribution that they make to Canadian society, Siksay appealed to Parliament stating: "That is why, plain and simple, we need this legislation. We must be absolutely and explicitly clear that trans Canadians are a valued part of our families and our communities."[36]

Redundant Protections

Countering claims and evidence that trans Canadians are not protected legally from discrimination and that explicit inclusion under the *CHRA* was necessary, objectors to the legislation argued that trans people were already protected and that explicit enumeration would be redundant. Raising the issue before the House of Commons, Sylvie Boucher, parliamentary secretary for the status of women, cautioned members, arguing that they "should think about whether adding 'gender identity' and 'gender expression' to the *Canadian Human Rights Act* [under Bill C-389] is really necessary."[37] Appealing to the principles of good law-making, opponents to the bill raised the issue of redundancy, citing several Canadian Human Rights Tribunal (CHRT) cases in which trans complainants received successful outcomes in their adjudication. In his examination of witnesses before the Justice and Human Rights Committee, Conservative party member Brent Rathgeber, raising the issue of gender dysphoria, remarked that in 2009 the CHRT said, in *Montreuil v Canadian Human Rights Commission and Canadian Forces* that "there's no longer any doubt that discrimination based on transsexualism is discrimination based on 'sex' or 'gender,' as well as discrimination based on 'disability.'"[38] Citing the 2001 CHRT ruling in *Kavanagh v Attorney General Canada (Correctional Services of Canada)*, he noted that the tribunal recognized in this case that discrimination on the basis of transsexualism constitutes "sex" discrimination as well as "disability" discrimination.[39]

Charging that proponents of Bill C-389 "played down the fact that transsexuals are already protected against discrimination based on 'sex' under the *Canada Human Rights Act*," Daniel Petit, parliamentary secretary to the Minister of Justice stressed that there was no need for such legislation and that to amend the *CHRA* and the *Criminal Code* by adding these two terms would bring redundancy and potential confusion to the law.[40] The introduction of the issue of "confusion" shifted the parameters of the political rhetoric from that of a rational objection to the necessity of duplication to that of an affective state of mind connoting anxiety, perturbation, and distress. Echoing the certainty of Rathgeber's contention that the *CHRA* protected trans people from discrimination, Conservative member Robert Goguen queried: "Do we completely *muddy the waters* with regard to what is otherwise a consistent ruling that there is no longer any doubt that in the issue of transgender, it's discrimination based on 'sex' and 'disability'?"[41] With respect to the metaphor of "mudding the waters," it is significant to note how the certainty of precedent and the consistency of federal jurisprudence double for something clear, consistent, and well defined. Whereas the proposed introduction of these terms, according to oppositional members, would serve only to obfuscate the law and to bring about a kind of legal muddiness and state of ambiguity.

Responding directly to the affective rhetorical strategy of muddiness and confusion, advocates of the proposed legislation remarked again and again how the introduction of the explicit terms "gender identity" and "gender expression" would remove any ambiguity about whether all trans people were protected under the *CHRA* and, by extension, under the hate crime statutes of the *Criminal Code*. Countering these comments and questions of committee members that claimed that transgender Canadians were protected under federal anti-discrimination law, Ian Fine, acting secretary general to the Canadian Human Rights Commission, stated that "parties still debate that issue before those very tribunals and courts and question whether or not transgender issues fall under 'sex' ... so for clarity reasons, we believe it would be a good thing to add these two grounds."[42] Resisting the inclination to lump transgender issues of discrimination under the protected category of "sex," Bloc Quebecois member Meili Faille shifted the terms of debate by suggesting that ambiguity lay not within the terms "gender identity" and "gender expression" but, rather, within the term "sex" for transgendered people: "It will no longer be necessary to refer to ambiguous interpretations of the term 'sex' to establish that all transgender people are protected by the law."[43]

Moreover, looking closely at the CHRT case examples provided by the objectors to the bill, the issue of confusion is embedded in their claims. It would be remiss not to point out that Rathgeber inaccurately identified "gender" as a ground of discrimination under the *CHRA*. Under the *CHRA*, the prohibited grounds of discrimination are race, national or ethnic origin, colour, religion, age, sex, sexual orientation, marital status, family status, disability, and conviction for an offence for which a pardon has been granted or in respect of which a record suspension has been ordered.[44] In that there is no explicit reference to "gender" under the *CHRA*, Rathgeber may have mistakenly confused the term "gender" for an equivalence with "sex," an anatomical distinction. However, as Irwin Cotler pointed out, "gender identity and gender expression do not refer to biological sex or sexual orientation. Rather, the terms refer to an inner feeling of being male, female, both or neither."[45]

Moreover, the Conservatives' unquestioning paradigmatic alignment of transsexuals and the transgendered problematically blends these identities and expressions of self. In an attempt to distinguish and contextualize the two terms, Paisley Currah remarks that the "diagnostic category" of transsexual has been critiqued by trans activist Sandy Stone as "an attempt by the 'body police' to homogenize "a vast heteroglossic account of difference,'" whereas transgender is an empowering "grassroots term ... crafted to resist the imposition of labels created by the psychiatric establishment to define and contain cross-gender identities and behaviors."[46] Responding to the labelling of gender identity as a disability, Senator Grant Mitchell admonished his honourable colleagues, stressing that "gender identity is not a disability. It is what someone simply is. It is who they are. The only thing that remotely 'disables' trans people is the discrimination, violence and bullying that inhibits them from having full, safe and fulfilling lives in Canadian society."[47] Addressing the problem of using a strategy that invokes "disability" or "sex" as a means to fight discrimination against trans

Canadians, Siksay stated: "Accessing these protections through a convoluted process using other possibly related categories, usually the categories of sex and disability, diminishes the protection and limits our understanding of the causes and effects of the particular discrimination."[48]

Ambiguity

"This bill continues to add more uncertainty and vagueness by using terms that are not commonly known and not clearly defined in the bill, providing more ambiguity to this poorly thought-out proposed legislation," argued Senator Don Meredith, "the Canadian courts have already recognized that discrimination against transsexuals is a form of sex discrimination. This bill will simply muddy the definitions of 'transsexualism,' weakening the laws that are in place."[49] As Meredith's statement makes clear, conservative objectors to the bill drew heavily on tropes of vagueness, uncertainty, and ambiguity to stress the ways in which the proposed legislation did not fit with good law-making practice.

From the initial introduction of Bill C-389 to the final Senate debates of Bill C-279, detractors rationally appealed to the good sense of concise and clear legislative language. Conservative MPs Kerry-Lynne Findlay, Brent Rathgeber, and Daniel Petit, for example, criticized the language of the proposed legislation as being "vague" or "undefined" on a number of occasions. Early on in the debates surrounding Bill C-389, Petit claimed that "the amendments proposed by Bill C-389 are vague and undefined."[50] Objecting directly to the terms "gender identity" and "gender expression" as being, in her words, "neither commonly understood nor defined," Findlay voiced particular concern with "the unclear term 'gender expression.'"[51] Responding to the way in which the proposed legislation was being characterized as being vague and ambiguous, Ryan Dyck, from EGALE, deliberately shifted the subject of ambiguity onto the state of the current law under which trans Canadians were offered no legal protections under the *CHRA* and the *Criminal Code*'s hate crime provisions. Speaking before the Justice and Human Rights Committee, Dyck argued: "I would argue that the current law is actually the law that is ambiguous and vague, because it is not in practice providing protection or recourse to our trans Canadians. More than being symbolic, this will make a real difference in the lives of our trans people and our trans communities across this country."[52]

The issue of definitional ambiguity tended to focus most sharply on the term "gender expression," with critics expressing unease about the potential for legal confusion with what was argued to be an overly broad and undefined term. Interestingly, with respect to law's unease with the term "gender expression," Currah notes the way in which American courts have responded to discrimination cases involving both issues of gender identity and gender expression: "The courts most often seemed to rely on 'seemingly fixed categories such as transgender or gender identity' rather than on 'concepts less anchored to identity categories, such as gender expression.'"[53] To Currah, as a means of garnering a few more crucial votes from the Conservatives, in the final draft of Bill C-279, the term "gender expression" was dropped and "gender identity" was formally defined based closely on the wording of the Yogyakarta Principles on the Application of International Human Rights Law in Relation to Sexual Orientation and Gender Identity, which were developed by the International Committee of Jurists and the International Service for Human Rights.[54] The newly amended draft of Bill C-279 thus included a definition of "gender identity": "In respect of an individual, the individual's deeply felt internal and individual experience of gender, which may or may not correspond with the sex that the individual was assigned at birth."[55] Despite this concession of removing "gender expression" from the proposed legislation and providing an internationally recognized and respected legal definition for "gender identity," a number of critics could not be satisfied.

Not surprisingly, REAL Women took objection to the proposed legislation suggesting that it would create "harm" for transgendered Canadians. Diane Watts, researcher for REAL Women, testifying before the Justice and Human Rights Committee claimed: "The consequences of the bill will be harmful to transgendered individuals themselves."[56] Specifically referencing the adoption of the Yogyakarta Principles, she remarked that "the Yogyakarta Principles, the source of the gender identity definition for Bill C-279, are vague and overbroad and can be interpreted to interfere with the rights of parents to provide gender-confused children with professional treatment."[57] According to the principle of harm conceptualized by REAL Women, harm would come about in a number of ways if the legislation were passed. First, by following the Yogyakarta Principles, parental rights would be in jeopardy by an overly zealous radicalized state. Second, REAL

Women believed that the apparent innateness of biology should be respected without medical or surgical intervention, particularly any medical treatment that was paid by "taxpayers." Appealing to an essentialist notion of a gendered self that was tied to a biological imperative, they argued that "persons with gender identity disorder should receive compassionate counselling rather than be encouraged in their dissatisfaction with the gender engrained in their DNA."[58]

Responding wryly to the general concerns expressed by REAL Women that this bill should not be supported because it would ultimately wreak havoc on Canadian society, NDP MP Françoise Boivin remarked: "I almost got a feeling of déjà vu with Ms. Watts. I do not think that anyone else was here at the meetings of the special committee on same-sex marriage, but I had the great pleasure to be part of that committee in 2005. I heard those kinds of remarks a lot."[59] Similarly, Senator Donald Plett, looking to Australian jurisprudence, was outraged by the broadly defined and inclusive understanding of "gender identity" listed by the Australian Human Rights Commission. Scoffing, he noted: "this list includes but is not limited to transgender, transsexual, intersex, androgynous, agendered, cross dresser, drag kind, gender fluid, gender queer, intergender, neutrois, pansexual, pan-gendered, third gender and third sex."[60] Bringing his objections back to Bill C-279, he stated: "The language in this bill is so vague that it begs the question: where do we draw the line?" Senator Plett's outrage, mockery, and dismissal of the human complexity of gender identity and gender expression heeds Thomas's critical observation that "the transgender rights movement thus faces the daunting challenge of raising the question of human rights under conditions in which the simple humanity of transgender publics is continually being called into question."[61]

Abjection and the "Bathroom Bill"

So in the context of this debate, which has at times been a vigorous debate and at times a debate with moments unworthy of this House, there are some who, contrary to evidence and facts, choose another path to make their case. They choose fear and innuendo, all the while claiming a moral high ground. They claim for themselves exclusivity to that which is right and decent, using language that is hurtful and demeaning. How can anyone claim to be of good heart or claim the virtue of "love thy neighbour" yet reduce this bill to gutter language when they call it "the bathroom bill"?

– Sean Casey, Member of Parliament, 27 February 2013

The most polemical objection to the proposed legislation took the form of an odd fear-mongering argument, one that was propagated by social conservatives and endorsed by Conservative party MP Rob Anders. As circulated in Ander's warning to constituents, the petition claimed that if "gender identity" and "gender expression" were added to the CHRA and to hate crime protections under the *Criminal Code*, men would be at legal liberty to disguise themselves in women's clothing and enter women's public washrooms where they would sexually assault women and girls: "[The bill's] goal is to give transgender me access to women's public washroom facilities."[62] "It is the duty of the House of Commons," argued Anders, "to protect and safeguard our children from any exposure and harm that would come from giving a man access to women's public washroom facilities."[63] The complete petition is reproduced exactly as it appeared:

PETITION TO THE HOUSE OF COMMONS
We, the undersigned, citizens of Canada, draw the attention of the House of Commons to the following:

That Bill C-279, also known as the "Bathroom Bill," is a Private Members Bill sponsored by B.C. NDP MP Randall Garrison and its goal is to give transgendered men access to women's public washroom facilities.

And that it is the duty of the House of Commons to protect and safeguard our children from an exposure and harm that will come from giving a man access to women's public washroom facilities.

Therefore your petitioners call upon the House of Commons to vote Nay on the "Bathroom Bill."

The extremity and illogicality of such an imaginative scenario is striking on a number of levels, not the least of which is the invocation of the public bathroom as a site of extreme threat. In a most profound way, the trope of ambiguity culminates most vividly in this scenario and indexes a number of fears and ideologies that reproduce trans people as less than human and as a threat to political and social stability.

If we look closely at what has been dubbed the bathroom prowler argument, there are three distinct sites or aspects of threat that are embedded in this scenario. The most obvious is that of the threat of sexual assault. What compounds this sexual threat is that it is directed at both adult women and female children – that is, little girls. As argued by Meredith, "Bill C-279 will not improve the lives of Canadians. It will confuse lawmakers and enforcers and place fear in the hearts of parents and grandparents who worry about the safety of their children."[64] By coding this threat as pedophilic, it is compounded in such a way that it is not simply a double threat. Rather, threat takes on a tenor of the disgusting, and it is this aspect of vile threat that situates it not only in the political and social world but also in the affective world as well, producing a disdain that evokes political disgust and moral revulsion.

The distaste and revulsion at such a scenario conjures up both Julia Kristeva's theory of the abject and Martha Nussbaum's discussion of the politics of disgust.[65] Deferring engagement with Kristeva's theory of the abject for the moment, Nussbaum's attribution of the Christian Right's rhetorical strategy of disgust in their political fight against gay and lesbian rights is particularly suggestive. It is a strategy that invokes deep visceral response to the political other in order to cast this other into the space of the abject, the untouchable, the disgusting, the inhuman. Highly affective and not able to withstand rational scrutiny, the politics of disgust is built upon a structure of projection in that "its tendency [is] to impute to others properties that are present but not confronted in the self."[66] Animality, baseness, mortality, and bodily decay are aspects of the self that seem unbearable, feared, loathsome, and reviled. Returning to Anders petition and the mechanism of the politics of disgust, the moral outrage and disgust directed at trans women, whom he misidentifies in his petition as transgendered men, is legitimated by the transphobic constituting of trans women as pedophilic "perverts." To the transphobic imagination, perversion is indexed by a number of behaviours: "cross-dressing," exhibitionism, voyeurism, and pedophilia. In the bathroom prowler scenario, exhibitionism and child molestation are the immediate threats.

However, a more sublime threat to the transphobic subject is revealed through this fantastic and offensive scenario: the mutability and indeterminacy of the sexed and gendered body. Insofar as the trans body is a sign of mutability and indeterminacy, it challenges and destabilizes heteronormative and cisgender-normative fantasies of the (supposedly) fixed and stable ontological categories of male and female and masculine and feminine. Such corporeal and ontological mutability and indeterminacy is an unbearable thought to the transphobic subject. Unable to accept such a possibility for the self, the transphobic subject rejects the ideation and projects the affect of disgust and fear onto the reviled other. Through these psychic mechanisms of displacement and projection, these highly affective emotions cast the transgender other as unassimilable, outcast, and abject. Once constituted as abject and outcast, the trans other is rendered outside of the protections of civil society and law's beneficence. As Nussbaum notes, "the politics of disgust is profoundly at odds with the abstract idea of a society based on the equality of all citizens, in which all have a right to the equal protection of the laws."[67]

The second site of threat is constituted by a sense of deception and artifice – the "disguise." Within this political message, transgendered and transsexual people are not authentic gendered beings; they have deceitfully altered themselves in such a way as to mask their true identity. "Disguised" as women, these supposed violators of gendered space – the public washroom – have malice in their hearts. This notion of transgendered people being in disguise regrettably has an ingrained presence in second-wave feminist discourse about transsexual identity. Perhaps the most notorious transphobic feminist diatribe was Janice Raymond's, *The Transsexual Empire*.[68] Published in 1979, Raymond's treatise polemically argues that transsexualism was "artifactual femaleness ... constructed, fashioned, and fabricated."[69] Highly essentialist in its argument, the distinction is made between the "natural" or biological woman and the fabricated one. Here, transsexual "becoming" is a kind of sexual violation via the transition to female corporality and being: "Transsexuals rape women's bodies by reducing the real female form to an artifact, appropriating this body for themselves."[70] "Loss of a penis," she writes, "however, does not mean the loss of an ability to penetrate women – women's identities, women's spirits, women's sexuality."[71] Remarking that rape is "a masculinist violation of bodily integrity," she claims that rape, although usually done by force, "can also be accomplished by deception."[72]

Described as a "'final solution' of women perpetrated by the transsexual empire," Raymond argues that male-to-female transsexuals attempt to "neutralize women by making the biological woman unnecessary – by invading both the feminine and feminist fronts."[73] The invocation to Hitler's "final solution" and the holocaust, to imperialism and militarism, and to the violation of corporeal integrity illustrate the way in which Raymond conceives of transsexuals as a dangerous artifice that has sought the invasion, penetration, and eradication of not only bio-women's (or cis-women's) bodies and sexuality but also their very ontology. Speaking to the way in which she perceives transsexual identity as a violation to "natural" femaleness, she contends that political support – specifically, lesbian feminist support – for male-to-female transsexuals "encourages the leveling of genuine boundaries of self-preservation and self-centering."[74] According to Raymond, the transsexual represents a vexatious state to essentialist order, challenging the very "boundaries of what constitutes femaleness," without which there is the "inability to distinguish the female Self and her process from the male-made masquerade."[75]

Returning to Kristeva's theory of the abject, I want to highlight the physical context of this fantastic fear of transgender assault, noting that "it is, in fact, transgendered Canadians who are most often at risk in public bathrooms."[76] The slight alliteration and play on words regarding the nomination of the proposed legislation as the "bathroom bill" signifies ambiguity most meaningfully in that the public bathroom is a site of in-between-ness where states of distinction – public/private, clean/dirty, male/female – are precarious and easily violated. Like the transgendered individual who transgresses gender boundaries and systems of regimented identity, public bathrooms represent a zone of indeterminacy where, in this case, public and private are blurred, where filth does not respect the boundaries of cleanliness, and where affective confrontation with waste matter and corporality comes into crisis for those whose very ontology rely on clear, demarcated boundaries and zones of distinction.

At the level of the psychic, Kristeva theorizes that "what disturbs identity, system, order. What does not respect borders, positions, rules. The in-between, the ambiguous, the composite" is the abject, the thing to be radically expelled.[77] It is confrontation with the abject that produces a visceral affective response of disgust, revulsion, a vomiting up, and a turning away. Insofar as Kristeva argues that abjection is a type of self-defence against unbearable indeterminacy, abjection signifies the fragility of the fantasy of the stable and self-determined subject. Thus, by situating trans-gender "threat" in the space of a public bathroom, the abject is ever present and over-determined. It is no coincidence that Conservative opponents to the bill managed to evoke the psychic unease of abjection and of the abject other in its appeal to constituents.

What I want to make clear is that this political strategy of disgust at the abject other only holds meaning if we adhere to a logic of limits, boundaries, and borders. One of the insights of Kristeva's theory of abjec-tion that is celebrated by queer scholars is that rigid distinctions are prod-ucts of psychic fantasy, fantasy that is unable to reconcile the messiness of human ontology. It is a fantasy in which rigid, taboo-like distinctions between self and other, inside and outside, clean and unclean are necessarily reproduced in order to protect the subject's fragile ego structure. How-ever, as queer theorist Diana Fuss remarks, "borders are notoriously un-stable."[78] Yet it is an instability that is perceived as fundamentally threatening and that must be radically eradicated. "In exposing the social artifice of 'gender' and 'humanity,'" Thomas writes, "transgender existence confronts our transphobic society with its most deep-seated fears and anxieties. Terrified by that fact, the transphobic imagination exorcises that terror through acts of political terrorism against the transgendered."[79]

Concluding with Liminality

The politics of trans dehumanization, including the appeal to a politics of disgust, anchor transgender variant people as politically abject, in an in-determinant space of citizenry. Thomas observes that "in the transphobic imaginary, [those who have] 'crossed over, cut across, move between, or otherwise queer socially constructed sex/gender boundaries' have, in effect, entered an indeterminate location somewhere between the human and the inhuman."[80] The stripping away of the human from transgendered experience reproduces a politics of dehumanization that allows and makes it "easy" for discrimination and violence to occur against trans people. To the transphobic imaginary, violence and legal exclusion both act in different ways to affirm the seemingly correct and unambiguous political citizen. They demarcate the seemingly proper citizen from its abject other. However, humanness is a messy business. As those engaged in both critical psychoanalysis and queer studies have revealed, the human condition is indeed an ambiguous state filled with contradiction and ambivalence, and these psychic defences and strategies to protect fragile ego fantasies are unstable and can actually have the capacity to absorb difference and otherness, which are always aspects of internalization and not of radical exteriority.

The contestation of political debate as to the place of "gender identity" and "gender expression" under Canadian law may be understood in a way that embraces and does exclude those at the political and social margins. Drawing on Victor Turner's[81] discussion of liminality, I wonder to what extent the ambiguity celebrated by trans people can be refigured from "the inhospitable territories in between ... the uninhabitable 'geographies of ambiguity'" to that of a liminal state in which liminality promises the movement of social and legal reintegration and the transformation to full citizen.[82] I see liminality working against abjection in that, although both are states of in-between-ness, liminality suggests a movement beyond, whereas abjection, to cite Kristeva, is ambiguity at its most psychically disturbing, a radical expulsion without a transformative return. Liminality suggests a transitioning that allows for reintegration and a re-assimilation back into cultural and, for our purposes, into a legal community.

A difficulty presents itself, of course, with the awareness that Bill C-279 dropped the term "gender expression" from the proposed legislation. With the dropping of "gender expression" from the final draft, the privileging of gender as an "identity" category became fixed. I suggest – and not without critique around identity as a fixed ontological state of being – that this imagined stability allowed for the potential reintegration of the now expanded (and stabilized) notion of the trans Canadian citizen to be recuperated legally under human rights law and hate crime protections. To quote Liberal MP Joyce Murray,

> it is essential that Parliament send a clear and unambiguous message that this is a crucial equality rights issue. Adopting the amendments proposed in Bill C-279 is not just about ensuring transgendered Canadians enjoy

the legal protections accorded to other targeted groups. It is also an opportunity for Parliament to send an unequivocal message of support to transgendered Canadians that we in this House affirm their identity and acknowledge their struggles. This would be a humanitarian step that would cost nothing. It is in alignment with the basic principles of fairness, humanity, equality, inclusion and respect. It is an opportunity for all parliamentarians to really look into their hearts and to express their values and principles of inclusion.[83]

5

The Baby and the Bathwater:
The Repeal of Section 13
of the *Canadian Human Rights Act*

> Eventually, honourable senators, there will come a time when complicity in the passage of this bill will be recognized for what it really is: a source of national regret and shame.
>
> – Senator Jim Munson, Senate Debates on Bill C-304, 23 October 2012

The invocation of freedom from tyranny is a powerful call to arms. It is one that rallies our democratic resolve and readies us against oppression. Calling for "a freer, more open society," Conservative party Member of Parliament (MP) Brian Storseth called on his colleagues to "resist ... the tyrannical instincts of bureaucracy" and vote for a repeal of section 13 of the *Canadian Human Rights Act* (*CHRA*).[1] The impugned section, a human rights mechanism that made it a "discriminatory practice for anyone to communicate by telephone, by a telecommunication undertaking, or by a computer-based communication, including the Internet, any matter repeatedly that is likely to expose anyone to hatred or contempt by reason of the fact that he or she is a member of a particular identifiable group," had been the subject of controversy, governmental study, reform, and repeal for almost twenty years.[2] Now before Parliament, the impugned section found itself as the subject of a private member's bill that sought its repeal. At the heart of the debate on Bill C-304, *An Act to Amend the Canadian Human Rights Act (Protecting Freedom)*, was the issue of free speech, discriminatory and hateful expression, and major shifts in lobbying efforts of agenda-driven groups. In some ways, it is fitting that this is the book's substantive final chapter as it draws attention to a growing backlash and resistance to hate speech regulation and to a partial dismantlement of human rights protections for minorities at the level of the federal government.

Framed in classically libertarian terms, arguments for the bill stressed a number of key factors. First, freedom of expression is the "bedrock" that all other democratic freedoms are built upon.[3] Without it, argued Storseth, all other freedoms would be moot, useless, and without efficacy and meaning. The impugned section, claimed Storseth, "eats away at this fundamental freedom."[4] Second, the human rights mechanism is a broken, tyrannical, and bureaucratic process that is ill-suited to investigate and adjudicate issues of hateful discriminatory telephonic messages, often catching legitimate expression in its net and stifling democratic public debate. And, lastly, the section is unconstitutional and, by its continued presence under law, threatens a nation built on the protection of fundamental freedoms and rights. Against these arguments, those who opposed the bill and sought to keep section 13 in the *CHRA* attempted valiantly, especially at the level of the Senate, to reclaim democratic freedoms and the protection of rights as being on the side of regulated speech and human rights law. They also attempted to clarify and set the record straight on a number of claims and issues surrounding the support of the section's repeal, including rebutting the claim that the courts ruled the section to be unconstitutional and identifying the motive of the bill as part of the government's political agenda. These attempts to defeat the bill proved ultimately unsuccessful, perhaps due to the persuasive and misleading arguments of bureaucratic abuses and political witch hunts and to the belief that the legitimate concerns regarding the problematic aspects to the section could not be amended and fixed.

The timing of the repeal, I believe, is not coincidentally connected to a larger political shift to the right and a growing influence of theocratic conservatism in Canadian politics. Embedded in a rhetoric of alarm and injury, theocratic conservatism is a shadowy presence in the debates surrounding the repeal of section 13. Cloaked behind legitimate concerns of rightful expression and the role, procedures, and remedies of the Canadian Human Rights Commission (CHRC) and its tribunal in section 13 cases, the theocratic conservative agenda is barely discernable. However, as in

Edgar Allan Poe's purloined letter, there are clues to its manifest presence. It is interesting how something can be both discreet and indiscreet at the same time. As a result of their increased usage in American politics, the words "God bless" (as in "God bless America," a staple phrase in US politics) can no longer be viewed in a purely benign or benevolent way. They are now primarily political words voiced to assure an anxious populous that god is on their side. Remarkably, Storseth concluded his arguments for the repeal of section 13 with the not-so-innocuous sign-off "God bless."[5] This public expression of religious language in Parliament is extremely unusual in Canadian politics. It is a discreet sign, but a sign nonetheless. Most notably, the freedom of speech polemic obliquely cites contentious debates about the freedom of religious expression and the notion of competing rights. Thus, my analysis of the arguments and language calling for the repeal of section 13 not only exposes a rhetorical strategy that attempts to mislead and obfuscate the realities of section 13 but also demonstrates the ways in which religious conservatism cloaked its agenda of political censorship in an appeal to liberal values of democratic expression and constitutional adherence.

Origin of Section 13

Written into law nearly thirty-five years earlier as a part of the *CHRA*, section 13 was originally enacted to proscribe the repeated dissemination of hate over the telephone, which is a federally regulated service. Then Minister of Justice Ron Basford stressed that the section dealing with telephone hate messages was designed to provide an "effective supplement" to the provisions of the *Criminal Code* "to combat the calculating traffickers in hate whose foul activities subvert the confidence of racial minorities in the protection that they are entitled to feel under the law."[6] Basford's reference to "calculating traffickers in hate" was directed at John Ross Taylor and his fascist, neo-Nazi party, the Western Guard, who in the mid-1970s were handing out cards on Toronto street corners, inviting passers-by to call a phone number to hear a pre-recorded message. Racist and anti-Semitic in their content, these messages typically spoke to white supremacy and the radical separation and extermination of non-Aryan races. One recording played the following message about the so-called evils of "race mixing":

Where large groups of different races mix in all phases of daily contact, race mixing or miscegenation is inevitable. Compared to race mixing an Atomic War with near total destruction is preferable as race mixing is permanent destruction of the higher values of each race whereas Atomic War will leave a remnant however small that can rebuild but a race mixed society is forever doomed.[7]

As a result of these recordings, complaints of anti-Semitism and racism were brought to the attorney general of Ontario, and since the Ontario *Human Rights Code* offered no remedy at that time, the attorney general took this matter to the federal minister of justice, Ron Basford.[8] Insofar as the telephone messages were, in effect, one-on-one private communications, there was worry that such hate lines "might not be caught by s. 319(2) of the *Criminal Code*, which by its terms does not apply to 'private' conversations."[9] Commenting in Parliament about the pre-recorded messages of the Western Guard party, Progressive Conservative MP Lincoln Alexander, the first African Canadian to be elected to the House of Commons, reflected: "I mentioned taped messages earlier which in my view, reflecting on the arsenal of hatred involved in which the taped voice is included, spilling forth malice and intolerance on the telephone, is the most insidious."[10] Commenting somewhat lightheartedly on the public response to the bill and to section 13 specifically, Basford noted:

The introduction of this bill seems to have attracted the attention of those hatemongers who use the telephone in this way, in that they have at least been diverted from the dirt they have disseminated about black people or people of the Jewish faith and have now instead directed their messages of hate to Roy McMurtry and myself – so at least we have provided protection for two minorities.[11]

Speaking about the purpose behind the *CHRA* bill – Bill C-25 – Basford noted that the principles of the act "rest upon the inherent dignity and the equal and inalienable rights of all members of the human family. These are principles as fundamental as freedom itself."[12] It was a highly significant statement, foreshadowing values under the *Canadian Charter of Rights and Freedoms*, in that there was no privileging of one right over others

– that is, there was no hierarchy of rights – and that dignity and equality were identified as fundamental values of Canadian democracy.[13] To the drafters of the legislation, the addition of section 13 posed no significant threat to the integrity of the *CHRA*. It was broadly felt that with careful crafting, section 13 would be an added measure to ensure the regulation, but not the criminalization, of telephonically communicated messages that were deemed hateful. As Senator Carl Goldenberg reminded Senate at seconding reading, the section was "intended to supplement the hate message provision in the *Criminal Code* ... and has been carefully crafted so as to avoid unjustifiable interference with legitimate expression of opinion."[14] In submissions before the parliamentary Standing Committee on Justice and Legal Affairs (Justice and Legal Affairs Committee), Basford stressed that section 13 was designed as a "balanced attempt" to deal with the new delivery system of hate speech via a pre-recorded telephone message by ensuring that the communication in question must "be communicated telephonically *repeatedly*."[15] Such assurances were welcomed unquestioningly by members, and comments on section 13 were, for the most part, perfunctory and praiseworthy. For instance, Alexander commended the bill as being part of the "great Canadian experiment" and stressed that "the political scalpel" of legislation was a necessary "treatment" for "the cancerous sore of racism, prejudice and discrimination which devours reasoning, love, compassion and tolerance."[16]

At the time, the section received little attention within the primary debates on the establishment of a federally enshrined human rights code. These debates largely concentrated on issues of gender equality, including amendments to the *Indian Act* and pension reform. However, one notable critic warned of its deleterious effects on democratic expression. Alan Borovoy, director of the Canadian Civil Liberties Association, appeared as a witness before the Justice and Legal Affairs Committee. As a respected advocate for free speech, Borovoy cautioned the committee that it was "not reasonable at this stage of history" to run the risks of catching legitimate expression of dissent and unpopular opinion within the proposed law's ambit.[17] Arguing that the section should be deleted from the bill, Borovoy acknowledged "the existence in this country of racist invective" but questioned the need for the ban on telephone hate messages.[18] Moreover, he pointed to the *Criminal Code* provisions that regarded the outlawing of hate propaganda as a more legitimate site for the censoring of hateful speech as it provided defences to expression that were not included under the proposed legislation. Despite Borovoy's trepidations regarding what he characterized as "risky legislation," the government moved the bill quickly through the two government houses, maintaining their belief that the section on telephonic hate messages fit well within a human rights paradigm.[19]

Political Correctness

At the heart of the move to repeal section 13 was a deep concern that, as Senator Doug Finley voiced, "political correctness ha[d] run amok."[20] Levelling serious accusations of mismanagement and corruption, Finley argued that Bill C-304 was "a response to the decrepit state of free speech in Canada that is a consequence in large part of the malpractices and censorship of human rights commissions ... These commissions have, in the last decade at least, run roughshod over the civil liberties of Canadians."[21] The picture of the state of free speech in Canada that he painted was alarming and abysmal. "The abuses of both provincial and federal human rights commissions," he admonished, "cannot be allowed to continue unabated. The censorship of politically incorrect statements in publications is not only wrong but also contrary to our democratic principles."[22] According to his perception of the CHRC and its tribunal, and to other provincial human rights commissions more broadly, the human rights commissions were hotbeds of vexatious and ideologically driven prosecutions by an unelected bureaucracy run afoul. His exaggerated claims of malfeasance and his flourish against the anti-discrimination mandate of the commission, as connoted by his slur towards the politically correct, signalled an unease with recent judgments and a worry about procedural abuse.

The charge of "political correctness" as a sign of the dogmatic restriction on speech and of the curtailment of democratic liberties has long been a strategy of conservative hegemony. "It is a clever ploy on the part of the neoconservatives," notes Herbert Kohl, "to insinuate that egalitarian democratic ideas are actually authoritarian, orthodox, and Communist-influenced when they oppose the right of people to be racist, sexist, and homophobic."[23] As Molefi Asante observes of the utilization of this term in the 1990s by detractors of gender-neutral and culturally progressive language, its invocation typically follows "a pattern of argumentation based upon political, masculine, and racial interests that distorts reality and overturns the commonly accepted principles of liberal democratic pluralism."[24] With respect to the origin of the expression, Kohl notes that the term was used by Socialists in the 1940s and 1950s to signal a blind, doctrinal obedience to Communist support for the Hitler–Stalin pact: "It was meant to separate out Socialists who believed in equalitarian moral ideas from dogmatic Communists who would advocate and defend party positions regardless of their moral substance."[25]

Since the 1990s, it was been used by conservatives as a disparaging and ironic term for those on the left whom they feel are ideologically orthodox and on the wrong side of the liberal ideals of democracy (read: majoritarian politics) and of freedom of expression. For those who level the term, "politically correct" is used ironically as they believe there is no accordance with truth or fact in their opponents' position. Often used as an "escape into hyperbole," the charge of political correctness attempts to alarm the speaker's audience and disparage the issue under attack.[26] With respect to Finley's remarks that the human rights commissions have run amok with political correctness, his remarks question the impartiality and neutrality of such commissions and allude to their dogmatic rigidness and blind left-wing leaning. Moreover, by describing the impugned speech brought before the commissions as being merely "politically incorrect statements," the wording suggests two things. First, the censured statements do not align with the commissions' ideological favour and left-leaning orthodoxy and are thus subject to vexatious prosecution. Second, from the perspective of the one levelling the characterization, the harm of these statements is trivial.

Thus, if we read the signifier "incorrect" to mean its ironic opposite, then the statements are possibly truthful and correct, and harm results not in the expression of these statements but, rather, in their censorship. Rising to support the bill, MP Brent Rathgeber stated: "Some of the ideas in that marketplace of ideas will not be popular and they will not be politically correct but they are important to further the debate."[27] Here, the left-socialist/right-capitalist metaphor continues its work, whereby the expression of such speech has valuable currency in the free marketplace of ideas. Reacting to the topsy-turvy word play of the terms "politically correct" and "politically incorrect," Senator Jim Cowan warned of "the dangers of turning language on its head."[28] Noting the ways in which the government under Stephen Harper was suppressing speech that contradicted its political agenda, he exclaimed: "We see freedom of speech routinely suppressed for those who should speak out – muzzled scientists, environmentalists, women's groups, international development NGOs – and yet, in the name of free speech, extolled here to allow hate speech."[29] Citing George Orwell's *1984* and the concept of doublespeak, the senator continued, stating:

> This bill has been presented to us as a defence of the right of freedom of speech. But let us not deceive ourselves. This is not a bill in defence of free speech. This is a bill in defence of hate speech. This is a freedom of hate speech bill. The bill is entitled *An Act to amend the Canadian Human Rights Act (protecting freedom)*. The more accurate title would be *Protecting Hatred*.[30]

Putting the hyperbole of political correctness aside, there were a number of critical claims made by the supporters of the bill that require exploration. First, there was a charge that section 13 of the *CHRA* had been deemed by the courts to be unconstitutional and that its continuance under the act was, in short, illegal. Second, the CHRC and the Canadian Human Rights Tribunal (CHRT) were operating beyond their mandate as human rights quasi-judicial bodies and engaging in vexatious prosecutions. And, finally, the bill itself was strictly a private member's bill that drew broad support across political party and ideological lines. Each of these claims, in some way, was misleading. The next sections of this chapter engage with these claims in order to verify their accuracy.

Section 13 as Unconstitutional

Reading Bill C-304 for a second time before Parliament, Storseth stated: "This conflict between section 13 of the *Canadian Human Rights Act* and paragraph 2(b) of the *Charter* has been reaffirmed by the Canadian Human Rights Tribunal, which found that section 13 was in fact unconstitutional in September 2009."[31] Nineteen months later, the honourable member would repeat his claim stating: "It has been widely acknowledged that it impedes section 2(b) of the *Charter of Rights and Freedoms*, which states that every individual has the freedom of thought, belief, opinion and expression, including freedom of press and other media communication."[32] The claim of constitutional infringement is a serious one and, if valid, a crucial argument for the impugned section's repeal. The effect of such a claim stirs those whose political sensibilities are grounded in the rule of law and in the belief of democratic liberalism as a fundamental Canadian characteristic. To raise such an alarm has the effect of garnering justifiable concern and legitimate support. However, what of this "widely acknowledged" infringement? What legal bodies have deemed the section to be constitutionally invalid and a violation of cherished *Charter* rights and freedoms? Is this claim, in fact, accurate?

The claim, at best, is muddled. To put Storseth's claim into perspective, the CHRT does not have the authority to strike down the law.[33] In that the CHRT members are not bound by previous tribunal decisions, they are obligated to follow decisions of the courts. Decisions of the CHRC and the CHRT are reviewable by the Federal Court of Canada, and a decision by the Federal Court may be appealed all the way to the Supreme Court of Canada.[34] In order to clarify the confusion over the constitutional status of section 13(1), it is prudent to go back to John Ross Taylor and the Western Guard party and their pre-recorded telephone message of racist and anti-Semitic invectives. Notably, the Western Guard telephone message was subject to the first section 13 complaint and was the first case heard by CHRT.[35]

Found to have breached section 13, Taylor and the Western Guard party were ordered by the CHRT in July 1979 to cease and desist the pre-recorded phone message. Despite the injunction, the pre-recorded message remained active. In 1981, a Federal Court judge found Taylor and his Western Guard party to be in contempt and imposed a fine of $5,000 and a one-year sentence of imprisonment.[36] Taylor's sentence was suspended on the condition that he discontinue his discriminatory activities.[37] He did not, and the sentence was enforced against him. Jeffrey Ian Ross notes that Taylor initially went into hiding but finally turned himself in to authorities.[38] Upon his release from jail, Taylor re-established the phone line. For a second time, the CHRC commenced contempt proceedings against him. However, shortly before the second contempt proceeding, the *Charter* came into force in 1982.[39] Using his right to a *Charter* challenge,

Taylor argued before the Trial Division of the Federal Court that the section violated section 2(b) of the *Charter* – the right to freedom of expression – and could not be justified under section 1, the limitations provision. The court rejected the argument, confirmed the contempt, imposed the fine, and made the commital order sought by the commission. The appellants' appeal to the Federal Court of Appeal was dismissed.

Concurrently, Taylor and the Western Guard party filed a complaint to the United Nations Human Rights Committee (UNHRC) in 1983, alleging a violation of the freedom of expression guarantee in the *International Covenant on Civil and Political Rights*.[40] Ruling against Taylor, the UNHRC stated that "the opinions which Mr. Taylor seeks to disseminate through the telephone system clearly constitute the advocacy of racial or religious hatred which Canada has an obligation under article 20(2) of the *Covenant* to prohibit."[41]

With respect to the constitutional challenge, the Supreme Court of Canada considered it in *Canada (Human Rights Commission) v Taylor*.[42] In a four-to-three decision, Chief Justice Brian Dickson, writing for the majority, ruled that section 13(1) of the *CHRA* did infringe upon section 2(b) of the *Charter* but that the infringement could be justified under section 1 of the *Charter*, which provides that the rights in the *Charter* are subject "to such reasonable limits prescribed by law as can be demonstrably justified in a free and democratic society." In its reasoning, the Court found that Parliament's objective of promoting equal opportunity unhindered by discriminatory practices is of "sufficient importance to warrant overriding a constitutional freedom." The Court stated that hate propaganda presents "a serious threat to society by undermining the dignity and self-worth of target group members and, more generally, contributes to disharmonious relations among various racial, cultural and religious groups, as a result eroding the tolerance and open-mindedness that must flourish in a multicultural society which is committed to the idea of equality." Concentrating on the idea of equality, the Court found that the section was proportionate to the government's objective, that it was rationally connected to the aim of restricting activities that were antithetical to the promotion of equality and tolerance in society, and that it was not overbroad or excessively vague. Speaking to the issue of breadth and vagueness, Dickson noted that "its terms, in particular the phrase 'hatred or contempt,' are sufficiently precise and narrow to limit its impact to those expressive activities which are repugnant to Parliament's objective."[43]

Following the reasoning in *R. v Keegstra*, the Court stated that the phrase "hatred or contempt" in the context of section 13(1) refers "only to unusually strong and deep-felt emotions of detestation, calumny and vilification."[44] The "absence in the *Act* of an interpretative provision" to protect freedom of expression, the Court opined, does not create in section 13(1) an overly wide scope. Addressing the differences between this human rights provision and those provisions in the *Criminal Code* that criminalize the wilful promotion of hatred and the public incitement of hatred, Dickson remarked that the absence of an intent component raised no problem of minimal impairment when one considers that the objective of the section requires an emphasis upon unintended and discriminatory effects. As in other human rights legislation, an intent to discriminate is not a precondition of a finding of discrimination. "To import a subjective intent requirement into human rights provisions, rather than allowing tribunals to focus solely upon effects," stated Dickson, "would defeat one of the primary goals of anti-discrimination statutes." Even though "the section may impose a slightly broader limit upon freedom of expression than does section 319(2) of the *Criminal Code*," he wrote, "the conciliatory bent of a human rights statute renders such a limit more acceptable than would be the case with a criminal provision."[45]

Writing for the dissent, Justice Beverley McLachlin took the opposite review. Despite the important legislative objectives "of preventing discrimination and of promoting social harmony and individual dignity," she found that the impugned section failed to meet the proportionality test. Describing section 13(1) as being too broad and too invasive, the dissent remarked that the section caught "more expressive conduct than can be justified by its objectives." Further to its overbreadth, the words "hatred" and "contempt" were deemed to be "vague, subjective and susceptible of a wide range of meanings." Addressing the human rights standard of unintended effect, she wrote that "while the chilling effect of human rights legislation is likely to be less significant than that of a criminal prohibition, the vagueness of the law may deter more conduct than can legitimately be targeted."[46] In the dissenting opinion, the infringement upon a "fundamental freedom" was deemed to be too great, particularly in that the provision targeted private speech and provided no defences and, in particular, no exemption for truthful statements. To these arguments, the majority would respond with the conclusion that the restriction of discriminatory telephonic communication was "not excessive" nor "fatally broad in scope."[47]

After Taylor

A key consideration in *Taylor* was the procedural and remedial provisions inherent in the *CHRA* to which section 13 was adherent. Dickson noted that section 13(1) "plays a minimal role in the imposition of moral, financial or incarceratory sanctions." As summarized by the CHRC's *Special Report to Parliament*, the tribunal offers mediation services to resolve complaints before a formal hearing is held, but it does not have the power to require respondents to apologize for their discriminatory behaviour, nor does it have the power to imprison respondents.[48] However, since *Taylor*, provisions added to the *CHRA* have, as the Canadian Bar Association has cited, "renewed concerns" about section 13's constitutionality.[49] In 1998, penalty provisions were added, allowing the tribunal to award a monetary penalty of up to $10,000 for a violation of section 13,[50] and, in 2001 as part of a package of anti-terrorism measures, a subsection was added to section 13 prohibiting the posting of hate messages on the Internet.[51]

Although subsection 13(2) was added in part as a response to the events of 9–11, the question of whether the *CHRA* should expressly prohibit hate messages on the Internet was raised by an independent panel established to review the act in 1999. In releasing its report entitled *Promoting Equality: A New Vision*[52] in June 2000, the panel recommended that the "prohibition of hate messages in the *Act* be broadened to encompass both existing and future telecommunications technologies in federal jurisdiction."[53] Chaired by Gérard La Forest, former justice of the Supreme Court of Canada, the panel considered whether broadening the scope of section 13 might be an undue limitation on freedom of expression. Considering the judgment in *Taylor* regarding the telephonic communication of hate messages, the panel noted the significance of the term "repeated" in the provision. Citing *Taylor*, the panel stated:

The use of the term "repeated" to describe the proscribed hate messages focused on the prohibition on the public, larger scale schemes for the dissemination of hate propaganda which most threatened the "admirable aim underlying the *Act*" ... We believe that the communication of hate messages by the Internet is just the kind of public and large-scale scheme for the dissemination of hatred that would come within the scope of the Supreme Court of Canada's ruling.[54]

Prior to this recommendation in *Promoting Equality*, the Toronto mayor's Committee on Community and Race Relations and Sabina Citron, a Holocaust survivor, lodged two parallel complaints against Ernst Zündel, a former Toronto resident, under section 13(1) of the *CHRA*, alleging that by posting discriminatory material on his website he "caused repeated telephonic communication that was likely to expose Jews to hatred and contempt."[55] The CHRC referred the complaint to the CHRT in 1997 for a hearing on the merits. The subject matter of the complaints was the Holocaust denial material posted by Zündel on the US-based Internet website Zündelsite. Zündelsite has been active for almost thirty years in the worldwide distribution of materials that deny the Holocaust and other Nazi atrocities against the Jews.

The CHRT's finding on this issue was precedent setting. Over fifty days of hearings were held.[56] The inordinate length of the hearing was due to the complexity of the issues raised and the fact that it was interrupted for approximately a year and a half as a result of Zündel's various attempts throughout the course of the hearing to have the proceedings stayed or declared invalid by the Federal Court. Dozens of procedural motions and judicial reviews were argued over the four-year period, which ended with the tribunal's decision in January 2002. After hearing technical evidence as to how the Internet works and how computers communicate "telephonically" (that is, using telephone lines and infrastructure within the legislative authority of Parliament), the tribunal determined that the scope of the section could now be interpreted as including advances in technology such as communication over the Internet by computers. The CHRT held that hate messages posted on a website are communicated "repeatedly" and that the Internet offers "an inexpensive means of mass communication."[57] On 18 January 2002, Zündel was ordered by the tribunal to cease and desist in his discriminatory practices. Just prior to the tribunal's decision, Parliament amended the *CHRA* to specify that section 13 included messages transmitted via the Internet. There have been no constitutional challenges to this 2001 amendment that includes the Internet as part of telephonic communications.

A number of claims have been made before Parliament, its Standing Committee on Justice and Human Rights (Justice and Human Rights Committee), and in Senate regarding the unconstitutionality of section 13. Some are murkier than others. Ezra Levant, appearing as a witness before the Justice and Human Rights Committee, gave evidence that, "section 13 of the *Canadian Human Rights Act*, the censorship provision, was declared unconstitutional."[58] In his arguments for the repeal of section 13, Conservative party MP Storseth stated a number of times throughout the debates on Bill C-304 that the impugned section had been ruled unconstitutional by the CHRT in 2009. Seeking to clarify this claim proffered by supporters of the section's repeal, New Democratic Party MP Craig Scott corrected Storseth, stating:

> On the *Lemire* decision in 2009 that you referenced from the Canadian Human Rights Tribunal, I may have misread, but it seems as if it focuses on the fact of a penalty being among the possible remedies as being the problem, not so much section 13 itself. Am I correct in that reading? If so, would you be open to an amendment to the act whereby the penalty provision gets removed, but not the actual section 13?"[59]

Similarly, Senator George Baker attempted to bring clarity to the claim by remarking: "However, I seem to remember that, just about six months ago, Justice Mosley of the Federal Court ruled in *Warman* that the penalty provisions were unconstitutional."[60] Citing the ruling by the Federal Court, Senator Lillian Dyck stressed the constitutional validity of section 13: "In addition, as pointed out by Senator Fraser, the Federal Court ruled a few months ago that the Canadian Human Rights Tribunal should have applied the section 13 provisions in the 2009 *Lemire* decision. The tribunal ruled that the penalties in the *Act* were inconsistent with *Charter* guarantees of freedom of thought, belief, opinion and expression. However, Federal Court Justice Richard Mosley indicated that the tribunal should have severed the penalty provisions and applied section 13 and its other remedies."[61]

The issue in question involved a ruling from the CHRT in the case of *Warman v Lemire*.[62] On 24 November 2003, Richard Warman filed a complaint with the CHRC alleging that Marc Lemire had communicated or caused to be communicated hate messages over the Internet in breach of section 13 of the *CHRA*. Lemire, a former leader of the white supremacist organization, the Heritage Front, was the webmaster and owner of the Freedomsite.org website. The message board, which operated from 1999 to 2003, was a forum for discussions at the website. An article on the Freedomsite.org website referred to in the complaint was removed after the complaint had been filed. Subsequent to the filing of the complaint, additional offending material was also allegedly found by Warman on the websites "JRBooksonline.com" and "Stormfront.org," whose banner displays the Celtic cross, a symbol of white supremacism, and the words "White Pride World Wide." These websites were run by Lemire and were referred to the commission's investigator in September 2004.

On 25 November 2005, Lemire filed a notice of constitutional question against the *CHRA* with every attorney general in Canada, in which he challenged the constitutionality of sections 13 and 54(1)(1.1) (fines). Specifically, he argued that they were in violation of sections 2(a) and (b), 7, 26, and 31 of the *Charter*. As a result of the constitutional challenge, the Canadian Free Speech League, the Canadian Association for Free Expression, the Attorney General of Canada, the Canadian Jewish Congress, B'nai Brith Canada, and the Simon Wiesenthal Centre all obtained "interested party status" in the case. Extensive evidentiary hearings were conducted by the CHRT between 29 January 2007 and 25 March 2008. Submissions were presented in September 2008. The tribunal rendered its decision on 2 September 2009.

Although the CHRT ruled that some of the materials did not breach section 13, it found that one of the articles that could be accessed by the public was in contravention. It stated that the article "AIDS Secrets" contained material that was likely to expose homosexuals and blacks to hatred or contempt and that Lemire had repeatedly communicated the matter within the meaning of section 13. The complaint was thus substantiated in respect of that one item. Addressing the issue of the constitutional violation, the tribunal found that *Taylor* was distinguishable from the case at hand. In their judgment, the scheme of the *CHRA* had been changed from "an exclusively remedial, preventive and conciliatory" regime at the time of *Taylor* to one that was quasi-penal. Based on the legislative changes and concerns about the CHRC's practices, the tribunal concluded that it was not bound by *Taylor* since it considered that the majority decision in that case had been premised on the assumption that the commission's procedures functioned in a conciliatory manner as intended by the statute. Thus, section 13 was no longer judged to minimally impair the right to freedom of speech and could not be saved under section 1 of the *Charter*. In arriving at this conclusion, the tribunal did not find that the compensation provisions in sections 53(3) and 54(1)(b), the cease-and-desist order power in sections 54(1)(a), or the other remedial measures in section 53 were constitutionally unsound but, instead, focused exclusively on sections 54(1)(c) and 54(1.1), the penalty sections. On 2 September 2009, CHRT member Athanasios Hadjis found section 13 to be unconstitutional and refused to impose a penalty on Lemire. On 1 October 2009, the commission appealed the decision in *Warman* to the Federal Court.

Writing for the Federal Court, the Justice Richard Mosley noted several places where the CHRT had erred.[63] The tribunal questioned the CHRC's decision to request that it hold an inquiry even though most of the impugned material had been removed from the Internet. Further, it commented on other complaints that had been referred to it in similar circumstances and remarked on the low settlement rate for section 13 complaints and on the fact that the commission did not generally offer to mediate such matters. The decision to hold an inquiry fell exclusively within the commission's jurisdictional discretion, and the proper way to challenge a commission decision in respect of such matters, noted Mosley, was through judicial review by the Federal Court. Furthermore, he regarded the tribunal's comments on low settlement rates as "compound[ing] the error" of jurisdiction. The court observed: "The Tribunal stepped over the line of its proper role – adjudication of the complaint – and assumed the role the Court would have upon an application for judicial review of the actions or decisions of the Commission."[64]

Speaking about the CHRT's own irregularities, Mosley noted that the tribunal's member, Athanasios Hadjis, had taken a critical view of the manner in which the commission's investigation was conducted, and he factored that into his conclusion that the scheme was constitutionally flawed. With respect to the issue of conciliation prior to a hearing, Hadjis had accepted Lemire's contention that the complainant and the commission had declined to mediate or conciliate a settlement to the complaint. As Mosley clarified,

> this is not borne out by the record of the Tribunal proceedings. Repeated efforts were made to engage Mr. Lemire in mediating or negotiating a settlement of the complaint. However, they were conditional on Lemire's acceptance of a cease and desist order, which he refused to accept. The Member's analysis that this complaint had not been handled in a sufficiently conciliatory and remedial fashion does not reflect the record.[65]

Zeroing in on the question of constitutional validity, Mosley remarked: "I start from the proposition, as did the Tribunal, that *Taylor* remains binding unless persuaded that it is no longer precedental authority due to changed factual and legal circumstances since it was decided." With respect to broadening the limitation on Internet communications, he took the opinion that a key word search or the entry of the URL in the browser address bar was "the modern equivalent of Mr. Taylor's little pieces of paper bearing the telephone number ... Is that reason enough to distinguish the Internet environment from that considered by the Supreme Court in *Taylor*? I don't think so."[66]

With respect to the amendment of the penalty provision, the tribunal ruled that the monetary penalty of section 54(1)(c) of the *CHRA* no longer minimally impaired section 2(b) of the *Charter*. The tribunal based this finding on the ground that one of the reasons for minimal impairment in *Taylor* was the conciliatory nature of the *CHRA*. The member found that this was no longer true based on the administration of the *CHRA* by the commission and based on what he considered to be the "now penal nature" of the act. Citing these issues, Mosley remarked on the fallacies of this interpretation:

> Moreover, the Tribunal appears to have interpreted *Taylor* as meaning that the only justification for s. 13 was that it was solely conciliatory and

remedial. However, this is not the case. Chief Justice Dickson indicated that the minimal impairment test was met because s. 13 was less penal and more conciliatory than criminal law ... What changed, as the Tribunal properly found, were the remedies.[67]

According to Mosley, the additions of paragraph 54(1)(c) and section 54(1.1) "fundamentally altered the nature of the s. 13 process and brought it uncomfortably close to the state's ultimate control measure, criminal prosecution." Insofar as the CHRC had abandoned its request for a financial penalty, the greater concern for Lemire, noted Mosley, "was always the possibility of a 'ccase and desist' order." Noting that the penalty was "inherently punitive," he agreed with the CHRT that these were all reasons to support a finding that the section 13 regime with these aspects "can no longer be considered exclusively remedial." However, he added: "I part company with the Tribunal on its conclusion that this applies to the regime as a whole ... I am satisfied that with severance of the problematic aspects, the regime can be preserved." In his ruling, he concluded that "the offending parts are not inextricably bound up with that part of the legislation held to be valid in *Taylor*. The remaining portion of the legislation is very significant and of a long-standing nature. It may safely be assumed that the legislator would have enacted s 13 without a penalty provision as it had done so at the time of its initial adoption in 1977."[68] Overturning the decision in *Lemire*, the Federal Court ruled that the CHRT had erred in refusing to apply section 13 and to exercise its discretion under paragraphs 54(1)(a) and/or (b) of the act to determine a remedy. Severing sections 54(1)(c) and 54(1.1) from the *CHRA*, Mosley declared those sections to be of no force or effect. Thus, section 13 was found not to be in breach of the *Charter* by the Federal Court.

Moreover, the characterization voiced by Storseth, Finley, and others, that the CHRT had found section 13 to be unconstitutional is also not accurate in that the tribunal's vice-chair Hadjis, who wrote the decision in *Lemire*, is not a judge and the tribunal is not a court. Hadjis' decision does not carry sufficient weight to strike down the section as unconstitutional, and, as a result, the ruling is not binding beyond *Lemire*. Noting the most recent ruling by the Supreme Court of Canada on the constitutionality of section 13, Dyck reminded the Senate that "this ruling was reinforced just a few weeks ago when the Supreme Court of Canada upheld key provisions against hate speech in the *Saskatchewan Human Rights Code* [which were consistent with and affirmed section 13 of the *CHRA* as well], but struck down some of the code's wording in a case prompted by flyers handed out by an anti-gay activist, William Whatcott."[69]

A "disgusting agency ... corrupted and diseased beyond salvation"

To a large extent, public and political scrutiny of section 13 and of the Canadian human rights regime resulted from a complaint against Mark Steyn, who wrote an article for *Maclean's* magazine in 2006.[70] This complaint and another one provincially directed at Ezra Levant provoked what Julian Walker has labelled "a particularly vigorous debate."[71] The fallout of these investigations can be clearly identified as resulting in a very public and media-savvy bombast about the issue of free speech and the place of human rights legislation in its regulation. Drawing together what Marci McDonald has named "mind-boggling bedfellows," "most of the country's mainstream media organizations scrambled aboard what had been largely a Christian bandwagon," the push to eradicate section 13(1) of the *CHRA*.[72]

The union of a well-organized lobby of Christian dissent with more mainstream organizations and political ideologies favouring free expression prompted the Harper government to consider the repeal of section 13 seriously. As noted by McDonald, party delegates voted at the 2008 Conservative policy convention to seek section 13's repeal by a huge margin, and, a year later, the Justice and Human Rights Committee held hearings into that possibility.[73] Spotlighting the agenda of the mover of the bill as well as more generally of the Conservative party, Liberal member Joe Comartin remarked that the bill was "an attempt to appease some of their right-wing ideologues, in the media in particular. It is also in keeping with their right-wing ideology of a society that has no government intervention."[74]

At one of these two hearings in October 2009, the chief commissioner for the CHRC, the late Jennifer Lynch, QC, reminded the Justice and Human Rights Committee that it was one "prominent" case that has "caused the current debate about the balancing of freedom of expression and freedom from discrimination based on hate messages."[75] The prominent complaint, to which Lynch was referring, was *Elmasry and Habib v Roger's*

Publishing and MacQueen, in which a lawyer for the Canadian Islamic Congress filed a multi-jurisdictional complaint, alleging that an article written by Mark Steyn, for the online edition of *Maclean's* magazine, exposed members of the Muslim community to hatred and contempt, pursuant to section 13.[76]

In Steyn's highly polemical and rhetorically colourful article "The Future Belongs to Islam," he argues that the demographic decline of Western Europe, along with "unsustainability of the social democratic state" and "the sense of civilizational ennui," will lead to the Islamization of Europe.[77] Remarking on the supposed demographic decline of Western European nations to due low birthrates and aging populations and casting this decline in stark contrast with the supposed young demographic of the Gaza Strip and other Muslim nations, he writes: "A people that won't multiply can't go forth or go anywhere. Those who do will shape the age we live in."[78] Noting the "serious global ambitions" of Islam, the article concludes with the prognostication that "in a few years, as millions of Muslim teenagers are entering their voting booths, some European countries will not be living formally under sharia, but – as much as parts of Nigeria, they will have reached an accommodation with their radicalized Islamic compatriots, who like many intolerant types are expert at exploiting the 'tolerance' of pluralistic societies."[79]

To Steyn, this was a foreseeable, foreboding, and terrifying future. As noted by Lynch, the CHRC dismissed the complaint, citing that the impugned content did not meet the narrow definition of hate as established under *Taylor*. Similarly, the Ontario Human Rights Commission dismissed the complaint, citing lack of jurisdiction and the BC Human Rights Tribunal dismissed the complaint after a hearing, citing that the article did not rise to the level of hatred and contempt as defined by the Supreme Court of Canada under section 7(1)(b) of the *BC Human Rights Code*.[80] Despite the dismissals, critics raised the issue of "procedural abuses" regarding the multi-jurisdictional filings against Rogers Publishing as a sign of malicious prosecution, despite the fact that human rights commissions are legally bound to investigate a complaint and tribunals are not prosecutorial but, rather, are remedial in their mandate.[81] Appearing before the Justice and Human Rights Committee in 2012, Marvin Kurz, legal counsel for B'nai Brith, used the case as an example of a system broken: "When you see a case like *Elmasry v. Rogers*, where Mark Steyn and *Maclean's* magazine were brought before three different human rights authorities and three different jurisdictions at the same time until they finally found a human rights authority that would allow them to bring a hearing without any screening, nothing could be more vexatious than that."[82]

The other source of intense public and political attack against the CHRC, and, more generally, against the provincial and federal human rights regimes that protected against hate speech discrimination, came from Ezra Levant, a journalist and lawyer who actively defended the Mark Steyn case. In 2006, Levant republished cartoons depicting the prophet Mohammed in the *Western Standard* that were originally published in the Danish newspaper *Jyllands-Posten*. Highly controversial, the cartoons ignited passions on multiple fronts, hitting on issues from freedom of the press and the censorious effect of blasphemy laws to Islamophobia, religious tolerance, and religious provocation, among other heated political and religious issues. Brought before the Alberta Human Rights Commission for an investigative meeting, Levant used the meeting as "an opportune stage," videotaping the session and posting it to YouTube.[83] The complaint was ultimately withdrawn after a lengthy process but not before incurring Levant's wrath. At the crosshairs of his objection was the CHRC and its chief commissioner, Jennifer Lynch, whom he described in his book *Shakedown: How Our Government Is Undermining Democracy in the Name of Human Rights*[84] as "chief commissar," a reference to a Communist official.[85] Characterizing Levant's media blitz on the CHRC, Senator Jim Munson exclaimed: "Levant is a rabid critic of the Canadian Human Rights Commission, a master at distorting facts and infiltrating mainstream discourse."[86]

Championing the *Warman* case and the tribunal's ruling, Levant stated before the Justice and Human Rights Committee in 2009 that "the commission is out of control" and "has become a threat to our human rights."[87] Referencing his own experience and that of Mark Steyn, he claimed that the focus of the CHRC was "targeted at publishers who publish cartoons or at columnists who have something to say about radical Islam."[88] Arguing that this whole thing has to be thrown out because it has been corrupted all the way through," Levant characterized the commission as having become "manifestly political."[89] "The commission, which was designed to be a conciliatory, mediating organization, has become 'aggressive and relent-less," he claimed, "it doesn't care about mediating. It's an attack organiza-tion."[90] Stating he was "shocked" to find this connection, he claimed that "the Human Rights Commission itself was the largest propagandist of anti-Semitic material in Canada."[91] The "awful revelation," which was never proven to be true, to which he alluded was the issue of Richard Warman, a former investigator for the CHRC who, as a private citizen and no longer an employee of the CHRC, allegedly posted on a number of racist websites material that would draw out invectives already ideologically indorsed by, and circulating on, the website.

The co-testimony of Mark Steyn added to these disturbing and un-proven accusations. "Richard Warman and his fellow dress-up Nazis at the Human Rights Commission," Steyn stated, "[are] salivating at the prospect of having found another witch to provide more bounty."[92] Drawing a com-parison of the seventeenth-century witch hunter, Matthew Hopkins, to that of Warman, Steyn stated:

I'm sure some of you are familiar with Matthew Hopkins, who in 1645 appointed himself England's witch-finder general and went around the country hunting down witches and turning them in for the price of one pound per witch. In 2002 Richard Warman appointed himself Canada's hate-finder general and went around the Internet hunting down so-called haters and turning them in for lucrative tax-free sums amounting to many thousands of dollars. Hate-finder Warman and his enablers at the commission abused the extremely narrow constitutional approval given to section 13 by the Supreme Court in the Taylor decision and instead turned it into a personal inquisition for himself and his pals.[93]

Thus, in Steyn's vexatious characterization, which was never proven to be true, the CHRC, by way of its employee, Warman, had engaged in the solicitation of anti-Semitic hate speech on various racist websites. It also held that Warman had "played at" being a Nazis, that the CHRC investigation was akin to a witch hunt lead by hysterical ideologues, that the "witches" were falsely accused individuals, and that the motivation for the investigation was both monetary and ideological. Members of the CHRC, including Lynch, were named as "Nazi fetishists" and "pseudo-human rights apparatchiks," nominations that respectively indexed perverse psychopathologies that were clearly anti-Semitic in their proclivity and hyper-feminist ideologues adherent to a disingenuous human rights regime.[94]

Responding to these attacks, Lynch attempted to set the record straight: "This committee has heard unsubstantiated allegations. Simply put, these are baseless ... unsubstantiated personal attacks."[95] Windsor law professor, Richard Moon, giving testimony to the Justice and Human Rights Committee after having prepared a comprehensive and balanced report in 2008 for the CHRC on section 13 was notably dismayed by the tone of the testimony directed against Lynch and the CHRC. Reflecting on the need for a serious debate on the restriction of speech by a human rights commission, noting the complexity and difficulty of such a debate, he criticized what was being said in the media and what had been levelled in the committee at the CHRC. "Unfortunately, the most vociferous and indeed the most media-amplified critics of the commission are not interested in this debate," he remarked, "it is easier and it seems more effective to invent injustices and engage in personal attacks."[96]

In that the statements of Steyn and Levant could be described as exaggerated, hyperbolic, and overstated with regard to the CHRC and its chief commissioner, other statements made in committee testimony came across as highly understated, overly banal, and misleadingly benign. For example, Steyn referenced Lemire's white supremacist and neo-Nazi website, Stormfront, as "an unread bit of nothing," wrongly persecuted by a zealous bureaucracy. However, according to the Southern Poverty Law Centre, the most prominent anti-hate advocacy and watchdog organization in the United States, Stormfront claims to have "more than 130,000 registered members (though far fewer remain active), [and] the site has been a very popular online forum for white nationalists and other racial extremists."[97] Referencing Christian Truth activist member William Whatcott and his flyer campaign against gays and lesbians as well as the Saskatchewan Human Rights Tribunal's 2005 decision fining Whatcott and his group and ordering them to cease such publications,[98] Steyn told the Justice and Human Rights Committee of "a man in Saskatchewan who is under a lifetime speech ban [for expressing] an honest opinion about homosexuality and gay marriage."[99] Such an opinion described "homosexuals" as predatory, corrupting, pedophilic, diseased, and unfit to teach in public schools.[100]

The CHRT's decision was affirmed by the Supreme Court of Canada in early 2013. In addition to a strategy of understatement, detractors of the CHRC used a strategy of rhetorical inversion whereby hate mongers were constituted as "innocents" and human rights regimes as punitive and persecutory.[101] In this game of inversion, which was designed to turn things on their head, offenders needed defending and human rights advocates were constituted as aggressors. In this strategy, affective reversal is often deployed as a tool – for example, white supremacists often claim that they do not "hate" people of colour, they just "love" white people. Overlooking his own vitriol and personal attacks against the CHRC's chief commissioner, Steyn claimed that "deep down, even Jennifer Lynch ... harbours a teensy-weensy little bit of hatred for Ezra and me."[102]

A Reversal of Position

> Mr. Kurz, three and a half years ago, in November 2008, your organization [B'nai Brith] issued a press release. You were quoted in it as saying that doing away with section 13 of the *Canadian Human Rights Act* governing hate speech "would be a step in the wrong direction." We've heard today that your position has changed. I guess my question for you is, what has happened in the last three and a half years to cause a 180-degree turn?
>
> – Sean Casey, Justice and Human Rights Committee, 26 April 2012

The committee member's question directed to Marvin Kurz, the national legal counsel for B'nai Brith's League of Human Rights, is pointed. The public and political reversal on the issue of discriminatory hate speech and its regulation by one of the most prominent Jewish advocacy groups in Canada is curious, if not somewhat shocking, and deserves scrutiny. As noted throughout this book, the Jewish community and its leadership have been at the forefront of Canada's hate speech and enhanced sentencing laws. Specifically, the Canadian Jewish Congress (CJC) has demonstrated a deep commitment to equality and human rights throughout its organizational lifespan. Regrettably, the CJC is no longer, having merged with several other Jewish advocacy groups in 2011 to form a new entity, the Centre for Israel and Jewish Affairs – "a move," reported the *Toronto Star*, "that has left the Jewish community divided."[103] How is it that an equally respected organization – B'nai Brith, which has been committed to fighting anti-Semitism, to promoting human rights, and to supporting the legal regulation of discrimination – has completely reversed its political position on the legal regulation of discriminatory speech? As Frank Diamant, executive vice-president of B'nai Brith, lamented: "We come with a heavy heart. We do not come to the decision lightly."[104]

One might not find a satisfactory answer. However, it may start with Marvin Kurz's response to the Liberal member. Referencing "an accumulation of factors," Kurz noted that B'nai Brith had suggested that the legislation "be fixed."[105] Two of the turning points that seemed to impress Kurz were "a frivolous and vexatious human rights complaint" to which B'nai Brith was subject and the *Elmasry and Habib* case. As noted by Kurz, a tipping point was "the *Elmasry and Rogers* case, which is a seminal case in the history of human rights commissions and human rights law dealing with hate speech, with the whole notion of Maclean's and Rogers, even as a big company, having to go through all of that."[106]

An apprehension expressed by David Matas regarding the CHRC centred on the complex and emotional politics of the Israel–Arab conflict. Referencing his experience of observing "the international human rights commission," an organization that he felt was "totally corrupted by people with an anti-Zionist agenda," he worried that Canada's commission may come to be "internally corrupted in the same way."[107] While there is no evidence that the CHRC has become, or will become, what Matas characterized as "an Israel-bashing organization rather than a human rights organization," there was a controversial decision made by the CHRC that is questionable. In 2008, the CHRC decided not to follow through on a section 13 complaint against Imam Abou Hammad Sulaiman al-Hayiti who was accused of inciting hatred against homosexuals, Western women, and Jews in a book he published on the Internet. Speaking to the issue of CHRC cases not pursued, Steyn noted in the Justice and Human Rights Committee that al-Hayiti, "who said far worse things than Mr. Keegstra," was not brought before the tribunal because of the issue being "multiculturally complicated."[108] When asked what he meant by this phrase – that is, whether he meant "politically correct" – he responded "yes." According to an opinion piece written in the *National Post*, al-Hayiti had written that Allah has taught that "if the Jews, Christians, and [Zoroastrians] refuse to answer the call of Islam, and will not pay the jizyah [tax], then it is obligatory for Muslims to fight them if they are able." Christianity, in particular, was denounced by al-Hayiti as a religion of lies, which is responsible for the West's "perversity, corruption and adultery." Al-Hayiti's book refers to "the incredible number of gays and lesbians (may Allah curse and destroy them in this life and the next) who sow disorder upon the Earth and who desire to increase their numbers."[109] The commission stated that they did not pursue the case because "infidel" was not an identifiable group covered under the CHRA and that the Iman's statements against gays did not reach the definitional threshold of hatred set out in *Taylor*.

This ruling imbalance has been identified by social and theocratic conservatives as resulting in the alliance of "strange bedfellows."[110] Heeding Val Jenness and Ryken Grattet's seminal observation about the politics of anti-hate crime movements – that politically disparate groups can come together, for different ideological reasons, to fight hate crime – it is both surprising and not that conservative Jews and conservative Christians have found some sort of middle ground regarding the repeal of section 13. However, this middle ground seems somewhat precarious. Noting the history of anti-Semitism in Canada, it has been conservative Christians who have tended to espouse anti-Semitic beliefs, and radical Christian groups have been extremely vocal about their anti-Semitism.[111] Moreover, white supremacists groups tend to identify ideologically as Christian, and both Taylor's Western Guard and Lemire's Stormfront, for example, have published expressive material that can be characterized as anti-Semitic. Nevertheless, with the dramatic shifts, both progressive and regressive, with the advance of lesbian and gay rights, and with the heightened levels of anti-Semitism, anti-Zionism, and Islamophobia as a result of the Middle East conflict and the North American aftermath of 9–11, the adage "the enemy of my enemy is my friend" might possibly make some sense here. That is, the focus of the political animosity of the Christian Right has shifted from an anti-Semitic bent to an orientation that is both anti-lesbian, gay, bisexual, and transgender and anti-Islam.

Finding allegiance with criticism directed at radical Islam and anti-Zionists might provide the common ground that forges this new relationship between the Christian Right and conservative Jews regarding the repeal of section 13.

With respect to more mainstream Christian conservatism in Canada, Marci McDonald makes the argument that the Christian Right and B'nai Brith, whose "constituency had shrunk to the most conservative and orthodox segments of the community," found commonality in their opposition to same-sex marriage, in their support for Israel, and in their criticism of the Canadian human rights commissions.[112] For many contemporary evangelicals and pre-millennialists, there must be religious Jews in Palestine as a precondition of the Second Coming.[113] Thus, there must be the state of Israel. According to McDonald, the "partnership between Canadian evangelicals and conservative Jews ... was forged nearly a decade ago, expressly with Middle East foreign policy in mind." McDonald writes that anxiety about a "shrink[ing]" Jewish community and growing anti-Israel faction required, according to Diamant, "a strategic ally, and that ally is the evangelicals."[114]

The Canadian Christian Right has long been a critic of human rights regimes that they have felt have restricted their religious freedom, which some may characterize as their freedom to discriminate. On the one hand, looking to influence government, education, and law, the Christian Right "very much wants the state [that is, a theocratic Christian state] to play an important role in people's lives."[115] And on the other hand, it seeks freedom from government control and regulation. The issue of hate speech, freedom of expression, and religious rights have been at the forefront of the Christian Right's legally active and politically vocal support of the repeal of any human rights restrictions on speech. A number of campaigns and Internet postings have labelled hate speech restrictions as attacks upon Christianity and as a banning of the Bible. For example, Tim Bloedow, the now former director of Equipping Christians for the Public-Square Centre, writes that the Alberta Human Rights Commission had issued "a ruthless decision against Mr. Boissoin [a pastor who wrote against the promotion of tolerance of homosexuality in schools], which in itself was an expression of hatred against Christianity."[116]

In a number of cases from *Vriend v Alberta* to *Whatcott v Saskatchewan Human Rights Tribunal*, the courts have generally ruled against discriminatory policies and actions of organizations and individuals that identify as Christian.[117] With respect to the issue of discriminatory hate speech against gays and lesbians, cases such as *Owens v Saskatchewan (Human Rights Commission)* and *Whatcott* received mixed judgments from the courts.[118] In one of these cases, the Saskatchewan Human Rights Board of Inquiry found that Hugh Owens, an evangelical Christian who paid the Saskatoon *StarPhoenix* to publish an advertisement of a bumper sticker displaying Biblical passages condemning homosexuals and advocating their destruction and an icon of two stick men holding hands in a red circle with a diagonal line running through it, violated the *Criminal Code* by exposing gays to hatred and ridicule.[119] In an article published in the *Western Catholic Reporter*, the writer exclaimed: "Activist courts and human rights commissions are no longer the thin edge of the wedge in the persecution of Christians for their faith ... they are the battering rams crashing through the door."[120] However, this ruling was eventually overturned by an unanimous Saskatchewan Court of Appeal.

It was a decision celebrated by the Christian Right. Responding to the question of support for the repeal, law professor Kathleen Mahoney noted that while "some groups are supportive of repealing the law ... there is a lot of self-interest involved."[121] Noting the strategic allegiance formed of unlikely allies, she remarked: "The media do not want to be troubled by limitations on what they say editorially, cartoon-wise or any other way. Similarly, some religious people do not want to be hampered in any way, so they see it as a self-interested thing."[122] With the Christian Right agitating for some time for the repeal of section 13 and other provincial provisions regulating hate speech, it is not surprising that with the discontent of major Jewish community human rights players around recent CHRC decisions a precarious new political agenda around speech and freedom of expression was forming.

Supposedly "not an issue of blue versus orange versus red"

From the beginning, the mover of Bill C-304 told members of the two government houses that the bill was non-partisan and that it was not a government bill.[123] "I see this not as an issue of left wing or right wing," stated Storseth, "I see this as an issue of importance to Canadians across the country, on both sides of the political spectrum."[124] Citing broad support from political divergent groups, Storseth said that the bill was "supported by B'nai Brith, the Muslim Canadian Congress, PEN Canada, the *Toronto Star*, Egale Canada, the *National Post*, and I could go on ... The fact of the matter is these are organizations that absolutely span the political spectrum."[125] To the members of the Justice and Human Rights Committee, he gave evidence stating: "I hope when we talk about the different groups that are endorsing my legislation ... I do bring up the Muslim Canadian Congress, the Canadian Jewish Congress, PEN Canada, the *Toronto Star*."[126] Similarly, he boasted: "I am proud that my private member's bill has received support from all different religious groups across the spectrum of ideological organizations."[127] Predictably, the Canadian Civil Liberties Association welcomed the bill, as did *Maclean's* magazine, which was the subject of the *Elmasry and Rogers* complaint. "We enthusiastically support the Parliamentarians," stated *Maclean's*, "who are calling for the legislative review of the commissions with regard to speech issues."[128] Insofar as Storseth presented the House of Commons with a partially true list of supporters, he did not name those who were not in favour of the repeal. While the Christian Right's support for the repeal has been well publicized, the position of more moderate Christian sects, like the United Church of Canada, are not known.

While the significant issue of freedom of expression, human rights, and hate speech span political and ideological spectra, the member's claim is misleading and misrepresentative on two fronts: as receiving broad support and as a private member's bill. With respect to the issue of broad support across the political spectrum, the claim about receiving support from Equality for Gays and Lesbians Everywhere (EGALE) is incorrect, as is the claim that it received support from the CJC. The endorsement by EGALE was a claim parroted by Conservative party member, Brian Jean, in the Justice and Human Rights Committee: "One particular group, a gay rights lobby group called Egale Canada, which you mentioned. They came out in favour of your position."[129] Failing to see EGALE as a witness at the committee hearings, I thought this statement was unusual. Disturbed and confused by his claim, I contacted Ryan Dyck, director of Research and Policy at EGALE. In a subsequent email correspondence, he assured me that EGALE did not officially support the repeal.[130] He also pointed me to an article written by Gilles Marchildon, the former executive director of EGALE. In it, Marchildon advocates for free speech.[131]

With respect to the position of the CJC, as mentioned, the organization disbanded in 2011, yet Storseth was making this claim of support in 2012. Bringing evidence against the bill, Senator James Cowan quoted from a letter written by Bernie Ferber, the former head of CJC, to the *Huffington Post*. Ferber's letter clearly supported the impugned provision and expressed incredulity and lack of confidence at the House of Commons in their vote to repeal it.[132] Similarly, Mark Freiman, past president of the CJC and current president of the Canadian Peres Center for Peace Foundation, addressed the Justice and Human Rights Committee as an expert on Canadian human rights law. Speaking, though, as a private citizen, he stated: "It is my view that subsection 13(1) of the *Canadian Human Rights Act* is an important resource in protecting vulnerable communities from the harm caused by hate propaganda. It is constitutionally appropriate in a free and democratic society because it deals only with dangerous and harmful speech and is not concerned simply with offensive speech."[133]

"While I would like to thank the grassroots members of the Conservative Party who identified this as an issue years ago, this is not a government bill," claimed Storseth, "this is a bill that was brought forward by me."[134] This dubious claim by Storseth provoked a number of challenges. One of the strongest was from Senator Munson. Naming it a "back-door private member's bill," he charged, "I am not saying that the promoters of this bill have a secret agenda. It is no secret at all. In fact, it has been blatantly obvious ... it was part of a policy platform in June of this year."[135] Similarly, Senator Terry Mercer stated: "I question why this bill was introduced as a private member's bill rather than as a government bill. It is what the government wants. In fact, it is what they campaigned on. Why is it not a government bill? They do not seem to have the guts to stand behind what they say their stated policy is."[136] Insofar as the government did not claim the bill as its own, Bill C-304's support did appear broad and non-partisan. The effect of a private member's bill, particularly one that would appeal to social conservatives, is that there seems to be little government interest, control, and intervention. As Munson suggests, it is a backdoor way of sneaking controversial political agenda into the legislature.

The Issue of Repeal

Without doubt, both critics and advocates have acknowledged that both the language of the provision and the process by which section 13 complaints are launched may be improved. As Munson observed, "section 13 is far from flexible, far from perfect, but it is fixable."[137] For the critics, as we have seen, the solution to these inadequacies and failings was the complete repeal of the section. Staunch advocates for the provision, however, recognized that it was a necessary tool in Canada's arsenal against hate speech and that it supplemented and complemented other provisions under the *Criminal Code*. Arguing passionately for the preservation of the provision, MP Irwin Cotler stated: "The solution is not through repeal of the legislation whose constitutional validity has been upheld by the Supreme Court, but to address the concerns and to offer proposals to modify the regime that is now in place."[138]

Arguments for repeal, beyond those legitimately connected to the section's wording and complaint process, tended to focus on the primacy of free speech in a truly democratic society first and foremost. In debate, this notion of free speech was frequently linked to historical memory. In Storseth's introduction of the bill, he selectively positioned the issue of the provision's repeal with Canadian sacrifice during our country's engagement in both World Wars and with its military mission in Afghanistan. Building on this notion of sacrifice for the preservation of democratic rights, Conservative party MP David Sweet orated:

> Freedom of speech is very much a Canadian concept, one that we should be very proud of and, most importantly, in this second week after Remembrance Day, let us never forget the ultimate sacrifice made by thousands of Canadians from the trenches of Europe to the hills of Afghanistan so that we could enjoy so many freedoms, not the least of

which is the freedom of speech but also so millions suffering in Europe during the two world wars and in other conflicts since could also be free.[139]

The evocation of such a steadfast nationalist myth was left wholly intact since challenging such a myth in Parliament would have been political suicide.

Some supporters of the repeal took an absolutist stance, citing the United States' First Amendment as evidence of the primacy of free speech above all other democratic freedoms. "Freedom of speech is a fundamental right that provides the basis for all other rights to thrive and succeed," stated Sweet, "without free speech, citizens could not assemble publicly to peacefully demonstrate their opposition to government policies, an act fundamental to our democracy."[140] The absolutist argument was quickly dismantled when he gave a long list of exceptions to absolute free speech under American law, including prohibitions against perjury, prohibitions against treasonous speech, prohibitions against pornography, and prohibitions respecting libellous and defamatory speech. Attempting to move the rhetoric away from an absolutist argument, noting that it was fallacious, Joe Comartin reminded his fellow parliamentarians that "this is not about a debate over free speech. This type of speech, like slander, defamation and libel, we have recognized historically people cannot do."[141]

Moreover, under Canadian jurisprudence, there is not such a hierarchy of rights as there is under American First Amendment doctrine. In its report to Parliament, the CHRC was clear to include this point, noting that "there is no hierarchy of rights"; rather, there is "a matrix with different rights and freedoms mutually reinforcing each other to build a strong and durable human rights system."[142] Citing the Supreme Court of Canada decision in *Dagenais v Canadian Broadcasting Corporation*, the CHRC's report included the section of the decision that addressed *Charter* values of balance when rights are in conflict: "A hierarchical approach to rights, which places some over others, must be avoided, both when interpreting the *Charter* and when developing the common law."[143]

Bringing the issue back to Canadian values, those resisting the private member's bill reminded colleagues that freedom together with equality is an articulated and legally entrenched Canadian democratic value. For those advocating reasonable limits on speech, hate speech is an attack upon those very principles that set out a just and equal society. Cotler, using his legal expertise as a former minister of justice and law professor, remarked pointedly: "Hate speech is an equality issue as well as a free speech issue."[144] Noting that hate speech targets those most vulnerable and effectively silences minorities, Dyck reiterated the well-established effects of hate propaganda: "Hate propaganda limits the freedom of belief, opinion and expression of the targeted group. How can one argue for the right to free speech and simultaneously ignore the fact that the intention of purveyors of hate messages is to take away the freedom of thought, belief, opinion and expression of their target?"[145]

In addition to these arguments, supporters of justifiably regulated speech resisted the abolishment of section 13(1) because they believed it to be an essential part of a legal "toolbox" that was designed so that criminal sanctions and civil remedies could work in conjunction with each other.[146] Committee witness Mark Toews, an executive member of the Canadian Bar Association, testified that "without section 13, the only tool the state will have to deal with this type of discrimination is the *Criminal Code*," which in some cases may be an inappropriate, ineffective, or overly onerous response to speech that is hateful. Originally designed as a complement to the *Criminal Code*, the legal standard and the resolution for section 13 cases are markedly different from those under the *Criminal Code*. "A criminal case requires proof beyond a reasonable doubt," noted MP Charmaine Borg, "while a case before the Canadian Human Rights Tribunal requires proof on a balance of probabilities."[147] With respect to resolution, the framework for human rights is mediation – and, in part, education – and the cessation of the discriminatory expression and acts, whereas, upon conviction, a *Criminal Code* resolution is fundamentally punitive, although there are other less punitive sentence principles that may also be involved, like rehabilitation. The arguments in support of keeping section 13 noted the importance of a two-system approach in that, first, all hateful speech may not reach the standard of criminal speech and thus should not be subject to its penalties and, second, hate speech that offends criminally should have a higher burden of proof, built-in mechanisms to guarantee the protection of legitimate expression, and a more onerous outcome upon conviction.

In preparing his report to the CHRC, Richard Moon, one of the leading Canadian legal scholars on freedom of expression, remarks that in his research he had come across "shocking misdescriptions of the CHRC's process."[148] Noting that these misdescriptions appear not only on marginal websites but also too often in mainstream media, he scolds: "This is a reminder that there are commentators who will say anything to support their larger agenda and have no particular interest in being accurate."[149] In his report, he offers three recommendations, his primary recommendation being the repeal of section 13. His other two recommendations offer ways to amend the impugned section while keeping it intact. His recommendations for amendment include tightening the language of the section and catching only the most extreme instances of discriminatory language. In the CHRC's own report to Parliament, they recommend providing a statutory definition of "hatred" and "contempt" following *Taylor*.

Moon also recommends that if amendment was the course of action, then the section should include an intention requirement, as it does under the *Criminal Code* provisions. However, this amendment works counter to human rights evaluations that focus on the effects of discrimination, rather than on the intent to discriminate. Despite some recommendations that paralleled protections under the *Criminal Code* provisions on hate propaganda, Moon did not suggest that a truth defence would be an appropriate amendment under discrimination law. Looking at the investigation process, he calls for the end to the complainant-driven process. The process, he writes, is "unavoidably time-consuming" since all complaints, unless "trivial, frivolous, vexatious or made in bad faith," must be investigated.[150] His chief concern here is that even if the complaint is dismissed after the investigative process, speech may have been chilled. Moreover, the complainant bears the responsibility of the complaint throughout the investigative and adjudicative process. Besides being time and financially consuming, the complainant may be subject to threats of violence by the respondent, as has been the case in some complaints. Lastly, Moon also considers the role that might be played by non-state actors (Internet service providers and the press) with respect to monitoring and the adherence to professional standards.

The CHRC itself provided Parliament with a report on freedom of expression and a comprehensive review of the current legislation in 2009.

It offered five recommendations. The first was to maintain the dual system of criminal and civil provisions already in place. The Canadian Bar Association, in their submission on Bill C-304, also recommended retaining section 13 and leaving the dual system in place.[151] As noted above, the CHRC recommended the addition of statutory definitions to key terms. If a party has abused the tribunal process, they recommended that there be an award of costs in exceptional circumstances. Recommendation 4 suggests a provision be included to allow early dismissal of section 13 complaints when messages do not meet the narrow definition of hatred or contempt. Last, in accordance with *Canada (Human Rights Commission) v Warman* and the recommendation of the Canadian Bar Association, they suggested that the penalty provisions be repealed.[152]

Perhaps the deck was stacked against the supporters of section 13(1) and their rational arguments for its revision. The clamour of outrage and the barrage of fury against so-called bureaucratic abuses and democratic violations were far too sensational and alarming to be ignored. The accusations hurtled at the CHRC jarred political sensibilities and destabilized a system of governance that called for adherence to the rule of law, respect for democratic values, and protections for legitimate speech. Perhaps the metaphors invoked by those urging repeal were too powerful to shake: Nazi fetishists and left-leaning feminists of a corrupt bureaucracy bent on the destruction of free speech, a liberal principle for which Canadians had fought and died. The dizzying characterization of human rights employees and officials as "dress-up Nazis" and "Nazi fetishists" worked to combine apprehension about anti-Semitism and fascism with a sexual proclivity that was labelled perverse. It was a disturbing image of a commission that was created as a governmental response to anti-Semitism and designed for the protection of human rights. Interestingly, it would be an offensive characterization that would draw together both those concerned about anti-Semitism and those fixated on issues of sexual difference. Designed to shock and confuse, this topsy-turvy constitution of Canadian human rights regimes as anti-Semitic had the effect of alienating a once supportive constituency. Moreover, the media blitz by Steyn and Levant criticizing the CHRC's so-called pro-Islamist stance would further the effects of alienation on some in the Jewish community. To the Christian Right, who had been agitating against the human rights commissions for years, labelling them anti-Christian and pro-"homosexualist," dissatisfaction from another religious community provided an opportunity to broaden its political support for the repeal of section 13. In addition to the making of strange bedfellows, the success of the repeal draws attention to a growing backlash and resistance to hate speech regulation and to a partial dismantlement of human rights protections for minorities at the level of the federal government.

Conclusion

What is the state of Canadian hate crime law? As this book goes into production, Bill C-279 appears to be in stasis, having been reintroduced to the second session of the forty-first Parliament. It remains referred to the Standing Senate Committee on Legal and Constitutional Affairs for the second time. The repeal of section 13(1) of the *Canadian Human Rights Act* (*CHRA*) will come into force within a few months.[1] On the political front, there seems to be little motivation to amend the enhanced sentencing provision or the hate propaganda statutes by adding or subtracting from the list of identifiable and protected groups. In some ways, thankfully, the push for hate crime laws seems to have abated.

I say "thankfully" not to disparage what has been termed a politics of hate. Clearly, there has been a legislative need to respond to acts of hate-motivated violence against minority groups and to hate speech that meets the threshold of *R. v Keegstra*.[2] Rather, the political and legislative silence reflects a large political quietude regarding hate-motivated violence. This is not to say that hate crime numbers have significantly diminished. As in the past, rates of hate-motivated violence and property destruction seem to follow alongside other political issues and tensions. Similarly, Internet hate speech activity tends to mirror larger political tensions. I speculate that anti-Semitic and anti-Islamic hate-motivated violence and hate propaganda may be on the rise here in Canada given the ethnic and religious geo-political tensions of the Middle East. I also wonder to what extent the current political push from Aboriginal communities and others for a federal commission into missing and murdered Aboriginal women and girls will spark a renewed discussion about systemic racism and gendered violence, which may take up a model of hate-motivated violence in addition to issues of poverty, the traumatic legacy of residential schools, domestic violence, and alcohol and drug use. Barbara Perry's seminal work on hate crimes against Native Americans may offer instruction on this issue if it gains Canadian political consideration.[3] However, for the meantime, a renewed call for additional legislative and political response to hate-motivated violence and extreme hateful speech appears unwarranted, although vigilance must remain.

I began this book with a comment that the language of debate in legislatures is a curious thing. It is literally a sign of the times, indexing and standing in for not only contemporaneous political currents and sensibilities but also larger and more abstract notions such as the limits of national identity and the affective undercurrents of political economies. The richness and hyperbole of the debates on hate, hate crime, and hate crime law demonstrate the way in which the meaning of those debates exceeds those very terms circulating among, and drawing from, the deep historical discourses on otherness, marginality, and difference. In that arguments for and against the creation and expansion of hate crime laws can be analyzed at the level of denotation, by way of rational legal analysis and the testing of the accuracy and validity of claims, my contribution seeks to explore and mine these arguments for deeper materials that index meaning beyond the literal. *Debating Hate Crime* attends to the denaturalizing of these arguments, locating them within power relations and exposing their affective materials.

Affect circulates between bodies, among speakers, across histories. Hate, as we have seen, circulates in specific ways, impacting some bodies and slipping off others. The affective power – its injury, in part – is produced by its history. In *Excitable Speech*, Judith Butler notes that the injury of name calling is contingent upon, and constituted by, interpolation.[4] That is, like the Fanonian hail, the power of injury has to do with the "sticking" power of the slur – its impact. The sticking power is contingent upon, and constituted by, the hated subject's relationship to the word. This relationship is personal in that there must be identification with the epithet, but the real force of injury comes from the historical force of that word and its circulation among bodies and power relations, across speakers and across time. Acknowledging the hail of history, Sara Ahmed remarks that some signs are repeated over time, not because those signs themselves contain hate but, rather, because "they are effects of histories that have stayed open."[5] As Roland Barthes would concur, a sign is arbitrary and empty until established relationally within a system of signs.[6] Once operating in a system of language and circulating through discourse, the epithet accumulates or loses the efficacy of injury depending upon whether the effects of history – subordination, marginalization, "spirit murder" – are maintained and reproduced by power relations.

And then there is physical violation and violence of hate reproduced from inequitable power relations and ideological systems that assign meaning to difference, valuing one sign of difference over another. Barbara Perry's apt nomination of this violence as "doing difference" affirms the way in which identities of difference are symbolically constituted through the violent act. In her model, the perpetrator utilizes violence as a means to separate and distinguish himself from the hated other.[7] As a kind of physical repudiation, the act of violence constitutes a radical ontological state of difference. For example, she remarks how in the act of a gaybashing the perpetrator utilizes violence as both a tool and index of hegemonic masculinity to assert that he is in opposition to – that is, the opposite of – the one who is perceived to violate sexual and gender norms. In that the act of violence is a type of punishment for the violation of hegemonic norms, it also serves to constitute and name subject positions. In the mind of the perpetrator, he is the righteous one restoring order and normativity, and the violator has been reduced from a dangerous threat to an impotent lower order – this might be evidenced by an accompanying linguistic slur like "you piece of sh*t!" However, as in any affective field, in the affective field of hate, some words stick to some bodies some of the times and some do not.

I would like to add to Perry's schema by suggesting that this field of violence is not only highly constitutive but also highly affective, circulating a number of emotive and affective states. Fear, hatred, revulsion, thrill, repulsion, anxiety, shame, regret, righteousness, empowerment, and justification are just a few emotive states circulating within this field. It is critical to note that anyone of these affective states could be attached to any one body within this field. For example, fear is not solely an emotion felt by the victim of the attack. Theories about the complex emotional states of hate crime, most notably explored by Brian Levin and Gregory Herek, Roy Gillis, and Jeanine Cogan provide that these emotions are not steadfastly attached to either perpetrator or victim.[8] For example, fear circulates between the attacker and the attacked. It is not simply an affective state assigned to the victim. Fear also resides in the attacker; however, this can shift and relocate in the expression of the attack so that it sticks to the victim. Speaking to the ways in which tolerance to difference operates, Wendy Brown notes that "a polity or culture certain of itself and its hegemony, one that does not feel vulnerable, can relax its borders and absorb otherness without fear."[9] From this statement, we can offer the opposite: for those not certain of themselves, for those who feel destabilized by difference, borders cannot be relaxed and otherness must be repudiated and destroyed in order to maintain and protect a vulnerable state, a fragile ego.

Debating Hate Crime takes the Canadian parliamentary debates and witness testimony on hate, hate propaganda, and hate crime as an affective field to be studied discursively. In recognizing these discursive sites as a rhetorical microcosm of an affective economy of hate, my question is: where does hate stick? How does it stick to, shift among, and slide between subjects, across bodies, and over time? What other affective states circulate within this discursive economy? Disturbingly, in the politics of hate, the hated has become a term of contestation. I mean two things by this suggestion. First, within a politics of hate, the hated are not merely subjects of violence and discrimination to be acknowledged, bestowed empathy upon, legitimized, and institutionally recognized. They are all of this as well as a subject position, or condition category, to cite Valerie Jenness – that is, contested by way of disparagement, scepticism, ridicule, disputation, and dismissal.[10] In the politics of hate, you have those working to entrench the condition category of legitimate victim in order to effect social and political results and benefits and you have those working to destabilize and resist it.

The work of identity politics with respect to hate crime has been to formidably establish the victim as a hated victim, who is unjustly targeted by no fault of his own and who is thus deserving of legal recognition and protection. However, as *Debating Hate Crime* has demonstrated, much of the work of the politics of hate has been to subvert this identity. As the Canadian example has demonstrated, social and religious conservatives have produced a concerted effort, in their rhetorical strategies and political mobilization, to challenge, reject, and eradicate this identity formation. They have done this by using two rhetorical strategies. In the first strategy, there is no crisis of hate. The very premise of James Jacob and Kimberly Potter's *Hate Crimes: Criminal Law and Identity Politics* has been to dispute and cast aspersion on the issue of hate as a particular social problem in need of legal redress.[11] For them, the politics of hate is structured upon questionable data collection, inflated statistics of violence and victimization, attention seeking by hysterical minority populations, and political hyperbole. It is not surprising to see these arguments reproduced by opponents to hate crime legislation. Oppositional response to the Special Committee on Hate Propaganda's call for criminal law regulating propaganda and hate speech questioned the need and urgency of such a response, citing little quantitative evidence of a rising crisis of hate propaganda directed at the Jewish and black communities. Similarly, the logic of exclusion deployed by the critics of Bill C-41's enhanced sentencing provision claimed that the need for such a provision was fuelled by a subversive and agenda-driven "homosexualist" lobby.

Alongside the arguments of there being no crisis of hate, opponents to the legislative response have used the retort of culpability. These arguments often took the position that if there was indeed violence and victimization directed at particular bodies and particular communities, then this affective expression was deserved. In that some arguments reproduced the trope of the "bad" victim who acted imprudently with respect to his own care and safety, other rhetorical strategies appealed to justification. The bathroom prowler argument invoked against the inclusion of gender identity and gender expression to the hate crime provisions and to the *CHRA* targeted unconscious fears associated with stealth and deception to produce transgendered citizens as a threat to sexual security. In that such subjects were constituted as a dangerous threat, the justification for suppression of that threat became both logical and tolerable.

In the questioning of victimization, figures like the "hysterical Jew," the "self-victimizing homosexual," and the "transgendered sexual predator" were introduced into parliamentary debate in an attempt to destabilize legitimate concerns for minority citizens. Hyperbole, stereotypes, misleading statements, and colourful language are used as an expressive toolkit designed to persuade, distract, and confuse not only fellow legislators but also the larger political body of the nation. Victimization itself is often turned on its head whereby victims of hateful assault or hateful language are stripped of their injury and repositioned as threats to socio-legal order and the nation at large. The rhetorical strategy of inversion, produced in part by topsy-turvy word play and fantastic expressions of terror and apprehension, reverse and realign subject positions of victim and offender.

My second meaning of "contestation" revolves around the awareness that the hated is a privileged signifier in the politics of hate. It is a paradoxical reality of hate that its affective and political value is sought after. Within which subjects does this value reside? Who is the hated? Much of the work of identity politics and hate crime has illustrated the way in which the politics of hate necessitates a subject of hate. To a large extent, this work has been structured around victim recognition and legitimization, political mobilization efforts by minority target groups, and legalization endeavours by those calling for hate crime and hate speech law. Where *Debating Hate Crime* makes a distinctive contribution is in its study and analysis of the way in which the contestation over hate and victimhood is played out and manifested in legislative debates and committee hearings. Critical discursive analysis of the politics of hate reveals not only a contest of whether the condition category of being hated exists but also who gets to claim it and how those narratives of legitimacy are constructed. Much of the analytical work involving a critical psychoanalytic reading of the opponents' objections to hate law unearthed deep-seated anxieties about victimization and identification with it. For the most part, the Christian Right's arguments against hate crime laws revealed a strangely inverted world order in which hate propaganda laws and the enhanced sentencing provision worked to discriminate against, and victimize, the Christian community. This fantastical apprehension of religious persecution by the state is an interesting and problematic byproduct of these debates around hate and victimization and is deserving of continued research and analysis.

Arguments for both the necessity and the non-necessity of hate crime law ran the gamut from rational argumentation to fantastical apprehension.

The commonality of these arguments for and against the creation, expansion, and repeal of hate speech statutes and the enhanced sentencing provision bears consideration. In the most philosophical and reasoned arguments for and against hate laws, the principle of liberty resounded. If Canada was to remain free and committed to civil rights, it must, on the one hand, curtail speech that jeopardizes the full participation of all citizens and, on the other hand, sustain liberty through minimal government restriction and interference in democratic expression. To both camps, Canada's liberty has been under threat and its citizenry in danger. Those who warned of the legal mechanism of enhanced sentencing also perceived dangers to a proportional system of punishment. Some argued that an increased sentence based on motivation had the troubling effects of criminalizing thought, while others felt that it decalibrated a rather measured and fair response to punishment. Those who advocated for the enhanced sentencing provision maintained that it would not necessarily produce harsher sentences but, rather, would be part of a symbolic statement that would have the effect of recuperating the violated victim of hate-motivated violence back into the Canadian imaginary, an imaginary of national polity stripped from the nation through the act of hate-motivated aggression.[12] Despite these compelling arguments driven by rational engagement with issues of citizenship, threats to Canadian democracy, and the merits of criminalization, legitimate fears about the restriction of free speech and the subversion of human rights principles in the name of criminal legal protections were often upstaged and subverted by arguments that had much more political flourish. It would be these rhetorical instances of flourish, excess, passion, defence, fear, and anxiety that would lend itself to a closer reading, involving not only legal rational analysis but also the tools of a critical hermeneutic.

Notes

Introduction: The Political and Affective Language of Hate

1 *Canadian Human Rights Act*, RSC 1985, c. H-6.
2 *Criminal Code*, RSC 1985, c. C-46.
3 Ahmed 2004.
4 Thomas 1993.
5 Silverman 1983, 3.
6 Benvensite 1971.
7 Barthes 1972 [1957].
8 Barthes 1972 [1957], 129.
9 Fairclough 2010, 30.
10 Qtd. in Silverman 1983, 37–88.
11 Eco 1989.
12 Barthes 1972 [1957], 111.
13 Silverman 1983, 3.
14 *Keegstra* 1990, 92.
15 Freud 1984 [1915].
16 Fanon 1967 [1952], 109.
17 Fanon 1967 [1952], 109.
18 Conrad 1969 [1902], 118.
19 Fanon 1967 [1952], 10.
20 Fanon 1967 [1952], 118, 151.
21 Fanon 1967 [1952], 111.
22 Ahmed 2004, 42.
23 Ahmed 2004, 43.
24 Ahmed 2004, 43.
25 Ahmed 2004, 45 (emphasis in original).

26 Ahmed 2004, 46.

27 Perry 2001.

28 Black 1983.

29 Perry 2001, 55.

30 Garafolo and Martin 1991; see also Levin and McDevitt 1993; McDevitt et al. 2001; Herek, Gillis, and Cohen 1999.

31 Mason 2002, 36.

32 Mason 2002, 36.

33 Mason 2002, 36.

34 Kristeva 1982; Grosz 1994.

35 Mason 2002, 45.

36 Butler 1993, 224.

37 Matsuda et al. 1993, 24; Williams 1992.

38 Matsuda et al. 1993, 25.

39 Moran 2001, 2004; Moran et al. 2004.

40 Moran et al. 2004, 29; Brown 1993, 2006.

41 Moran 2004, 940, 941.

42 Ahmed 2004, 57.

43 Ahmed 2004, 12.

44 Jenness and Broad 1997; Jenness and Grattet 2001.

45 Jacobs and Potter 1998; Jacobs and Henry 1996.

46 Jacobs and Potter 1998, 3.

47 Jacobs and Potter 1998, 64.

48 Jenness and Grattet 2001, 6.

49 Stanko and Curry 1997, 516, 519.

50 Giddens 1998.

51 Stanko and Curry 1997, 518, quoting from an observation by Jenness and Broad 1994.

52 Stanko and Curry 1997, 519.

53 Garland 1996, 452, 453.

54 Moran et al. 2004, 44.

55 Rose 2000, 324.

56 Rose 2000, 328.

57 Moran et al. 2004, 47.

58 Stanko and Curry 1997, 519. They are drawing on the work of Pat O'Malley on crime prevention through risk management.

59 Mason 2002, 87.

60 Stanko and Curry 1997, 519.

61 Stanko and Curry 1997, 526.

62 Jenness and Grattet 2001, 21–32.

63 Jenness and Broad 1997, 23. See also Jenness and Grattet 2001.

64 Jenness and Grattet 2001, 31.

65 Roach 1999, 4.

66 M. Smith 2005.

67 Roach 1999, 222.

68 See Iganski 2008.

69 Spade 2012, 7.

70 Spade 2012, 7.

71 Brown 1993, 390.

72 Roach 1999, 239.

73 Roach 1999, 239.

74 Carter 2001.

75 See, for example, Anand 1998b; Backhouse 1999; Cohen-Almager 2006; Gilmour 1994; Janoff 2005; J. Walker 2010.

76 This was later amended to include telephonic messages communicated via computer or the Internet. S. 13 in its entirety was repealed in 2013.

77 Steyn 2006. The now defunct *Western Standard* republished cartoons of the prophet Mohammad (13 February 2006) originally published in the Danish newspaper *Jyllands-Posten* 30 September 2005.

78 Daniels, Macklem, and Roach 2001, 3.

79 Toronto Police Service 2002, 4.

80 Sarmite Bulte, House of Commons Debates, 16 October 2001, 1230.

81 Daniels, Macklem, and Roach 2001, 93.

82 Daniels, Macklem, and Roach 2001. *Anti-Terrorism Act*, SC 2001, c. 41.

83 See Daniels, Macklem, and Roach 2001.

84 Sarmite Bulte, House of Commons Debates, 16 October 2001, 1230.

85 Anand 1998a; Braun 2004; *Citron* 2002; *Keegstra* 1990; Moon 1992.

86 Moon 2000; Sumner 2004.

87 Moon 1992, 2000; Sumner 2004.

88 Anand 1998b; Backhouse 1999; B. Walker 2008; J. Walker 1997.

89 Kinsella 2001.

90 Backhouse 1999.

91 Kinsella 2001.

Chapter 1: Hate Propaganda and the Spectre of the Holocaust

1 Palmer 2009, 15.

2 M. Cohen 1966, 1.

3 *Criminal Code*, RSC 1985, c. C-46.

4 M. Cohen 1966, 69–71. Note the important changes, additions, and omissions regarding what was recommended by the Cohen Committee with respect to the final legislation.

5 M. Cohen 1971, 103.

6 The Allan Gardens riot in 1965.

7 Canada became a signatory to the *Convention on the Prevention and Punishment of the Crime of Genocide*, 1948, 78 UNTS 277, and the *Convention on the Elimination of All Forms of Racial Discrimination*, 1965, 660 UNTS 195. See also *The Queen v. Drybones* 1970, a Supreme Court of Canada decision that gave effect to the *Canadian Bill of Rights*, SC 1960, c. 44, and the power to override legislation inconsistent with it. See Tarnopolsky 1971. The 1960s was a decade marked by the enactment of five provincial human rights codes: Ontario in 1962, Nova Scotia in 1963, Alberta in 1966, New Brunswick in 1967, and Prince Edward Island in 1968.

8 See McLuhan's (1962) theories of a "global village."

9 Kayfetz 1970, 5.

10 Bialystok 1996–97, 5.

11 1963 amendment to Toronto Bylaw 21379; see MacGuigan 1966, 233.

12 MacGuigan 1966, 234.

13 Bialystok 1996–97, 15.

14 A number of the protestors, and mainly its organizing force, were N3 Fighters against Racial Hatred, a number of whom were Jewish Holocaust survivors. N3 was an acronym that stood for Newton's third law of motion – for every action there is an equal and opposite reaction. See Bialystok 1996–97; MacGuigan 1966.

15 Tulchinsky 2008.

16 See Davies 1992; Delisle 1993; MacFadyen 2004; Tulchinsky 2008.

17 MacFadyen 2004, 75.

18 Tulchinsky 2008, 141.

19 MacFadyen 2004, 76.

20 See Perry and Schweitzer 2002.

21 Tulchinsky 2008, 142.

22 MacFadyen 2004, 77.

23 Macfadyen 2004, 75.

24 MacFadyen 2004, 81.

25 Stingel 2001, 3.

26 Tulchinsky 2008, 307.

27 Tulchinsky 2008, 313.

28 Quoted in Cook 2011, 13.

29 MacFadyen 2004, 89.

30 Tulchinsky 2008; J. Walker 2002, 4.

31 MacGuigan 1966, 232.

32 See J. Walker 2002. Fair Employment Practices Act, RSO 1951, c. 24; Fair Accommodations Practices Acts, SO 1954, c. 131.

33 J. Walker 2002, 14.

34 See MacFadyen 2004; Stingel 2001; Tulchinsky 2008; J. Walker 2002. Various members of the Jewish community also responded to hate propaganda and anti-Semitism through frustration and retaliatory violence. The Christie Pits riot in August 1933 would be an example. The Allan Gardens riot of 1965 would be another example of frustration vented by Holocaust survivors who witnessed John Beattie's neo-Nazi anti-Semitic tirade. Bialystok 1996–97; M. Cohen 1966, 32.

35 Kayfetz 1970, 5. *Boucher* 1951.

36 Kaplan 1993, 244.

37 Kayfetz 1970, 5; Bialystok 1996–97, 5.

38 S. Cohen 1971, 768; Kayfetz 1970, 5; M. Cohen 1966, 12–24.

39 M. Cohen 1966.

40 See M. Cohen 1966, 14–24.

41 Kayfetz 1970, 5.

42 Quoted in Bialystok 1996–97, 7.

43 Kaplan 1993, 245; Kayfetz 1970, 5.

44 Quoted in Kaplan 1993, 245–6; Kayfetz 1970, 5. *Canadian Bill of Rights*.

45 John Diefenbaker, House of Commons Debates, 9 April 1970, 5679.

46 M. Cohen 1966, Appendix IV; Suriya 1998, 29.

47 Kaplan 1993, 246.

48 Kaplan 1993, 246. Two other private members' bills were given first reading in 1965: Bill C-16, *An Act to Amend the Criminal Code* (disturbing the public peace) and Bill C-117, re-introduced in 1966 as Bill C-164, *An Act to Amend the Criminal Code* (group defamation libel). See M. Cohen 1966, Appendix IV.

49 Kaplan 1993, 247.

50 Kaplan 1993, 247.

51 Hage 1970, 66; Valois 1992, 379.

52 M. Cohen 1966, 3.

53 See Kaplan 1993.

54 Qtd. in Kaplan 1993, 249.

55 Qtd. in Kaplan 1993, 249.

56 M. Cohen 1966, 3.

57 M. Cohen 1966, 29–30.

58 M. Cohen 1966, 29.

59 M. Cohen 1966, 29.

60 M. Cohen 1966, 30.

61 Cohen-Almagor 2006, 157.

62 M. Cohen 1966, 32.

63 M. Cohen 1966, 59.

64 M. Cohen 1966, 59.

65 M. Cohen 1966, 59.

66 M. Cohen 1966, 59.

67 M. Cohen 1966, 59.

68 M. Cohen 1966, 59.

69 M. Cohen 1966, 8.

70 M. Cohen 1966, 8.

71 See McLuhan 1964, 5.

72 McLuhan 1964.

73 McLuhan 1994, 15.

74 M. Cohen 1966, 8.

75 Blackman and Walkerdine 2001, 32.

76 M. Cohen 1966, 9.

77 M. Cohen 1966, 25.

78 Kayfetz 1970, 6.

79 M. Cohen 1966, 24.

80 Senator Daniel Lang, Senate Hearings on Bill C-3, 12 April 1970, 944.

81 M. Cohen 1966, 24.

82 Gerald William Baldwin, House of Commons Debates, 7 April 1970, 5578.

83 Graham Park, Standing Senate Committee on Legal and Constitutional Affairs, 22 April 1969, 142.

84 John Diefenbaker, House of Commons Debates, 9 April 1970, 5685.

85 René Matte, House of Commons Debates, 17 November 1969, 892.

86 David Lewis, House of Commons Debates, 9 April 1970, 5694.

87 Lionel Choquette, Special Committee on the Criminal Code (Hate Propaganda), 29 February 1968, 24.

88 David Walker, Senate Standing Committee on Legal and Constitutional Affairs, 25 February 1969, 43.

89 Saul Hayes, Senate Standing Committee on Legal and Constitutional Affairs, 25 February 1969, 41, 44. Deputations supporting the bill came from the Canadian Jewish Congress, the Manitoba Human Rights Association, the Canadian Council of Christians and Jews, the Canadian Polish Congress, a Chinese–Canadian group, the United Nations Association of Canada, the

Canadian Labour Congress, the Association of Survivors of Nazi Oppression, and the United Black Front of Nova Scotia.

90 Senate Standing Committee on Legal and Constitutional Affairs, 18 March 1969, 94.

91 Josie Quart, Senate Standing Committee on Legal and Constitutional Affairs, 19 May 1970, 1060.

92 Barthes 1972 [1957].

93 See Perry and Schweitzer 2002.

94 Gilman 1985, 151.

95 Gilman 1985, 150–62, 154.

96 Gilman 1985, 155; von Krafft-Ebing 1905.

97 Qtd. in Gilman 1988, 169; see also Gilman 1985, 154–55. Insofar as Gilman has remarked on the racialized constitution of the nineteenth-century hysteric, feminist scholars, including Elaine Showalter, have critiqued the manifestly gendered constitution of the hysteric as a political discourse. Hysteria, historically and clinically, belies any singular definition. Beizer 1994, 34; Bernheimer 1990, 2. It was, however, "virtually without contestation a female disease, a uterine disorder" from Egyptian antiquity until the nineteenth century, during which Jean-Martin Charcot and other scientists of the time stressed its etiology as neurological. Beizer 1994, 3.

98 Qtd. in Beizer 1994, 6.

99 Harry Arthurs, Senate Standing Committee on Legal and Constitutional Affairs, 22 April 1969, 148.

100 Melvin McQuaid, House of Commons Debates, 27 October 1969, 906.

101 Patrick Mahoney, House of Commons Debates, 6 April 1970, 5530.

102 Robert Thompson, House of Commons Debates, 8 April 1970, 5644.

103 John Turner, House of Commons Debates, 6 April 1970, 5557.

104 Andrew Brewin, House of Commons Debates, 7 April 1970, 5588.

105 Fred Catzman, Special Committee of the Criminal Code, 29 February 1968, 40.

106 *Universal Declaration on Human Rights*, UN Doc A/810 (1948), 71.

107 See George White, Senate Debates, 17 June 1968, 1613.

108 See David Walker, Senate Debates, 17 June 1968, 1620.

109 Eldon Woolliams, House of Commons Debates, 6 April 1970, 5543.

110 Stanley Haidasz, House of Commons Debates, 17 November 1969, 914.

111 Arthur Roebuck, Senate Debates, 17 December 1968, 1610.

112 Harry Arthurs, witness, Senate Standing Committee on Legal and Constitutional Affairs, 22 April 1969, 146.

113 George White, Senate Debates, 17 June 1969, 1611.

114 George White, Senate Debates, 17 June 1969, 1611.

115 Harry Arthurs, witness, Senate Standing Committee on Legal and Constitutional Affairs, 22 April 1969, 145.

116 Michael Rubenstein, Senate Standing Committee on Legal and Constitutional Affairs, 11 March 1969, 82.

117 Paul Goldstein, Senate Standing Committee on Legal and Constitutional Affairs, 25 March 1969, 130.

118 Philip Givens, House of Commons Debates, 8 April 1970, 5654.

119 *Canadian Charter of Rights and Freedoms,* Part 1 of the *Constitution Act, 1982,* being Schedule B to the *Canada Act 1982* (UK), 1982, c. 11.

120 See Adam 1995; Rayside 1998; M. Smith 1999, 2005; Warner 2002.

121 M. Smith 2005, 328.

122 See Commission des Droits de la Personne du Quebec 1994; Faulkner 1997; New Brunswick Coalition for Human Rights Reform 1990; Julian Roberts, *Disproportionate Harm: Hate Crime in Canada — An Analysis of Recent Statistics* (Ottawa: Department of Justice Canada, 1995).

123 See Toronto Police Service 1999, 2000, 2002. See also Petersen 1991; Samis 1995; Suriya 1998.

Chapter 2: Legislating Victims of Hate

1 Jacobs and Potter 1998, 3.

2 Major 1996; Petersen 1991; Roberts 1995; Shaffer 1995.

3 This is the first time "sexual orientation" was written into the proposed legislation. Valverde (2003, 87) notes: "Examining a large number of rights-oriented cases, one finds that new knowledges and different authorities are required by law to investigate and legally certify the existence of the object, invented for legal purposes, but quickly adopted by many as a descriptor of experience, that has come to be called 'sexual orientation.'"

4 *Act to Amend the Criminal Code (sentencing) and Other Acts in Consequence thereof,* SC 1995, c. 22. It received royal assent on 13 July 1995 and was proclaimed in force (except for ss. 718.3(5) and the provisions dealing with hospital orders, ss. 747–747.8) on 3 September 1996. It included amendments on national or ethnic origin, language, or similar factors.

5 Daubney and Parry 1999.

6 The words seemed so diminutive against the rest of the content of the bill that Russell MacLellan, parliamentary secretary to the minister of justice and attorney general), described them as "just a little itsy-bitsy part of a section." Russell MacLellan, Bill C-41, House of Commons Debates, 13 June 1995,

120–25. For an interesting discussion of American hate crime legislative domain expansion to include "sexual orientation," see Jenness 1999; Jenness and Grattet 2001.

7 Allan Rock, Bill C-41, House of Commons Debates, 15 June 1995, 1525. These sentencing reforms included, but were not limited to, providing direction to the courts on the purpose and principles of sentencing, creating a new sentencing option called a conditional sentence, providing a provision for alternative measures (diversion) for adult and Aboriginal offenders, modernizing probation provisions, codifying rules of evidence and procedure, and establishing various reforms to victim restitution and presentation at early parole hearings. See Daubney and Parry 1999.

8 Allan Rock, Bill C-41, House of Commons Debates, 15 June 1995, 1525.

9 The first characterization was offered by Stan Keyes, Bill C-41, House of Commons Debates, 14 June 1995, 1545 and the second was uttered by Roseanne Skoke, Bill C-41, House of Commons Debates, 20 September 1994, 1630.

10 In this election, the Liberals under Jean Chrétien won a "significant parliamentary majority." Rayside 1998, 111.

11 Liberal Party of Canada 1992, 11.

12 Liberal Party of Canada 1992, 86.

13 Liberal Party of Canada 1992, 86.

14 Allan Rock, House of Commons Debates, 20 September 1994, 1215 [emphasis added].

15 Sheila Finestone, House of Commons Debates, 20 September 1994, 1515.

16 Walt Lastewka, House of Commons Debates, 15 June 1995, 1935.

17 *Canadian Charter of Rights and Freedoms,* Part 1 of the *Constitution Act, 1982,* being Schedule B to the *Canada Act 1982* (UK), 1982, c. 11.

18 Rayside 1998, 111.

19 Ménard came out publicly during these debates.

20 Roseanne Skoke, House of Commons Standing Committee of Justice and Legal Affairs, 7 February 1995 minutes 75:36. *Criminal Code,* RSC 1985, c. C-46.

21 Myron Thompson, House of Commons Debates, 15 June 1995, 2015.

22 In reported judgments, judicial consideration of bias motivation makes its first appearance in 1977 in *R. v Ingram and Grimsdale* (1977), a racially motivated attack, and again in 1979 with *R. v Atkinson, Ing and Roberts* (1978), an attack motivated by hatred of sexual orientation.

23 Myron Thompson, House of Commons Debates, 15 June 1995, 2015.

24 Mark Sandler, House of Commons Standing Committee of Justice and Legal Affairs, 14 February 1995, minutes 78:13 [emphasis added].

25 Dick Harris, House of Commons Debates, 15 June 1995, 2045.

26 In May 1981, it was reported that then UK Prime Minister Margaret Thatcher stated that "a crime is a crime is a crime." Rejecting the political nature of the actions of members of the Internal Revenue Agency (IRA), she is reported to have said, such crimes are not political. See Nationmaster http://www.nation master.com/. So this phrase used by opponents to s. 718.2(a)(I) mimics Thatcher's characterization of IRA action. It is also Thatcherite in that it articulates a particular law and order politics popularized under Thatcher's government. Mawby and Walklate argue that the economic and social unrest of Britain in the 1980s fertilized the socio-political environment in which a neo-conservative ideology of "authoritarian populism" flourished. In the 1980s, the United Kingdom saw a "continuing rise in crime, escalating unemployment, and a growing gap between rich and poor." Stuart Hall, qtd. in Mawby and Walklate 1994, 81. Among other neo-conservative agendas, including the promotion of racialized national and traditional family values (Smith 1994), Thatcherism employed a range of political, economic, and ideological mechanisms that were put in place to secure social order. The Tory campaign of the 1980s responded to a sensationalized "crime problem" by advocating a tougher approach to enforcement and punishment. At the same time, however, the fiscal politics of neo-conservatism produced cutbacks in public expenditure, widespread privatization, and a discourse of self-sufficiency and efficacious government spending. The United States, under Presidents Ronald Reagan and George Bush senior, respectively, also advocated and practised an enforcement crackdown by increasing police response, prosecutions, convictions, and punishments.

27 Stein 1998 [1913], 387–96.

28 Gomes 1996, 43.

29 Gomes 1996, 45.

30 Gwendolyn Landolt, House of Commons Standing Committee of Justice and Legal Affairs, 22 November 1994, minutes 64:37. See also Elwin Hermanson, House of Commons Debates, 13 June 1995, 2300: "a crime is a crime." John Williams, House of Commons Debates, 22 September 1994, 1720: "A victim is a victim."

31 Garry Breitkreuz, House of Commons Debates, 14 June 1995, 1555.

32 Jacobs and Potter 1998, 131.

33 Perry makes a similar observation, critically rebuking Jacobs and Potter for their position that hate crime law creates intergroup hostilities and their failure to recognize fully that "structural exclusions and cultural imagining leave minority members vulnerable to systemic violence." Perry 2002, 486.

34 Derek Lee, House of Commons Standing Committee of Justice and Legal Affairs, 9 February 1995, minutes 77:24.

35 Jack Ramsay, House of Commons Debates, 15 June 1995, 1615–30.

36 Spoken as part of Philip Mayfield's (Cariboo-Chilcotin, Reform) response to s. 718.2(a)(i), which he felt divided and retrenched racism in Canada. Philip Mayfield, House of Commons Debates, 15 June 1995, 2130.

37 Ian McClelland, House of Commons Debates, 13 June 1995, 2140.

38 Myron Thompson, House of Commons Standing Committee of Justice and Legal Affairs, 1 December 1994, minutes 69:28. For other criticism around identity, see Jack Ramsay, House of Commons Debates, 15 June 1995, 1640. He cites comment by member for Wild Rose party on obesity.

39 Hedy Fry, House of Commons Debates, 15 June 1995, 1655.

40 John Williams, House of Commons Debates, 15 June 1995, 2030.

41 Diane Ablonczy, House of Commons Debates, 15 June 1995, 2215. To this outrageous scenario, Torsney responded: "Men have a gender. They are male." Paddy Torsney, House of Commons Debates, June 15, 1995, 2215).

42 Morris Bodnar, House of Commons Standing Committee of Justice and Legal Affairs, 16 February 1995, minutes 81:19.

43 Morris Bodnar, House of Commons Standing Committee of Justice and Legal Affairs, 16 February 1995, minutes 81:20 [emphasis added]. This issue of a "backlash" against heterosexuals in the form of "heterosexual bashing" was raised earlier in the committee and was responded to by Fisher of Equality for Gays and Lesbians Everywhere (EGALE) who claimed that the term "sexual orientation" offered equal protection to heterosexuals even though "the reality is that heterosexuals don't live in a society where they are targeted as heterosexuals when they walk out the door." John Fisher, House of Commons Standing Committee of Justice and Legal Affairs, 1 December 1994, minutes 69:26.

44 Allan Rock, House of Commons Debates, 15 June 1995, 1530.

45 Stan Dromisky, House of Commons Debates, 15 June 1995, 2010.

46 Appearing before the committee, Chérif stated that the Centre for Research Action on Race Relations "categorically rejected the unreasonable and unsubstantiated arguments that the protection of hate crime victims will create more class inequities between citizens and destabilize the foundations of our pluralistic and democratic society." Mohamed Chérif, House of Commons Standing Committee of Justice and Legal Affairs, 14 February 1995, minutes 78:18. In debate, Fry stated: "I do not know if the member knows what he means by special interest groups. The bill deals with women, children, elders, and victims. Now we are being told by members of the third party

that women are a special interest group. Actually they said that already. Now children are special interests and victims are special interests. Everyone is a special interest as far as members of the third party are concerned. They do not speak for Canadians. I do not know who they speak for." Hedy Fry, House of Commons Debates, 15 June 1995, 1700.

47 Val Meredith, House of Commons Standing Committee of Justice and Legal Affairs, 14 February 1995, minutes 78:32.

48 In my research of the Hansard debates and the committee evidence, I had noted this metaphoric term, "backdoor," several times to connote a deceitful Liberal political strategy. In order to verify my observations, I performed an electronic "search" of the debates and committee testimony, all of which I had transferred electronically onto my computer's hard drive. This term was used in this exclusive context by the following members (all emphasis is added). Val Meredith, House of Commons Standing Committee of Justice and Legal Affairs, 14 February 1995, minutes 78:32 (epigraph above) and 65:31: "A *back-door* approach to having sexual orientation added to the *Charter*"; Jack Ramsay, House of Commons Debates, 13 June 1995, 1920: "We object to the minister's *back door* attempt through the bill to keep his word to provide added protection for certain groups of people and thereby create a semblance of special status for those groups"; Ian McClelland, House of Commons Debates, 13 June 1995, 2150: "It [the government] should show the courage of its convictions and do it through the *front door* honestly and honourably, not try to slide it in the *back door* through this legislation"; Elsie Wayne, House of Commons Debates, 14 June 1995, 1605: "I also fear the inclusion of the words sexual orientation in the statement of principle is a *back door* attempt at eventually legalizing same sex benefits and same sex marriages. It has been reported that on March 30, 1995 in New York City at a UN meeting the top Canadian officials at the United Nations were pushing for homosexual rights internationally so they can compel domestic compliance in Canada and justify the route they are taking with Bill C-41. The government should be *up front* about its agenda and should also listen to Canadians." This term was not used in any other context in debates surrounding the other content of Bill C-41.

Warning of such inclusion, Dennis Mills, parliamentary secretary to the minister of industry, voiced: "I hope I have made it clear why I, without any personal disrespect or malice toward homosexual persons, do not feel it would be prudent to include the words sexual orientation in this legislation. We are *opening the door* to the use of this language in other contexts that may lead to legitimizing other forms of sexual orientation we would not want to approve or to the use of the concept of sexual orientation to harm the rights of religious and other groups to freedom of religion, freedom of expression and freedom of association." Dennis Mills, House of Commons Debates, 14 June 1995, 1610 [emphasis added]. I cannot but help think that this metaphor has a richer reading, one that indexes the very act of sodomy. I explore this idea further in the chapter when I discuss REAL Women's use of the term "piggybacking" with respect to gays and lesbians wanting equity with "the legitimate claims of genuinely discriminated people." Gwendolyn Landolt, House of Commons Standing Committee of Justice and Legal Affairs, 22 November 1994, minutes 64:10.

49 Jay Hill, House of Commons Debates, 14 June 1995, 2315.

50 Rayside 1998, 111. *Canadian Human Rights Act*, RSC 1985, c. H-6. The inclusion of "sexual orientation" to the CHRA would prohibit discrimination against gays and lesbians in areas covered by federal jurisdiction. As Bill C-33, the amendment was passed on 9 May 1996, "ending the long and tortuous campaign commenced by gay and lesbian activists over two decades earlier" (Warner 2002, 214).

51 Rayside 1998, 109.

52 *Charter of Human Rights and Freedoms*, RSQ 1977, c. C-12. S. 15 of the *Canadian Charter of Rights and Freedoms*, the equality section, only came into effect in 1985 in order "to allow the federal and provincial governments enough time to review all legislation and to introduce any amendments necessary to ensure compliance." Warner 2002, 193). My use of the "door" metaphor seems quite apropos here as it both accurately reflects the tangible and symbolic effects of the *Charter* and continues the play of the "backdoor" trope used extensively around this issue. Interestingly, both Rayside and Warner respectively use the same language to describe the expansion of gay and lesbian rights. According to Rayside, the *Charter*'s "final wording included enumeration of specific grounds on the basis of which discrimination was prohibited, and the vitally important general wording that would provide courts with flexibility, in addition to a subsection explicitly opening the door for affirmative action" (Rayside 1998, 109). Warner wrote that the 1985 discussion paper, *Equality Issues in Federal Law*, "opened the door" to gay and lesbian activists seeking equality rights. Unlike the "backdoor" metaphor, the sign "door" used in these ways does not connote a devious, indirect, or concealed approach to rights-seeking activism.

53 Warner 2002, 191. See also Miriam Smith (1999, 109–10), who writes that "the *Charter* fundamentally altered the equation. For the first time, there was

the possibility that lesbians and gays could obtain actual legal protection and defence of their rights in a broad range of areas ... the *Charter* also created a new discourse of rights talk. The defining feature of rights talk is its positivistic approach to law, meaning that the law is taken seriously on its own terms as a means of achieving social change."

54 Five provinces and one territory amended their human rights codes before 1996. They were: Ontario in 1986, the Yukon and Manitoba in 1987, New Brunswick and British Columbia in 1992, and Saskatchewan in 1993. In 1990, the Nova Scotia Human Rights Commission "directed that in all places where the act referred to *sex* it would be interpreted to mean *sexual orientation*, citing s. 15 of the *Charter* and the recommendation of the parliamentary subcommittee [that inquired into equality rights and whose 1985 report, *Equality for All*, recommended that federal and provincial human rights codes be amended to include sexual orientation explicitly." See Rayside 1998, 109; Warner 2002, 202.

55 The Conservative government made such a promise but included a provision stipulating marital status, including common law relationships, in exclusively heterosexual terms (see Rayside 1998, 110–11).

56 See *Haig and Birch* 1992. Both Warner (2002) and Smith (1999) respectively track major equality-seeking litigation during this period. Three critical cases that festered in the imagination of social conservatives of the times were *Egan and Nesbit* (1995), whereby a majority of the Supreme Court of Canada confirmed that "sexual orientation" could be an analogous ground of discrimination for s. 15 *Charter* purposes; *M. v H.* (1996), where the Court of Appeal upheld the decision that exclusion of same-sex couples in s. 29 of the *Family Law Act*, RSO 1990, c. F-3, infringes s. 15 of the *Charter*; and the Alberta Court of Queen's Bench's decision in *Vriend et al.* (1994), which found that the omission of protection against discrimination on the basis of sexual orientation from the Alberta *Individual's Rights Protection Act*, RSA 1980, c. I-2, was an unjustified violation of s. 15(1). During the parliamentary debates on Bill C-41 in 1994–96, the Supreme Court of Canada had not yet ruled on *M. v H.* (1999) or *Vriend v Alberta* (1998); these judgments would be delivered in 1999 and 1998 respectively.

As evidence of agitation felt by socially conservative members of the House of Commons, I offer two accounts. The first was by Roseanne Skoke and the second by Dennis Mills; both were Liberal members. "To endorse or to include the words sexual orientation in any federal legislation would confer on homosexuals the ability to obtain special legal status, allow them to redefine the family, to enter into the realm of the sanctity of marriage, to adopt children, to infiltrate the curriculum of schools and to impose an alternative lifestyle on youth. All these demands are encroaching on and undermining the inherent and inviolable rights of family and the rights of the church." Roseanne Skoke, House of Commons Debates, 13 June 1995, 2040. "I fear that by including the words sexual orientation in federal law for the first time without clarification or definition, we are extending an invitation to the courts to read sexual orientation into other statutes as they have done with the Canadian and Alberta bill of rights in previous provincial court decisions. The legitimacy of this reading has not yet been ruled on by the Supreme Court of Canada. By including these words in a s. 15 like list in a federal statute we are saying as federal legislators that what we did not want to include in 1981 we want to include today. The courts may well turn to this wording for guidance on other matters. What we have already seen is not encouraging. The Alberta Court of Queen's Bench ruled the Alberta human rights code had to be read as if sexual orientation was included in the *Vriend* case, which meant a private Christian Reformed college had to hire a teacher who was a practising homosexual despite its religious objections to his behavior." Dennis Mills, House of Commons Debates, 14 June 1995, 1610.

57 Myron Thompson, House of Commons Debates, 15 June 1995, 2110. See also Jay Hill, House of Commons Debates, 13 June 1995, 2325.

58 Art Hanger, House of Commons Debates, 13 June 1995, 2200–5.

59 This reading of a seemingly innocuous statement – "unhealthy relationships" – is supported by my extensive reading of right-wing Christian media during this historic period. For example, REAL Women of Canada's newsletter, *REALity*, republished a controversial commentary from a lawyer commenting on the *Vriend* case. Marking out the "fundamental differences" between homosexuals and heterosexuals, William Somerville remarked that gays are a "high risk to life and health" and that they cannot contribute to "the regeneration of society." See REAL Women of Canada, http://www.realwomenca.com/newsletter/2000_Sept_Oct/article_9.html. Accessed November 2002.

60 The avalanche quotation was provided by Elsie Wayne, House of Commons Debates, 14 June 1995, 1605, and the larger quotation by Art Hanger, House of Commons Debates, 13 June 1995, 2205.

61 Dick Harris, House of Commons Debates, 15 June 1995, 2040.

62 Jim Abbott, House of Commons Debates, 14 June 1995, 1535.

63 Roseanne Skoke, House of Commons Debates, 13 June 1995, 2040. Insofar as natural law is constructed as being both anterior and superior to positive law, natural law typically provides an absolute and (on its own terms) indisputable

grounding for positions, especially in contrast to the positive law generated by the conventional or legal sovereignty of the state. I am rather fond of Jerome Frank's (1949, 351) indictment of natural law: "Eloquent verbal adherence to Natural Law gives no assurance of moral practices, may indeed furnish a smoke-screen for highly questionable activities ... Pragmatically, such devotion is no guaranty against injustice and immorality." Bill Graham responding to Skoke stated: "When I hear comments from members of the House about relativism and about characterizing one group as being outside the bounds of protection afforded by civilized society and refer to natural law, I think of that quote and I shudder. My natural law is found in the Supreme Court of Canada in *Egan v. Nesbitt* which holds that discrimination is outlawed in the country." Bill Graham, House of Commons Debates, 15 June 1995, 1705.

64 Roseanne Skoke, House of Commons Debates, 14 June 1995, 1540; she has repeatedly used the term, "homosexualist," to describe gays and lesbians (see 20 September 1994, 1630). It was reported in the media that members of the Reform attempted to deliver a wheelbarrow full of petitions against adding sexual orientation to the bill.

65 Roseanne Skoke, House of Commons Debates, 13 June 1995, 2045.

66 Carolyn Parrish, House of Commons Debates, 13 June 1995, 2255. See also Sue Barnes, House of Commons Debates, 14 June 1995, 1705: "I have also heard it said that the new bill will make it a crime to speak out publicly against homosexuality. Again, let us be perfectly clear. It is the right of every Canadian to be able to speak his or her mind. A church sermon expressing a moral view is not a crime. Freedom of speech and religion are both specifically protected under our *Charter of Rights and Freedoms*." Even Liberal Don Boudria, who was not a proponent of gay and lesbian equality rights, noted his displeasure with the content and volume of public misinformation: "Never, since first arriving in this House a long time ago, have I read letters from constituents and others expressing such disturbing grievances. Let us remember that the bill is about sentencing with regard to crimes already committed. I received letters and postcards from people in other ridings, like this one, which talk about the government wanting to legitimize the lifestyle of a group that undermines basic family values. I have here another letter I have received. Another letter says Bill C-41 would harm the rights of parents to protect their children, the rights of institutions to have a preference over adoption policy, historical rights of freedom of religion, the right of religious institutions to have hiring practices consistent with their religious belief and so on." Don Boudria, House of Commons Debates, 14 June 1995, 1630.

67 William Gilmour, House of Commons Debates, 14 June 1995, 1640.

68 Dennis Mills, House of Commons Debates, 14 June 1995, 1610.

69 Similarly, in their submission to the committee, Victims of Violence's research director, Steve Sullivan, citing the opinion of Dr. David Greenberg, a psychiatrist with the sexual behaviour clinic at Royal Ottawa Hospital, stated that sexual orientation is "a descriptive term about what turns a person on … it does include pedophilia."

70 Paul Forseth, House of Commons Debates, 14 June 1995, 1615. He used the same statement in House of Commons Standing Committee of Justice and Legal Affairs on 24 November 1994, minutes 65:18.

71 Robert Wakefield, House of Commons Standing Committee of Justice and Legal Affairs, 9 February 1995, minutes 76:54.

72 John Conroy, House of Commons Standing Committee of Justice and Legal Affairs, 24 November 1994, minutes 65:18.

73 Dick Harris, House of Commons Debates, 15 June 1995, 2040: "Bill C-41 does not reflect the views of the average Canadian because the Liberals did not pursue a broad sampling of the views of average Canadians … Instead they selected people to attend the committees, to submit briefs from groups and organizations, not individuals views, so they could mould them into the real Liberal agenda of the bill, something politically expedient for that party."

74 See EGALE Communiqué, 16 November 1994.

75 Wappel 1994. Wappel's citation to medical authority falls short in that, according to the Queer Resources Directory, "Paul Cameron is both the best known, and the least credible, of the various psychologists, medical doctors, and associated professionals which actively collaborate with the Religious Right, and attempt to lend a veneer of scientific respectability to the Religious Right's anti-gay propaganda" (http://www.qrd.org/QRD/www/RRR/cameron.html), In 1984, Cameron was expelled from the American Psychological Association; see http://facultysites.dss.ucdavis.edu/~gmherek/rainbow/html/facts_cameron_sheet.html#note5. In an internal ASA resolution dated August 1985, the resolution stated: "Dr. Paul Cameron has consistently misinterpreted and misrepresented sociological research on sexuality, homosexuality, and lesbianism" (see http://facultysites.dss.ucdavis.edu/~gmherek/rainbow/html/ASA_resolution_1985.PDF).

76 Allan Rock, House of Commons Standing Committee of Justice and Legal Affairs, 17 November 1994, minutes 62:30. Rock's interpretation of sexual orientation was supported by John Fisher, executive director of EGALE, who stated that "in our view there is no chance whatsoever that sexual orientation

will be interpreted by the courts to include pedophilia" (minutes 69:15). Pierrette Venne, Bloc Québécois member for Saint-Hubert, similarly argued that "in the *Egan* case, the federal court seems to indicate that a sexual tendency or orientation can be heterosexual, homosexual or bisexual. This case made a challenge under s. 15 of the *Canadian Charter of Rights and Freedoms*. The court concluded that, although the Supreme Court has never issued an opinion on the issue, the fact that sexual tendencies can be invoked as motives constituting discrimination such as those prohibited under ss. 15(1) had become a matter of settled law." Pierrette Venne, House of Commons Debates, 13 June 1995, 2035.

77 Jim Slater, House of Commons Standing Committee of Justice and Legal Affairs, 16 February 1995, minutes 81:5.

78 Gwendolyn Landolt, House of Commons Standing Committee of Justice and Legal Affairs, 22 November 1994, minutes 64:10.

79 John Fisher, House of Commons Standing Committee of Justice and Legal Affairs, 1 December 1994, minutes 69:22. See also Hardisty and Gluckman in which they write that anti-homosexual literature in addition to portraying gays and lesbians as "immoral, disease-ridden child molesters [are further] described as superwealthy, highly-educated free spenders." Hardisty and Gluckman 1997, 218.

80 Rigdon 1991.

81 Didi Herman (1996, 349) notes the methodology is flawed citing that "self-selecting readers of a glossy gay men's magazine are likely to be amongst the most affluent members" of the gay and lesbian community, that in the rare data that has been collected on lesbian income "lesbian households earn anywhere from far below, to somewhat above, the national [American] average" (349), and that the comparative statistic of gay to African-American household is misleading noting that "the gay average is not being contrasted with the African-American average, but with the average of the *poorest* black households" (350, emphasis in original). Another observer notes that respondents were "self-selected ... and that there was no means to prevent multiple responses in the survey" Wilke 2001.

82 Herman 1996. See also Hardisty and Gluckman (1997, 218), who note that the slogan of "special rights" implies that "the movement to ensure civil rights for lesbians and gay men is usurping and destroying the African American civil-rights agenda."

83 Kinsey et al. 1948 and Kinsey et al. 1953.

84 For example, citing American Focus on the Family research, Landolt of REAL Women stated: "There has been absolutely no proof to indicate a convincing pattern of oppression causing them, as an entire class, to experience abuse –

physical or verbal abuse. It's true that some individual homosexuals have been subject to verbal or physical abuse, but of course so have many heterosexuals. However, no matter how loudly proclaimed, allegations of oppression against them *as a class* simply do not hold up." Gwendolyn Landolt, House of Commons Standing Committee of Justice and Legal Affairs, 22 November 1994, minutes 64:10 [emphasis added]. Landolt was adamant about the issue that sexual orientation was not a historically discriminated class, arguing that gays and lesbians had not suffered economically, socially, or culturally as had other minority groups. Coupling this argument with another that rejected the notion that, as she rephrased it, "sexual behaviour" was "an analogous group to gender, ethnicity and race," she concluded that "homosexuals" could not be perceived to be "victims" (minutes 64:19).

85 Jim Slater, House of Commons Standing Committee of Justice and Legal Affairs, 16 February 1995, minutes 81:5. Queer legal scholar, Did Herman, in her excellent article on America's Christian Right anti-gay discourse cited a 1993 Christian Right document written by Tony Marco which claimed that "[g]ays are no minority; gay militants constitute a rich, powerful *special interest.* And, to coin a phrase, enough money makes anyone a "majority" (1996: 350, emphasis in the original).

86 I am convinced that Landolt's inclusion of "gender" is not produced out of a feminist understanding of gender oppression but, rather, as an obligatory mention insofar as she represents REAL Women, a national, Christian-based, socially conservative movement that is "pro-family." Gwendolyn Landolt, House of Commons Standing Committee of Justice and Legal Affairs, 22 November 1994, minutes 64:8.

87 Herman's article on the anti-gay strategies and rhetoric of the American Christian Right (CR) is illuminating and her findings parallel many of the arguments of exclusion voiced by Reform and its supporters. For example, with respect to the construction of gays as deceitful, she writes: "Often using lesbian and gay theorizing and 'queer' politics, several CR pragmatists argue that the notion of 'gay' is meaningless; that lesbians and gays themselves are discarding these labels, and that civil rights protections based on gay sexuality will actually be open to anyone claiming any sort of sexual identity at all (for example, paedophiles, necrophiliacs, and so on). Furthermore, this fluidity, the CR suggests, is additional evidence of the *deceit* of the gay community; on the one hand, they persist in advocating immutability, and on the other, they insist on the shifting terrain of sexuality signified by the word 'queer.'" Herman 1996, 354 [emphasis added].

88   See for example, Staver 2002.

89   Several incidents of gaybashing and anti-gay/lesbian victimization were mentioned in the House of Commons debates. Notably, Svend Robinson raised the issue early stating: "Just last weekend in Toronto two men on a downtown street walking home from a café, the Second Cup coffee shop, were attacked. Six young men piled out of a van and beat these two men with fists, boots, and beer bottles, right in the heart of downtown Toronto." Svend Robinson, House of Commons Debates, 18 October 1994, 1115. After the committee hearings, other members spoke of anti-gay/lesbian victimization, often speaking in a highly personalized way. For example, Hedy Fry, parliamentary secretary to the minister of health, recounted gay victimization through her experience as an emergency physician: "When I was a physician I saw many young men come into the emergency room with injuries from beatings inflicted because they were gay. Gay bashing in my riding is a favourite Friday and Saturday night sport when brave, macho males drive into town and identify men who are gay, or even worse, who they think are gay, and in bullying, frightened, drunken bravado afflict brutal harm on these people." Hedy Fry, House of Commons Debates, 15 June 1995, 1650. Bill Graham, the Liberal member for Rosedale, a riding that includes the Church-Wellesley village, spoke personally of knowledge that was conveyed to him by his constituents: "In my own riding of Rosedale, like the member for Vancouver Centre [Hedy Fry], I know of people walking down Church Street and having cars pull up and people jump out who have been beaten them up, crying that they were gay." Bill Graham, House of Commons Debates, 15 June 1995, 1705.

90   John Nunziata, House of Commons Debates, 13 June 1995, 2155.

91   EGALE 1994.

92   EGALE 1994, 7.

93   Shirley Maheu, member for St. Laurent-Cartierville, brought forward Bill C-455, *Bias Incidents Statistics Act*. It had its first reading on 8 June 1993 but did not receive a second reading: "An *Act* to provide for the collection of statistics respecting incidents investigated by police forces where those incidents manifest evidence of bias against certain identifiable groups" (cited in Roberts 1995). *Hate Crimes Statistics Act*, 28 USC § 534 and the 1992 British Crime Survey as cited in Roberts 1995.

94   Respectively, these studies were New Brunswick Coalition for Human Rights Reform 1990; Nova Scotia Public Interest Research Group 1994; and the preliminary findings of Samis 1995.

95 EGALE 1994, 7. See also Commission des droits de la personne 1994.

96 Allan Rock, House of Commons Debates, 15 June 1995, 1530; Sue Barnes, House of Commons Debates, 14 June 1995, 1705.

97 Myron Thompson, House of Commons Standing Committee of Justice and Legal Affairs, 24 November 1994, minutes 66:27.

98 Roberts 1995; Perry 2001.

99 See, for example, Berrill 1991; Herek, Gillis, and Cogan 1999.

100 Matsuda et al. 1993.

101 Roberts 1995, 1, 2.

102 Julian Roberts, House of Commons Standing Committee of Justice and Legal Affairs, 7 February 1995, minutes 75:12.

103 Qtd. in Roberts 1995.

104 Sepejak 1977.

105 Roberts 1995.

106 Myron Thompson, House of Commons Standing Committee of Justice and Legal Affairs, 24 November 1994, minutes 65:29.

107 Paul Forseth, Reform, House of Commons Standing Committee of Justice and Legal Affairs, 22 November 1994, minutes 64:32 [emphasis added].

108 Gwendolyn Landolt, House of Commons Standing Committee of Justice and Legal Affairs, 22 November 1994, minutes 64:32–33.

109 Von Hentig 1967.

110 Bayer 1987; Bieber 1962.

111 With respect to this notion of defence, Bristow notes that the inference is that "repressed homosexual desire is the cause of ... homophobia [and that] such an argument gives the impression that gay men are the culprits" of their own victimization. Bristow 1989, 63–64.

112 Both Freud and his epigones believed that femininity was psychically structured around masochistic tendencies. Freud 1977a; Freud 1977b.

113 Bieber 1962; Bayer 1987.

114 Maghan and Sagarin 1983, 158–59.

115 Maghan and Sagarin 1983, 160–61.

116 Weinberg 1972.

117 Crew and Norton 1974, 275.

118 This literature spans widely from the psychological (see Berrill and Herek 1992) to the philosophical (see Butler 1993; Foucault 1990 [1976]; Fuss 1991).

119 Mason 2002; Tomsen and Mason 2001. Perry (2001, 110) adopts the phrase "doing gender appropriately" to describe the heteronormative ideal of adhering to a strict code of gender performance; "doing gender inappropriately"

would be a violation of these codes and subject to punishment or opprobrium.

120 Stanko and Curry 1997, 514.

121 Miller and Humphreys (1980) labelled Rupp's article in this way. See Rupp 1970.

122 Quoted in Miller and Humphreys 1980, 180.

123 Miller and Humphreys 1980, 180.

124 Miller and Humphreys 1980, 182.

125 Johnson and Ferraro 2000; Puzone, Saltzman, Kresnow, Thompson, Mercy 2000; Turell 2000.

126 Bryden 1994, 1.

127 The first characterization was offered by Stan Keyes, House of Commons Debates, 14 June 1995, 1545, and the second was uttered by Roseanne Skoke, House of Commons Debates, 20 September 1994, 1630.

Chapter 3: Bill C-250: A Censoring of Religious Freedom or a Protection against Hate?

1 The hearings of the Senate Standing Committee on Legal and Constitutional Affairs were conducted on 10–25 March 2004. The first reading of Bill C-250 was 24 October 2002.

2 *Criminal* Code, RSC 1985, c. C-46.

3 37th Parliament, 3rd Session, 10–25 March 2004.

4 The panel of witnesses opposing Bill C-250 was composed, principally, by Gwendolyn Landolt from REAL Women of Canada, Derek Rogusky from Focus on the Family (Canada), Janet Epp Buckingham from the Evangelical Fellowship of Canada, Dr. André Lafrance from the Canadian Family Action Coalition, Dr. Charles McVety, president of Canada Christian College, and Dawn Stefanowicz, a certified management accountant.

5 Libertarian arguments are two-fold: free expression is intrinsic to the autonomy, self-development, and self-expression of the rational citizen and the social collective and free expression is instrumental insofar as it promotes autonomy and self-expression, and contributes to the advancement of democracy in that opposing ideas, particularly the political, circulate and are debated in the public forum (see Kallen 1991; Moon 2000). Posited against libertarian ideas are egalitarian notions on freedom of expression. These state that there are reasonable limits to expression, particularly with respect to hate propaganda, that advancement of truths is not always the inevitable outcome of expression and that the state, in its duty to protect all citizens, must reasonably limit extreme expression that vilifies targeted groups.

6 See J. Cohen 2000; Major 1996; Ross 1994.

7 Prior to the inclusion of "sexual orientation" to the list of identifiable groups, the list consisted only of "any section of the public distinguished by colour, race, religion or ethnic origin." *Criminal Code*, RSC 1985.

8 Svend Robinson, House of Commons Debates, 27 June 1990, 1400. Bill C-326, *An Act to Amend the Criminal Code (Hate Propaganda)*, 2nd Session, 34th Parliament, died in the House of Commons.

9 In this same session of Parliament, Peter Milliken sought to expand the list further by adding "age, sex, sexual orientation, or mental or physical disability" to two subsequent bills – Bill C-350 and Bill C-429 respectively. Both bills died in the House of Commons.

10 Svend Robinson, House of Commons Debates, 26 October 1999, 1735.

11 Svend Robinson, House of Commons Debates, 29 May 2002, 1735.

12 Information on prorogation and Standing Order 86.1, http://www.parl.gc.ca/ information/about/process/house/Prorogation/prorogation-e.htm.

13 Svend Robinson, House of Commons Debates, 24 October 2002, 830.

14 Svend Robinson, House of Commons Debates, 24 October 2002, 830. A motion was carried and accepted in the House of Commons that an additional clause be added to the amendment. To the defences of s. 3(b) – "No person shall be convicted of an offence under subsection (2), (b) if, in good faith, the person expressed or attempted to establish by an argument an opinion on a religious subject" – was added the phrase "or an opinion based on a belief in a religious text."

15 Charles McVety, Senate Standing Committee on Legal and Constitutional Affairs, 24 March 2004, Issue 4.

16 Gwendolyn Landolt, Senate Standing Committee on Legal and Constitutional Affairs, 17 March 2004, Issue 4.

17 Gwendolyn Landolt, Senate Standing Committee on Legal and Constitutional Affairs, 17 March 2004, Issue 4.

18 Janet Buckingham, Senate Standing Committee on Legal and Constitutional Affairs, 17 March 2004, Issue 4.

19 *Canadian Charter of Rights and Freedoms,* Part 1 of the *Constitution Act, 1982,* being Schedule B to the *Canada Act 1982* (UK), 1982, c. 11.

20 David Smith, Senate Standing Committee on Legal and Constitutional Affairs, 24 March 2004, Issue 4.

21 Gwendolyn Landolt, Senate Standing Committee on Legal and Constitutional Affairs, 17 March 2004, Issue 4.

22 Gwendolyn Landolt, Senate Standing Committee on Legal and Constitutional Affairs, 17 March 2004, Issue 4.

23 Richard Parkyn, Senate Standing Committee on Legal and Constitutional Affairs, 17 March 2004, Issue 4.

24 Svend Robinson, Senate Standing Committee on Legal and Constitutional Affairs, 10 March 2004, Issue 3. *Charter of Human Rights and Freedoms*, RSQ 1977, c. C-12.

25 Serge Joyal, Senate Standing Committee on Legal and Constitutional Affairs, 24 March 2004, Issue 4. The term under Canadian law means heterosexuality, homosexuality, and bisexuality. No specific *philia* are recognized nor are sexual acts or behaviours that are illegal under Canadian law. *Vriend* 1998, 61.

26 Gwendolyn Landolt, Senate Standing Committee on Legal and Constitutional Affairs, 17 March 2004, Issue 4.

27 *Keegstra* 1990.

28 *Keegstra* 1990, 163–64.

29 *Keegstra* 1990, 84.

30 Richard Parkyn, Senate Standing Committee on Legal and Constitutional Affairs, 17 March 2004, Issue 4.

31 Trevor Fenton, Senate Standing Committee on Legal and Constitutional Affairs, 11 March 2004, Issue 3. See also Webking 1995, 7. S. 318 was only used once, unsuccessfully, to prosecute a number of Manitoba Knights of the Ku Klux Klan in December 1991, Suriya 1998, 51, n. 110.

32 As of 2009, there were six reported cases under s. 319(2). Four cases were successful: *R. v Harding* (2001b), 57 OR (3d) 333 (Ont. CA); *Keegstra* 1990; *Andrews* 1990; *Safadi* 1994. See Suriya 1998. The other two were unsuccessful at appeal: *Buzzanga and Durocher* 1979; *Ahenakew* 2009.

33 Janet Buckingham, Senate Standing Committee on Legal and Constitutional Affairs, 17 March 2004, Issue 4.

34 Svend Robinson, Senate Standing Committee on Legal and Constitutional Affairs, 10 March 2004, Issue 3.

35 Gwendolyn Landolt, Senate Standing Committee on Legal and Constitutional Affairs, 17 March 2004, Issue 4.

36 Charles McVety, Senate Standing Committee on Legal and Constitutional Affairs, 24 March 2004, Issue 4.

37 Tommy Banks voiced the same sentiment when he addressed a witness: "Do you take any comfort from the fact that in order to protect against all prosecutions under the *Criminal Code*, one must convince an attorney general that the bringing of a charge is likely to result in a conviction and that absent that, the kinds of frivolous things that you are talking about would not likely obtain?" Tommy Banks, Senate Standing Committee on Legal and Constitutional Affairs, 17 March 2004.

38 Trevor Fenton, Senate Standing Committee on Legal and Constitutional Affairs, 11 March 2004, Issue 3.

39 Derek Rogusky, Senate Standing Committee on Legal and Constitutional Affairs, 17 March 2004, Issue 4.

40 *Harding* 2001a; Janet Buckingham, Senate Standing Committee on Legal and Constitutional Affairs, 17 March 2004, Issue 4.

41 *Harding* 2001b. Examples of Harding's published statements are the following: "[Muslims are] violent and hateful towards Jews, Christians and anyone else that denies or objects to their false religion" and Muslims masquerade as pacifists "but underneath their false sheep's clothing are raging wolves, seeking whom they may devour and Toronto is definitely on their hit list" (3).

42 *Harding* 2001b, para. 11.

43 *Harding* 2001a, para. 66.

44 Clair Schnupp, Senate Standing Committee on Legal and Constitutional Affairs, 17 March 2004, Issue 4.

45 *Owens* 2002.

46 *Vriend et al.* 1996, 1.

47 *Individual's Rights Protection Act*, R.S.A. 1980, c. I-2.

48 *Vriend* 1998.

49 *Owens* 2002.

50 *Owens* 2002, para. 7.

51 *Owens* 2002, para. 3. *The Saskatchewan Human Rights Code*, S.S. 1979, c. S-24.1

52 Janet Buckingham, Senate Standing Committee on Legal and Constitutional Affairs, 17 March 2004, Issue 4. As a point of interest, *Owens* was overturned by Saskatchewan's Court of Appeal in 2006: "The Board of Inquiry and the Chambers judge both took these passages at face value, making no allowance for the fact they are ancient and fundamental religious text. In other words, the passages referred to by Mr. Owens were assessed by the Board and the Chambers judge in the same way as one might consider a contemporary poster, notice or publication saying 'Homosexuals should be killed.' In my view, that was an error." *Owens* 2006, para. 77.

53 Moon 2000, 144.

54 See Moon 2000, 144. *Canadian Human Rights Act*, SC 1976–77, c. 33. In 1996, "sexual orientation" was added as a prohibited ground of discrimination.

55 *Human Rights Code*, RSBC 1996, c 210.

56 Qtd. in Moon 2000, 144. *Canada (Human Rights Commission)* 1990.

57 Moon 2000, 145.

58 Moon 2000, 145.

59 Trevor Fenton, Senate Standing Committee on Legal and Constitutional Affairs, 11 March 2004, Issue 3.

60 Trevor Fenton, Senate Standing Committee on Legal and Constitutional Affairs, 11 March 2004, Issue 3.

61 David Smith, Senate Standing Committee on Legal and Constitutional Affairs, 24 March 2004, Issue 4.

62 Serge Joyal, Senate Standing Committee on Legal and Constitutional Affairs, 17 March 2004, Issue 4.

63 Serge Joyal, Senate Standing Committee on Legal and Constitutional Affairs, 17 March 2004, Issue 4.

64 "Mr. Speaker, in my 10 years as a member of Parliament, I have never seen an issue that has led to so many letters, e-mails and phone calls from across Canada. I have heard from hundreds of constituents and close to 10,000 Canadians from across the country, almost all opposed." Murray Calder, House of Commons Debates, 6 June 2003, 1445.

65 Charles McVety, Senate Standing Committee on Legal and Constitutional Affairs, 24 March 2004, Issue 4.

66 Dawn Stefanowicz, Senate Standing Committee on Legal and Constitutional Affairs, 17 March 2004, Issue 4.

67 Dawn Stefanowicz, Senate Standing Committee on Legal and Constitutional Affairs, 17 March 2004, Issue 4.

68 Dawn Stefanowicz, Standing Senate Committee on Legal and Constitutional Affairs, 17 March 2004, Issue 4.

69 Dawn Stefanowicz, Standing Senate Committee on Legal and Constitutional Affairs, 17 March 2004, Issue 4.

70 Dawn Stefanowicz, Senate Standing Committee on Legal and Constitutional Affairs, 17 March 2004, Issue 4.

71 Dawn Stefanowicz, Senate Standing Committee on Legal and Constitutional Affairs, 17 March 2004, Issue 4.

72 Dawn Stefanowicz, Senate Standing Committee on Legal and Constitutional Affairs, 17 March 2004, Issue 4.

73 Dawn Stefanowicz, Senate Standing Committee on Legal and Constitutional Affairs, 17 March 2004, Issue 4.

74 Dawn Stefanowicz, Senate Standing Committee on Legal and Constitutional Affairs, 17 March 2004, Issue 4.

75 Dawn Stefanowicz, Senate Standing Committee on Legal and Constitutional Affairs, 17 March 2004, Issue 4.

76 Dawn Stefanowicz, Senate Standing Committee on Legal and Constitutional Affairs, 17 March 2004, Issue 4.

77 Dawn Stefanowicz, Senate Standing Committee on Legal and Constitutional Affairs, 17 March 2004, Issue 4.

78 Ahmed 2004, 51 [emphasis in original].

79 Ahmed 2004, 50.

80 Dawn Stefanowicz, Senate Standing Committee on Legal and Constitutional Affairs, 17 March 2004, Issue 4.

81 Dawn Stefanowicz, Senate Standing Committee on Legal and Constitutional Affairs, 17 March 2004, Issue 4.

82 André Lafrance, Senate Standing Committee on Legal and Constitutional Affairs, 17 March 2004, Issue 4.

83 André Lafrance, Senate Standing Committee on Legal and Constitutional Affairs, 17 March 2004, Issue 4.

84 André Lafrance, Senate Standing Committee on Legal and Constitutional Affairs, 17 March 2004, Issue 4.

85 André Lafrance, Senate Standing Committee on Legal and Constitutional Affairs, 17 March 2004, Issue 4.

86 André Lafrance, Senate Standing Committee on Legal and Constitutional Affairs, 17 March 2004, Issue 4.

87 Grant Hill, *Homosexuality and Health.* Reference to the Canadian Medical Association responding to Hill's claims quoted in *The Free Library.* 2002 Catholic Insight. http://www.thefreelibrary.com/Grant+Hill,+homosexuality+and+health.+(News+in+Brief%3A+Canada).

88 Lafrance 1993.

89 André Lafrance, Standing Senate Committee on Legal and Constitutional Affairs, 17 March 2004, Issue 4.

90 André Lafrance, Standing Senate Committee on Legal and Constitutional Affairs, 17 March 2004, Issue 4.

91 André Lafrance, Senate Standing Committee on Legal and Constitutional Affairs, 17 March 2004, Issue 4 [emphasis added].

92 André Lafrance, Senate Standing Committee on Legal and Constitutional Affairs, 17 March 2004, Issue 4 [emphasis added].

93 Anne Cools, Senate Standing Committee on Legal and Constitutional Affairs, 17 March 2004, Issue 4: "Would Dr. Lafrance tell us about the medical consequences to individuals who involve themselves in activities such as 'rimming' if you know the word, sado-masochism and so on?"

94 Raynell Andreychuk, Senate Standing Committee on Legal and Constitutional Affairs, 17 March 2004, Issue 4.

95 André Lafrance, Standing Committee on Legal and Constitutional Affairs, 17 March 2004, Issue 4.

96 Tommy Banks, Senate Standing Committee on Legal and Constitutional Affairs, 17 March 2004, Issue 4.

97 John Lynch-Staunton, Senate Standing Committee on Legal and Constitutional Affairs, 17 March 2004, Issue 4.

98 John Lynch-Staunton, Senate Standing Committee on Legal and Constitutional Affairs, 17 March 2004, Issue 4 [emphasis added].

99 André Lafrance, Senvate Standing Committee on Legal and Constitutional Affairs, 17 March 2004, Issue 4.

100 John Lynch-Staunton, Senate Standing Committee on Legal and Constitutional Affairs, 17 March 2004, Issue 4.

101 Freud 1979b [1910]. For an in-depth analysis of Freud's theory of paranoia and homophobia, see Lunny 1997.

102 Freud 1979b [1910], 143, 150.

103 Freud 1979b [1910], 142.

104 Freud 1979b [1910], 150.

105 Freud 1979b [1910], 196.

106 Freud 1979b [1910] 196–97.

107 Freud 1979b [1910], 200.

108 Freud 1979b [1910], 200–1.

109 Freud 1979b [1910], 201.

110 Freud 1979b [1910], 201.

111 Freud 1979b [1910], 201 [emphasis in the original]. In "Some Neurotic Mechanisms in Jealousy, Paranoia and Homosexuality," Freud (1977a [1925], 201) reiterates his theory of paranoia and its roots in the unbearable homosexual wish, stating "the enmity which the persecuted paranoic sees in others is the reflection of his own hostile impulses against them." Speaking to the reversal of affect, he notes that "this ambivalence thus serves the same purpose for the persecuted paranoic as jealousy served for my patient – that of a defence against homosexuality" (201).

112 Charles McVety, Senate Standing Committee on Legal and Constitutional Affairs, 24 March 2004, Issue 4.

Chapter 4: The Trans "Bathroom Bill"

1 *Canadian Human Rights Act*, RSC 1985, c. H-6 (*CHRA*); *Criminal* Code, RSC 1985, c. C-46.

2 Terms "gender identity" and "gender expression" were in Bill C-392, *An Act to Amend the CHRA ("gender identity" and "gender expression")* (2005); Bill C-326, *An Act to Amend the CHRA ("gender identity" and "gender expression")* (2006);

Bill C-494, *An Act to Amend the Criminal Code ("gender identity" and "gender expression")* (2007).

3 Significantly, Cabinet ministers Jim Flaherty, Lisa Raitt, and John Baird voted in favour of the bill.

4 By request of the government, the governor-general prorogued Parliament on 13 September 2013. The bill was re-instated at the 41st Parliament, 2nd Session, and referred to the Senate Standing Committee on Legal and Constitutional Affairs. The Senate gave consideration to the committee report only to adjourn debate on 9 June 2015. The 41st Parliament was dissolved on 2 August 2015. With the newly elected Liberal government, there was talk that the bill may be revived.

5 Bill Siksay, House of Commons Debates, 15 May 2009, 1100.

6 Irwin Cotler, House of Commons Debates, 5 April 2012, 1400. *Canadian Charter of Rights and Freedoms,* Part 1 of the *Constitution Act, 1982,* being Schedule B to the *Canada Act 1982* (UK), 1982, c. 11.

7 Jeremy Garrison, House of Commons Debates, 5 April 2012, 1350.

8 Thomas 2006, 316.

9 Bill Siksay, House of Commons Debates, 10 May 2010, 1105.

10 Thomas 2006, 311.

11 Bill Siksay, House of Commons Debates, 10 May 2010, 1105.

12 Qtd. Irwin Cotler, House of Commons Debates, 27 February 2013, 1905.

13 Noa Mendelsohn Aviv, Senate Standing Committee on Human Rights, 10 June 2013, Issue 28, http://www.parl.gc.ca/Content/SEN/Committee/411/ridr/28ev-50227-e.htm?Language=E&Parl=41&Ses=1&comm_id=77.

14 Robert Peterson, Senate Standing Committee on Human Rights, 10 June 2013, Issue 28, http://www.parl.gc.ca/Content/SEN/Committee/411/ridr/28ev-50227-e.htm?Language=E&Parl=41&Ses=1&comm_id=77.

15 Juang 2006, 706.

16 Perry 2001.

17 Jack Levin, Gail Mason, and Leslie Moran to cite a few.

18 Hershel Russell, House of Commons Standing Committee on Justice and Human Rights, 20 November 2012, 1640.

19 Thomas 2006, 318.

20 Perry 2001.

21 Ryan Dyck, House of Commons Standing Committee on Justice and Human Rights, 20 November 2012, 1715.

22 Berrill and Herek 1992; Herek, Gillis, and Cogan 1999.

23 Ginsberg 1996, 5.

24 Sara Buechner, House of Commons Standing Committee on Justice and Human Rights, 20 November 2012, 1545.

25 Ginsberg 1996, 4.

26 Ginsberg 1996, 4.

27 Jeremy Garrison, House of Commons Standing Committee on Justice and Human Rights, 20 November 2012, 1530.

28 Greta Bauer, Senate Standing Committee on Human Rights, 3 June 2013, Issue 27, http://www.parl.gc.ca/Content/SEN/Committee/411/ridr/28ev-50227-e.htm?Language=E&Parl=41&Ses=1&comm_id=77.

29 Mario Silva, House of Commons Debates, 8 June 2010, 1745.

30 Greta Bauer, Senate Standing Committee on Human Rights, 3 June 2013, Issue 27, http://www.parl.gc.ca/Content/SEN/Committee/411/ridr/28ev-50227-e.htm?Language=E&Parl=41&Ses=1&comm_id=77.

31 Bill Siksay, House of Commons Debates, 10 May 2010, 1105.

32 Jeremy Garrison, House of Commons Standing Committee on Justice and Human Rights, 20 November 2012, 1530.

33 Sara Buechner, House of Commons Standing Committee on Justice and Human Rights, 20 November 2012, 1545.

34 Hershel Russell, House of Commons Standing Committee on Justice and Human Rights, 20 November 2012, 1640.

35 Hershel Russell, House of Commons Standing Committee on Justice and Human Rights, 20 November 2012, 1645.

36 Bill Siksay, House of Commons Debates, 10 May 2010, 1110.

37 Sylvie Boucher, House of Commons Debates, 10 May 2010, 1125.

38 Brent Rathgeber, House of Commons Standing Committee on Justice and Human Rights, 20 November 2012, 1555. In 2004, Montreuil filed a complaint with the Canadian Human Rights Commission (CHRC) alleging that the Canadian Forces Grievance Board discriminated against her on the basis of sex (transgender) and ethnic origin (language). In 2006, she withdrew her complaint of language discrimination. *Montreuil* 2009.

39 Ms. Kavanagh, at that time a pre-operative transsexual woman housed in a male prison, filed complaints with the CHRC against the Correctional Service of Canada in relation to the withholding of hormone treatment, the denial of sex reassignment surgery, and her placement in a male institution. Each complaint alleged discrimination on the basis of sex and disability. *Kavanagh* 2001.

40 Daniel Petit, House of Commons Debates, 8 June 2010, 1810.

41 Robert Goguen, House of Commons Standing Committee on Justice and Human Rights, 6 December 2012, 1555 [emphasis added].

42 Ian Fine, House of Commons Standing Committee on Justice and Human Rights, 27 November 2012, 1600.

43 Meili Faille, House of Commons Debates, 10 May 2010, 1140.

44 *CHRA*, s. 3.

45 Irwin Cotler, House of Commons Debates, 5 April 2012, 1405.

46 Currah 2006, 4.

47 Grant Mitchell, Senate Standing Committee on Justice and Human Rights, 16 April 2013, 1810.

48 Bill Siksay, House of Commons Debates, 10 May 2010, 1835.

49 Don Meredith, Senate Standing Committee on Justice and Human Rights, 29 May 2013, 1530. Meredith is also an ordained Pentecostal minister.

50 Daniel Petit, House of Commons Debates, 8 June 2010, 1810.

51 Kerry-Lynne Findlay, House of Commons Debates, 5 April 2012, 1355.

52 Ryan Dyck, House of Commons Debates, 20 November 2012, 1655.

53 Qtd. in Thomas 2006, 319.

54 The Yogyakarta Principles define gender identity as referring to "each person's deeply felt internal and individual experience of gender, which may or may not correspond with the sex assigned at birth, including the personal sense of the body (which may involve, if freely chosen, modification of bodily appearance or function by medical, surgical or other means) and other expressions of gender, including dress, speech and mannerisms." Yogyakarta Principles on the Application of International Human Rights Law in relation to Sexual Orientation and Gender Identity, November 2006, http://www.yogyakarta principles.org/principles_en.htm.

55 Bill C-279, *An Act to amend the Canadian Human Rights Act and the Criminal Code (gender identity)* R.S., c. H-6, 2(2).

56 Diane Watts, Senate Standing Committee on Justice and Human Rights, 10 June 2013, Issue 28, http://www.parl.gc.ca/Content/SEN/Committee/411/ridr/28ev-50227-e.htm?Language=E&Parl=41&Ses=1&comm_id=77.

57 Diane Watts, Senate Standing Committee on Justice and Human Rights, 10 June 2013, Issue 28, http://www.parl.gc.ca/Content/SEN/Committee/411/ridr/28ev-50227-e.htm?Language=E&Parl=41&Ses=1&comm_id=77.

58 Diane Watts, Senate Standing Committee on Justice and Human Rights, 10 June 2013, Issue 28, http://www.parl.gc.ca/Content/SEN/Committee/411/ridr/28ev-50227-e.htm?Language=E&Parl=41&Ses=1&comm_id=77.

59 Françoise Boivin, Senate Standing Committee on Justice and Human Rights, 27 November 2012, 1610.

60 Donald Plett, Senate Standing Committee on Justice and Human Rights, 23 May 2013, 1540.

61 Thomas 2006, 311.

62 Anders misidentifies transgender women as transgender men; those who would be using the women's public facilities under this bill would identify as "women," not as "men." Transgender men would use the men's public facilities. Both transgender women and transgender men, the utilization of public washroom facilities presents a grave risk of negative confrontation, hostility, aggression, harassment, and even violence. Rob Anders, House of Commons Debates, 20 March 2013, 1515. Cavanagh 2010.

63 Rob Anders, House of Commons Debates, 20 March 2013, 1515.

64 Dan Meredith, Senate Standing Committee on Justice and Human Rights, 29 May 2013, 1530.

65 Kristeva 1982; Nussbaum 2010.

66 Nussbaum 2010, 21.

67 Nussbaum 2010, xiv.

68 Raymond 1979. I write "notorious" because as Stryker and Whittle (2006, 131), the editors of *The Transgender Studies Reader*, note of Raymond's book: "It did more to justify and perpetuate [anti-transsexual prejudice] than perhaps any other book ever written." Comparing it to the anti-Semitic *Protocols of the Elders of Zion* and "other notorious works of propaganda," they argue that it was a "profoundly polemical book [structured] upon falsifiable fantasies [that had] the power ... to demonize transgender people" (131).

69 Raymond 1979, xvi. Raymond primarily railed against male-to-female transsexualism and incorrectly named this transition as "male transsexualism."

70 Raymond 1979, 103.

71 Raymond 1979, xix.

72 Raymond 1979, 104.

73 Raymond 1979, xxiv–xxv.

74 Raymond 1979, 110.

75 Raymond 1979, 110.

76 Jeremy Garrison, Senate Standing Committee on Justice and Human Rights, 3 June 2013, Issue 27, http://www.parl.gc.ca/Content/SEN/Committee/411/ridr/28ev-50227-e.htm?Language=E&Parl=41&Ses=1&comm_id=77.

77 Kristeva 1982, 4.

78 Fuss 1991, 3.

79 Thomas 2006, 317.

80 Thomas 2006, 316.

81 Turner 1969.

82 Bhanji 2012, 170.

83 Joyce Murray, House of Commons Debates, 1 June 2012, 1335.

Chapter 5: The Baby and the Bathwater: The Repeal of Section 13 of the *Canadian Human Rights Act*

1 Brian Storseth, House of Commons Debates, 30 September 2011, 1205. Under the terms of the bill's coming into force clause, the act would be effective one year after receiving royal assent. *Canadian Human Rights Act*, RSC 1985, c. H-6, s. 12 (*CHRA*).

2 Walker 2010, 1. In the *Special Report to Parliament*, the Canadian Human Rights Commission (CHRC) (2009, 1) acknowledged that "section 13 has always been controversial, but particularly so since it was amended in 2001 to include hate on the internet." On 30 January 2008, Liberal, and former Reform, MP Keith Martin brought forward a private member's motion calling for the deletion of s. 13(1) of the *CHRA*.

3 Brian Storseth, House of Commons Debates, 22 November 2011, 1830.

4 Brian Storseth, House of Commons Debates, 22 November 2011, 1830.

5 Brian Storseth, House of Commons Debates, 30 September 2011, 1205; 4 April 2012, 1105. David Sweet, House of Commons Debates, 22 November 2011, 1910.

6 Ron Basford, House of Commons Debates, 11 February 1977, 1220. *Criminal Code*, RSC 1985, c. C-46.

7 *Smith and Lodge* 1979. This message was found to contravene s. 13.

8 *Human Rights Code*, RSO 1990, c. H-19.

9 Moon 2008, 5.

10 Lincoln Alexander, House of Commons Debate, 17 February 1977, 1545.

11 Ron Basford, House of Commons Debates, 11 February 1977, 1220.

12 Ron Basford, House of Commons Debates, 11 February 1977, 1215.

13 *Canadian Charter of Rights and Freedoms,* Part 1 of the *Constitution Act, 1982,* being Schedule B to the *Canada Act 1982* (UK), 1982, c. 11.

14 Carl Goldenberg, Senate Debates, 8 June 1977, 1420.

15 CHRC, "Section 13," http://www.chrc-ccdp.ca/proactive_initiatives/hoi_hsi/qa_qr/page1-eng.aspx. Accessed May, 2007.

16 Lincoln Alexander, Senate Standing Committee on Justice and Legal Affairs, 17 February 1977, 1550.

17 Alan Borovoy, Senate Standing Committee on Justice and Legal Affairs, 28 April 1977, Issue 10, 5.

18 Alan Borovoy, Senate Standing Committee on Justice and Legal Affairs, 28 April 1977, Issue 10, 4.

19 Alan Borovoy, Senate Standing Committee on Justice and Legal Affairs, 28 April 1977, Issue 10, 5.

20 Doug Finley, Senate Standing Committee on Justice and Legal Affairs, 27 June 2012, 1540.

21 Doug Finley, Senate Standing Committee on Justice and Legal Affairs, 27 June 2012, 1540.

22 Doug Finley, Senate Standing Committee on Justice and Legal Affairs, 27 June 2012, 1540. It should be noted that s. 13 of the *CHRA* does not include "publications," although speech on the Internet falls within its ambit.

23 Kohl 1992, 1–2.

24 Asante 1992, 141.

25 Kohl 1992, 1.

26 Asante 1992, 145.

27 Brent Rathgeber, House of Commons Debates, 22 November 2011, 1920.

28 Jim Cowan, Senate Debates, 26 June 2013, 1410.

29 Jim Cowan, Senate Debates, 26 June 2013, 1410.

30 Jim Cowan, Senate Debates, 26 June 2013, 1390–1400.

31 Brian Storseth, House of Commons Debates, 22 November 2011, 1835. Conservative party MP Rick Dykstra also made this claim in Parliament: "This is why section 13's overly broad hate speech provision was ruled to be unconstitutional in 2009." Rick Dykstra, House of Commons Debates, 14 February 2012, 1830.

32 Brian Storseth, Senate Standing Committee on Justice and Human Rights, 25 June 2013, Issue 29.

33 J. Walker 2010, 9.

34 J. Walker 2010, 2.

35 *Smith* 1979. See Moon 2008, 5–6; Canadian Human Rights Commission, n.d.

36 Ross 1994, 163.

37 Moon 2008, 6.

38 Ross 1994, 163.

39 Moon 2008, 6.

40 *International Covenant on Civil and Political Rights*, 1966, 999 UNTS 171.

41 Moon 2008, 19; Canadian Human Rights Commission, n.d.

42 *Canada (Human Rights Commission)* 1990.

43 *Canada (Human Rights Commission)* 1990, 895.

44 *Keegstra* 1990.

45 *Canada (Human Rights Commission)* 1990, 928.

46 *Canada (Human Rights Commission)* 1990, 964.

47 *Canada (Human Rights Commission)* 1990, 895.

48 *Canadian (Human Rights Commission)* 2009, 21.

49 Canadian Bar Association 2012, 6.

50 *CHRA*, para. 54(1)(c), s. 54(1.1).

51 *CHRA*, s. 13(2).

52 Canadian Human Rights Act Review Panel 2000.

53 Canadian Human Rights Commission, n.d, Recommendation 143.

54 Canadian Human Rights Commission, n.d.

55 *Citron* 2002. In 1983, Sabina Citron filed a private criminal complaint against Zündel. In 1984, the Ontario government joined the criminal proceedings against Zündel based on Citron's complaint. Zündel was charged under the *Criminal Code*, s. 181, of spreading false news for publishing "Did Six Million Really Die?" The case reached the Supreme Court of Canada, which ruled that the limitation was not constitutionally sound and the section was ruled to be of no force and effect. The two complaints were dated 18 July 1996 and 25 September 1996 respectively. See Webking 1995, 14–15.

56 Canadian Human Rights Commission, n.d.

57 See Moon 2008, 9; Canadian Human Rights Commission 2009, 30.

58 Ezra Levant, Senate Standing Committee on Justice and Human Rights, 5 October 2009, 1530.

59 Craig Scott, Senate Standing Committee on Justice and Human Rights, 24 April 2012, 1110.

60 George Baker, Senate Standing Committee on Justice and Human Rights, 25 June 2013, Issue 29.

61 Lillian Dyck, Senate Debates, 26 March 2013, 1810.

62 *Warman* 2009. Unless otherwise identified, factual information regarding *Lemire* was obtained from *Canada (Human Rights Commission)* 2012.

63 *Canada (Human Rights Commission)* 2012.

64 *Canada (Human Rights Commission)* 2012, para. 62.

65 *Canada (Human Rights Commission)* 2012, para. 61.

66 *Canada (Human Rights Commission)* 2012, para. 93.

67 *Canada (Human Rights Commission)* 2012, para. 65.

68 *Canada (Human Rights Commission)* 2012, para. 134.

69 Lillian Dyck, Senate Debates, 26 March 2013, 1810.

70 Steyn 2006. The quotation in the section title is from Mark Steyn, House of Commons Standing Committee on Justice and Human Rights, 5 October 2009, 1535. Complaint filed in December 2007 by Mohamed Elmasry of the Canadian Islamic Congress with the Canadian Human Rights Commission, the British Columbia Human Rights Tribunal and the Ontario Human Rights Commission.

71 J. Walker 2010, 10.

72 McDonald 2010, 302–3.

73 McDonald 2010, 303.

74　Joe Comartin, House of Commons Debates, 14 February 2012, 1815.

75　Jennifer Lynch, House of Commons Standing Committee on Justice and Human Rights, 26 October 2009, 1625. The committee was convened, in part, for the purpose of examining s. 13, despite that at the time neither the government of Canada nor the opposition parties had announced firm plans to repeal or amend s. 13; see J. Walker 2010, 15.

76　The complaint was lodged with the CHRC, the Ontario Human Rights Commission, and the British Columbia Human Rights Tribunal (BCHRT). The article under complaint before the BCHRT was titled "The New World Order," *Elmasry and Habib* 2008.

77　Steyn 2006, para. 19.

78　Steyn 2006, para 10.

79　Steyn 2006, para. 50.

80　*Human Rights Code*, SBC 1973 (2d Sess.), c. 19. In 2003, with the abolishment of the code, the responsibilities of the BCHRT were expanded to include "accepting, screening, mediating and adjudicating human rights complaints."

81　Marvin Kurz, House of Commons Standing Committee on Justice and Human Rights, 26 April 2012, 1110.

82　Marvin Kurz, House of Commons Standing Committee on Justice and Human Rights, 26 April 2012, 1110.

83　McDonald 2010, 300.

84　Levant 2009.

85　Qtd. in McDonald 2010, 301.

86　Jim Munson, Senate Debates, 23 October 2012, 1520.

87　Ezra Levant, House of Commons Standing Committee on Justice and Human Rights, 5 October 2009, 1530 and 1535 respectively.

88　Ezra Levant, House of Commons Standing Committee on Justice and Human Rights, 5 October 2009, 1550.

89　Ezra Levant, House of Commons Standing Committee on Justice and Human Rights, 5 October 2009, 1615, 1625.

90　Ezra Levant, House of Commons Standing Committee on Justice and Human Rights, 5 October 2009, 1625.

91　Ezra Levant, House of Commons Standing Committee on Justice and Human Rights, 5 October 2009, 1600.

92　Mark Steyn, House of Commons Standing Committee on Justice and Human Rights, 5 October 2009, 1535.

93　Mark Steyn, House of Commons Standing Committee on Justice and Human Rights, 5 October 2009, 1535.

94 Mark Steyn, House of Commons Standing Committee on Justice and Human Rights, 5 October 2009, 1540, 1535 respectively.

95 Jennifer Lynch, House of Commons Standing Committee on Justice and Human Rights, 26 October 2009, 1535.

96 Richard Moon, House of Commons Standing Committee on Justice and Human Rights, 26 October 2009, 1640.

97 Southern Poverty Law Centre, https://www.splcenter.org/fighting-hate/extremist-files/group/stormfront.

98 See Warner 2010, 21617.

99 Mark Steyn, House of Commons Standing Committee on Justice and Human Rights, 5 October 2009, 1630.

100 William Whatcott's flyer, entitled "Keep Homosexuality out of Saskatoon's Public Schools," stated: "Our children will pay the price in disease, death, abuse and ultimately eternal judgement if we do not say no to the sodomite desire to socialize your children into accepting something that is clearly wrong." The flyer titled "Sodomites in our Public Schools" stated that "Sodomites are 430 times more likely to acquire Aids [sic] and 3 times more likely to sexually abuse children!" In addition, this flyer claimed that "our acceptance of homosexuality and our toleration of its promotion in our school system will lead to the early death and morbidity of many children." See *Whatcott* 2007.

101 David Matas, House of Commons Standing Committee on Justice and Human Rights, 26 April 2012, 1110.

102 Mark Steyn, House of Commons Standing Committee on Justice and Human Rights, 5 October 2009, 1550.

103 Kidd 2011.

104 Frank Diamant, House of Commons Standing Committee on Justice and Human Rights, 26 April 2012, 1105.

105 Marvin Kurz, House of Commons Standing Committee on Justice and Human Rights, 26 April 2012, 1130.

106 Marvin Kurz, House of Commons Standing Committee on Justice and Human Rights, 26 April 2012, 1130.

107 David Matas, House of Commons Standing Committee on Justice and Human Rights, 26 April 2012, 1110. His reference was no more specific than this.

108 Mark Steyn, House of Commons Standing Committee on Justice and Human Rights, 5 October 2009, 1620.

109 "Two-tiered Thought Police" 2008.

110 Jenness and Grattet 2001, 21.

111 See, for example, McDonald 2010.

112 McDonald 2010, 320.

113 Herman 1997, 39–41.

114 McDonald 2010, 322.

115 Herman 1997, 171.

116 Bloedow 2009.

117 *Vriend* 1998; *Whatcott* 2007.

118 *Owens* 2002, 2006.

119 See Warner 2010, 215.

120 Qtd. in Warner 2010, 216.

121 Kathleen Mahoney, Senate Standing Committee on Human Rights, 25 June 2013, Issue 29.

122 Kathleen Mahoney, Senate Standing Committee on Human Rights, 25 June 2013, Issue 29.

123 The quotation in the section title is from Brian Storseth, House of Commons Debates, 22 November 2011, 1840.

124 Brian Storseth, House of Commons Standing Committee on Justice and Human Rights, 24 April 2012, 1115.

125 Brian Storseth, House of Commons Debates, 30 May 2012, 1910.

126 Brian Storseth, House of Commons Standing Committee on Justice and Human Rights, 24 April 2012, 1145.

127 Brian Storseth, Senate Standing Committee on Human Rights, 25 June 2013, Issue 29.

128 Brean 2008.

129 Brian Jean, House of Commons Standing Committee on Justice and Human Rights, 24 April 2012, 1150.

130 Email from Ryan Dyck, 9 December 2013 [on file with the author].

131 Marchildon 2005.

132 Senator Cowan, Senate Debates, 26 June 2013, 1410.

133 Mark Freiman, House of Commons Standing Committee on Justice and Human Rights, 24 April 2012, 1215.

134 Brian Storseth, House of Commons Debates, 30 May 2012, 1910.

135 Jim Munson, Senate Debates, 23 October 2012, 1510, 1520.

136 Terry Mercer, Senate Debates, 26 June 2013, 1440.

137 Jim Munson, Senate Debates, 23 October 2012, 1510.

138 Irwin Cotler, House of Commons Debates, 22 November 2011, 1905.

139 David Sweet, House of Commons Debates, 22 November 2011, 1200.

140 David Sweet, House of Commons Debates, 22 November 2011, 1905.

141 Joe Comartin, House of Commons Debates, 14 February 2012, 1820.

142 Canadian Human Rights Commission 2009, 1.
143 *Dagenais* 1994. Qtd. in Canadian Human Rights Commission 2009, 7, n. 4.
144 Irwin Cotler, House of Commons Debates, 22 November 2011, 1900.
145 Ryan Dyck, Senate Debates, 26 March 2013, 1800.
146 Jim Munson, Senate Standing Committee on Human Rights, 25 June 2013, Issue 29.
147 Charmaine Borg, House of Commons Debates, 22 November 2011, 1920.
148 Moon 2008, 12.
149 Moon 2008, 12.
150 Moon 2008, 38.
151 Canadian Bar Association 2012, s. IV.
152 *Canada (Human Rights Commission)* 2012.

Conclusion

1 *Canadian Human Rights Act*, RSC 1985, c. H-6.
2 *Keegstra* 1990.
3 Perry 2008.
4 Butler 1997.
5 Ahmed 2004, 59.
6 Barthes 1972.
7 Perry 2001.
8 Levin 1999; Herek, Gillis, and Cogan 1999.
9 Brown 2006, 187–88.
10 Jenness 1999.
11 Jacob and Potters 1998.
12 To some extent, this bears out in the Canadian context. Reflecting on an unpublished paper of mine comparing, both in terms of quantitative measure and symbolic pronouncements, the sentencing of offenders convicted of violent offences that identified bias or hatred in the commission of the offence, before and after the codification of s. 718.2(a)(i), there was little difference in the length of the sentence under the enhanced sentencing provision. My results showed that the penalty increased marginally for first-time offenders sentenced under the provision, usually resulting in what would have been a conditional sentence to a conditional sentence with higher restrictions or, in some cases, a short term at a provincial jail facility. What was most evident in the judicial statements attached to these judgments guided by s. 718.2(a)(i) was a generalized condemnation of these acts and a statement about how Canada as a multicultural, democratic, and tolerant society would not countenance such behaviour. Since my conclusion was somewhat observational, the study does call for renewed research and analysis utilizing statistical as well as qualitative data analysis.

References

Adam, Barry. 1995. *The Rise of a Gay and Lesbian Movement*. New York: Twayne.

Ahmed, Sara. 2004. *The Cultural Politics of Emotion*. New York: Routledge.

Anand, Sanjeev. 1998a. "Beyond *Keegstra*: The Constitutionality of the Wilful Promotion of Hatred Revisited." *National Journal of Constitutional Law* 9: 117.

–. 1998b. "Expressions of Racial Hatred and Racism in Canada: An Historical Perspective." *Canadian Bar Review* 77 (1–2): 181–97.

Asante, Molefi Kete. 1992. "The Escape into Hyperbole: Communication and Political Correctness." *Journal of Communication* 42 (2): 141–47. http://dx.doi.org/10.1111/j.1460-2466.1992.tb00786.x.

Backhouse, Constance. 1999. *Colour-Coded: A Legal History of Racism in Canada, 1900–1950*, Osgoode Society for Canadian Legal History. Toronto: University of Toronto Press.

Barthes, Roland. 1972 [1957]. *Mythologies*. New York: Hill and Wang.

Bayer, Ronald. 1987. *Homosexuality and American Psychiatry: The Politics of Diagnosis*. Princeton, NJ: Princeton University Press.

Beizer, Janet. 1994. *Ventriloquized Bodies: Narratives of Hysteria in Nineteenth-Century France*. Ithaca, NY: Cornell University Press.

Benveniste, Emile. 1971. *Problems in General Linguistics*. Coral Gables: University of Miami Press.

Bernheimer, Charles. 1990. "Introduction: Part One." In *In Dora's Case: Freud – Hysteria – Feminism*, edited by C. Bernheimer and C. Kahane, 1–18. New York: Columbia University Press.

Berrill, Kevin. 1991. "Anti-Gay Violence: Causes, Consequences, and Responses." In *Bias Crime: The Law Enforcement Response*, edited by N. Taylor, 113–25. Chicago: Office of International Criminal Justice, University of Illinois at Chicago.

Berrill, Kevin, and Gregory Herek. 1992. "Primary and Secondary Victimization in Anti-gay Hate Crime: Official Response and Public Policy." In *Hate Crimes: Confronting Violence against Lesbians and Gay Men*, edited by G. Herek and K. Berrill, 289–305. Newbury Park: Sage.

Bhanji, Nael. 2012. "Trans/Scriptions: Homing Desires, (Trans)sexual Citizenship and Racialized Bodies." In *Transgender Migrations: The Bodies, Borders, and Politics of Transition*, edited by T. Cotten, 157–75. New York: Routledge.

Bialystok, Franklin. 1996-97. "Neo-Nazis in Toronto: The Allan Gardens Riot." *Canadian Jewish Studies* 4–5: 1–38.

Bieber, Irving. 1962. *Homosexuality: A Psychoanalytic Study*. New York: Basic Books.

Black, Donald. 1983. "Crime as Social Control." *American Sociological Review* 48 (1): 34–45. http://dx.doi.org/10.2307/2095143.

Blackman, Lisa, and Valerie Walkerdine. 2001. *Mass Hysteria: Critical Psychology and Media Studies*. Basingstoke, UK: Palgrave Macmillan.

Bloedow, Tim. 2009. "ECP Centre Celebrates Victory." *News n Blues*, 4 December, http://newsnblues.ca/articles/1049-ecp-centre-celebrates-victory-for-stephen-boissoin-and-canadian-liberty

Braun, Stefan. 2004. *Democracy Off Balance: Freedom of Expression and Hate Propaganda Law in Canada*. Toronto: University of Toronto Press.

Bristow, Joseph. 1989. "Homophobia/misogyny: Sexual Fears, Sexual Definitions." In *Coming On Strong: Gay Politics and Culture*, edited by S. Shepherd and M. Wallis, 54–75. London: Unwin Hyman.

Brown, Wendy. 1993. "Wounded Attachments." *Political Theory* 21 (3): 390–410. http://dx.doi.org/10.1177/0090591793021003003.

–. 2006. *Regulating Aversion: Tolerance in the Age of Identity and Empire*. Princeton, NJ: Princeton University Press.

Brean, Joseph. 2008. "Rights Organization Dismisses Complaint against *Maclean's*." *National Post*, 27 June.

Bryden, Joan. 1994. "Predictions That the Liberal Caucus Could Split." *CanWest News*, 23 November.

Butler, Judith. 1993. *Bodies That Matter: On the Discursive Limits of 'Sex*. New York: Routledge.

–. 1997. *Excitable Speech: A Politics of the Performative*. New York: Routledge.

Canadian Bar Association. 2012. *Bill C-304 Canadian Human Rights Act Amendments (Hate Messages)*. Ottawa: Canadian Bar Association.

Canadian Human Rights Act Review Panel. 2000. *Promoting Equality: A New Vision*. Ottawa: Dept. of Justice.

Canadian Human Rights Commission. 2009. *Special Report to Parliament: Freedom of Expression and Freedom from Hate in the Internet Age*. Ottawa: Minister of Public Works and Government.

–. n.d. *Expanding Knowledge: Hate on the Internet*. http://www.chrc-ccdp.ca/proactive_initiatives/hoi_hsi/qa_qr/page1-eng.aspx. Accessed May, 2007.

Carter, Mark. 2001. "Addressing Discrimination through the Sentencing Process: *Criminal Code* s. 718.2(a)(i) in Historical and Theoretical Context." *Criminal Law Quarterly* 44: 399–436.

Cavanagh, Sheila. 2010. *Queering Bathrooms: Gender, Sexuality, and the Hygienic Imagination*. Toronto: University of Toronto Press.

Cohen, Jonathan. 2000. "More Censorship or Less Discrimination? Sexual Orientation Hate Propaganda in Multiple Perspectives." *McGill Law Journal. Revue de Droit de McGill* 46: 69–104.

Cohen, Maxwell. 1966. *Report to the Minister of Justice of the Special Committee on Hate Propaganda in Canada (Cohen Report)*. Ottawa: Queen's Printer.

–. 1971. "The Hate Propaganda Amendments: Reflections on a Controversy." *Alberta Law Review* 9: 103–17.

Cohen, Stephen. 1971. "Hate Propaganda: The Amendments to the *Criminal Code*." *McGill Law Journal*. 17: 740–91.

Cohen-Almagor, Raphael. 2006. *The Scope of Tolerance: Studies on the Costs of Free Expression and Freedom of the Press*. New York: Routledge.

Commission des Droits de la Personne du Quebec. 1994. *From Illegality to Equality: Public Consultation Report on Violence and Discrimination Against Gays and Lesbians*. Quebec City: Commission des droits de la Personne du Quebec.

Conrad, Joseph. 1969 [1902]. *Heart of Darkness and The Secret Sharer*. New York: Bantam Books.

Cook, Ramsay. 2011. "Homegrown Fascism: A Quebec Newspaperman's Transformation into One of Canadian History's Disturbing Footnotes." *Literary Review of Canada* 19 (10): 12–14.

Crew, Louie, and Rictor Norton. 1974. "The Homophobic Imagination: An Editorial." *College English* 36 (3): 272–90. http://dx.doi.org/10.2307/374839.

Currah, Paisley. 2006. "Gender Pluralisms under the Transgender Umbrella." In *Transgender Rights*, edited by P. Currah, R. Juang, and S. Price Minter, 3–31. Minneapolis: University of Minnesota Press.

Daniels, Ronald, Patrick Macklem, and Kent Roach, eds. 2001. *The Security of Freedom: Essays on Canada's Anti-Terrorism Bill*. Toronto: University of Toronto Press.

Daubney, David, and Gordon Parry. 1999. "An Overview of Bill C-41 (The Sentencing Reform Act)." In *Making Sense of Sentencing*, edited by J. Roberts and D. Cole, 31–47. Toronto: University of Toronto Press.

Davies, Alan, ed. 1992. *Antisemitism in Canada: History and Interpretation.* Waterloo: Wilfrid Laurier University Press.

Eco, Umberto. 1989. *The Open Work.* Cambridge, Mass. Harvard University Press.

EGALE. 1994. *Submissions to the House of Commons Standing Committee of Justice and Legal Affairs.* Ottawa: EGALE.

Fairclough, Norman. 2010. *Critical Discourse Analysis: The Critical Study of Language.* 2nd ed. Harlow, UK: Pearson Education.

Fanon, Frantz. 1967 [1952]. *Black Skin White Masks.* New York: Grove Weidenfeld.

Faulkner, Ellen. 1997. *Anti-Gay/Lesbian Violence in Toronto: The Impact on Individuals and Communities.* Ottawa: Department of Justice Canada.

Frank, Jerome. 1949. *Courts on Trial: Myth and Reality in American Justice.* Princeton, NJ: Princeton University Press.

Foucault, Michel. 1990 [1976]. *The History of Sexuality: An Introduction,* vol. 1. New York: Vintage Books.

Freud, Sigmund. 1977a [1925]. "Some Psychical Consequences of the Anatomical Distinction between the Sexes." In *Sigmund Freud: 7. On Sexuality,* edited by Angela Richards, 323–43. London: Penguin Books.

–. 1979a [1914]. "From the History of an Infantile Neurosis (The 'Wolf Man')." In *Sigmund Freud: 7. Case Histories II,* edited by Angela Richards, 227–366. London: Penguin Books.

–. 1979b [1922]. "Some Neurotic Mechanisms in Jealousy, Paranoia and Homosexuality." In *Sigmund Freud: 10. On Psychopathology,* edited by Angela Richards, 195–208. London: Penguin Books.

–. 1984 [1915]. "Instincts and Their Vicissitudes." In *Sigmund Freud: 11. On Metapsychology,* edited by Angela Richards, 105–38. London: Penguin Books.

Fuss, Diana. 1991. "Inside/Out." In *Inside/Out: Lesbian Theories, Gay Theories,* edited by D. Fuss, 1–12. New York: Routledge.

Garland, David. 1996. "The Limits of the Sovereign State: Strategies of Crime Control in Contemporary Society." *British Journal of Criminology* 36 (4): 445–71. http://dx.doi.org/10.1093/oxfordjournals.bjc.a014105.

Garofolo, James, and Susan Martin. 1991. "The Law Enforcement Response to Bias-Motivated Crimes." In *Bias Crime: The Law Enforcement Response,* edited by Nancy Taylor, 17–31. Chicago: Office of International Criminal Justice, University of Illinois at Chicago.

Giddens, Anthony. 1998. *The Third Way: The Renewal of Social Democracy.* Cambridge: Polity.

Gilman, Sander. 1985. *Difference and Pathology: Stereotypes of Sexuality, Race, and Madness.* Ithaca, NY: Cornell University Press.

–. 1988. *Disease and Representation: Images of Illness from Madness to AIDS.* Ithaca, NY: Cornell University Press.

Gilmour, Glenn A. 1994 May. Hate-Motivated Violence, Working Document WD1994-6e. Ottawa: Department of Justice Canada.

Ginsberg, Elaine. 1996. "Introduction: The Politics of Passing." In *Passing and the Fictions of Identity*, edited by E. Ginsberg, 1–18. Durham, NC: Duke University Press. http://dx.doi.org/10.1215/9780822382027-001.

Gomes, Peter J. 1996. *The Good Book: Reading the Bible with Mind and Heart.* New York: William Morrow and Company.

Grosz, Elizabeth. 1994. *Volatile Bodies.* Bloomington, IN: Indiana University Press.

Hage, Robert. 1970. "The Hate Propaganda Amendment to the *Criminal Code.*" *University of Toronto Faculty of Law Review* 28: 63–73.

Hardisty, Jean, and Amy Gluckman. 1997. "The Hoax of 'Special Rights': The Right Wing's Attack on Gay Men and Lesbians." In *Homo Economics: Capitalism, Community, and Lesbian and Gay Life*, edited by A. Gluckman and B. Reed, 209–22. New York: Routledge.

Herek, Gregory, J. Roy Gillis, and Jeanine C. Cogan. 1999. "Psychological Sequelae of Hate-Crime Victimization Among Lesbian, Gay, and Bisexual Adults." *Journal of Consulting and Clinical Psychology* 67 (6): 945–51. http://dx.doi.org/10. 1037/0022-006X.67.6.945.

Herman, Didi. 1996. "(Il)legitimate Minorities: The American Christian Right's Anti-Gay-Rights Discourse." *Journal of Law and Society* 23 (3): 346–63. http:// dx.doi.org/10.2307/1410716.

–. 1997. *The Antigay Agenda: Orthodox Vision and the Christian Right.* Chicago: University of Chicago Press. http://dx.doi.org/10.7208/chicago/9780226327 693.001.0001.

Iganski, Paul. 2008. *Hate Crime and the City.* Bristol, UK: Policy Press. http:// dx.doi.org/10.1332/policypress/9781861349408.001.0001.

Jacobs, James B., and Jessica Henry. 1996. "The Social Construction of a Hate Crime Epidemic." *The Journal of Criminal Law and Criminology* 86 (2): 366–91.

Jacobs, James B., and Kimberly Potter. 1998. *Hate Crimes: Criminal Law and Identity Politics.* New York: Oxford University Press.

Janoff, Douglas. 2005. *Pink Blood: Homophobic Violence in Canada.* Toronto: University of Toronto Press.

Jenness, Valerie. 1999. "Managing Differences and Making Legislation: Social Movements and the Racialization, Sexualization, and Gendering of Federal Hate Crime Law in the U.S., 1985–1998." *Social Problems* 46 (4): 548–71. http:// dx.doi.org/10.2307/3097075.

Jenness, Valerie, and Kendal Broad. 1994. "Anti-violence Activism and the (In) Visibility of Gender in the Gay/Lesbian Movement and the Women's Movement." *Gender & Society* 8 (3): 402–23.

–. 1997. *Hate Crimes: New Social Movements and the Politics of Violence.* New York: Aldine de Gruyter.

Jenness, Valerie, and Ryken Grattet. 2001. *Making Hate a Crime: From Social Movement to Law Enforcement.* New York: Russell Sage.

Johnson, M.P., and K.J. Ferraro. 2000. "Research on Domestic Violence in the 1990's: Making Distinctions." *Journal of Marriage and the Family* 62 (4): 948–63. http://dx.doi.org/10.1111/j.1741-3737.2000.00948.x.

Juang, Richard. 2006. "Transgendering the Politics of Recognition." In *The Transgender Studies Reader,* edited by S. Stryker and S. Whittle, 706–19. New York: Routledge.

Kallen, Evelyn. 1991. "Never Again: Target Group Responses to the Debate Concerning Anti-hate Propaganda Legislation." *Windsor Yearbook of Access to Justice* 11: 46–73.

Kaplan, William. 1993. "Maxwell Cohen and the Report of the Special Committee on Hate Propaganda." In *Law, Policy, and International Justice: Essays in Honour of Maxwell Cohen,* edited by W. Kaplan and D. McRae, 243–74. Montreal and Kingston: McGill-Queen's University Press.

Kayfetz, B.G. 1970. "The Story behind Canada's New Anti-Hate Law." *Patterns of Prejudice* 4 (3): 5–8. http://dx.doi.org/10.1080/0031322X.1970.9968910.

Kidd, Kenneth. 2011. "The Canadian Jewish Congress Has Been Replaced." *Toronto Star,* 30 August. https://www.thestar.com/news/canada/2011/08/30/the_canadian_jewish_congress_has_been_replaced_by_the_centre_for_israel_and_jewish_affairs.html.

Kinsella, Warren. 2001. *Web of Hate: Inside Canada's Far Right Network.* Toronto: Harper Collins.

Kinsey, Alfred, Wardell B. Pomeroy, and Clyde E. Martin. 1948. *Sexual Behavior in the Human Male.* Philadelphia: W.B. Saunders.

–. 1953. *Sexual Behavior in the Human Female.* Philadelphia: W.B. Saunders.

Kohl, Herbert. 1992. "Uncommon Differences: On Political Correctness, Core Curriculum and Democracy in Education." *Lion and the Unicorn* 16 (1): 1–16. http://dx.doi.org/10.1353/uni.0.0216.

Kristeva, Julia. 1982. *Powers of Horror: An Essay on Abjection.* New York: Columbia University Press.

Lafrance, André. 1993. *The Deadly Con Game: How Relying on Condoms for Protection Can Mean Lifelong Disease, Suffering, and Even Death for You or Someone You Love.* Toronto: Life Ethics Centre.

Levant, Ezra. 2009. *Shakedown: How Our Government Is Undermining Democracy in the Name of Human Rights.* Toronto: McClelland and Stewart.

Levin, Brian. 1999. "Hate Crimes: Worse by Definition." *Journal of Contemporary Criminal Justice* 15 (1): 6–21. http://dx.doi.org/10.1177/10439862990150 01002.

Levin, Brian, and Jack McDevitt. 1993. *Hate Crimes: The Rising Tide of Bigotry and Bloodshed.* New York: Plenum Press. http://dx.doi.org/10.1007/978-1-4899-6108-2.

Liberal Party of Canada. 1992. *Creating Opportunity: The Liberal Plan for Canada.*

Lunny, Allyson M. 1997. "Psychoanalysis and Homosexuality: Que(e)rying the Trope of Inversion." MA thesis, Centre for the Study of Theory and Criticism, University of Western Ontario.

MacFadyen, Joshua. 2004. "'Nip the Noxious Growth in the Bud': *Ortenberg v. Plamondon* and the Roots of Canadian Anti-hate Activism." *Canadian Jewish Studies* 12: 73–96.

MacGuigan, Mark. 1966. "Hate Control and Freedom of Assembly." *Saskatchewan Bar Review* 31: 231–50.

Maghan, Jess, and Edward Sagarin. 1983. "Homosexuals as Victimizers and Victims." In *Deviants: Victims or Victimizers?* edited by D. MacNamara and A. Karmen, 147–62. Beverly Hills, CA: Sage.

Major, Marie-France. 1996. "Sexual-Orientation Hate Propaganda: Time to Regroup." *Canadian Journal of Law and Society* 11 (01): 221–40. http://dx.doi.org/10.1017/S0829320100004646.

Marchildon, Giles. 2005. "Freedom for All Means Freedom for Each." *InQueeries,* 3 November.

Martin, James. 2014. *Politics and Rhetoric: A Critical Introduction.* New York: Routledge

Mason, Gail. 2002. *The Spectacle of Violence: Homophobia, Gender and Knowledge.* London: Routledge. http://dx.doi.org/10.4324/9780203360781.

Matsuda, Mari, Charles Lawrence, III, Richard Delgado, and Kimberlé Williams Crenshaw, eds. 1993. *Words That Wound: Critical Race Theory, Assaultive Speech, and the First Amendment.* Boulder, CO: Westview Press.

Mawby, R.I., and S. Walklate. 1994. *Critical Victimology: International Perspectives.* London: Sage.

McDevitt et al. 2001. "Consequences for Victims: A Comparison of Bias- and Non-bias Motivate Assaults." *American Behavioral Scientist* 45 (4): 697–713.

McLuhan, Marshall. 1962. *The Gutenberg Galaxy: The Making of Typographic Man.* Toronto: University of Toronto Press.

–. 1964. *Understanding Media: The Extensions of Man*. New York: McGraw-Hill.

McDonald, Marci. 2010. *The Armageddon Factor: The Rise of Christian Nationalism in Canada*. Toronto: Random House Canada.

Miller, Brian, and Laud Humphreys. 1980. "Lifestyles and Violence: Homosexual Victims of Assault and Murder." *Qualitative Sociology* 3 (3): 169–85. http://dx.doi.org/10.1007/BF00987134.

Moon, Richard. 1992. "Drawing Lines in a Culture of Prejudice: *R. v. Keegstra* and the Restriction of Hate Propaganda." *UBC Law Review* 26: 99–143.

–. 2000. *The Constitutional Protection of Freedom of Expression*. Toronto: University of Toronto Press.

–. 2008. Report to the Canadian Human Rights Commission Concerning Section 13 of the Canadian Human Rights Act and the Regulation of Hate Speech on the Internet. Ottawa: Canadian Human Rights Commission.

Moran, Leslie. 2001. "Affairs of the Heart: Hate Crime and the Politics of Crime Control." *Law and Critique* 12 (3): 331–44. http://dx.doi.org/10.1023/A:1013758417185.

–. 2004. "The Emotional Dimensions of Lesbian and Gay Demands for Hate Crime Reform." *McGill Law Journal* 49: 925–49.

Moran, Leslie, Beverley Skeggs, Paul Tyrer, and Karen Corteen. 2004. *Sexuality and the Politics of Violence*. London: Routledge.

Nova Scotia Public Interest Research Group. 1994. *Proud but Cautious: Homophobic Abuse and Discrimination in Nova Scotia*. Halifax: Nova Scotia Public Interest Research Group.

New Brunswick Coalition for Human Rights Reform. 1990. *Discrimination and Violence Encountered by Lesbian, Gay and Bisexual New Brunswickers*. Fredericton, NB: New Brunswick Coalition for Human Rights Reform.

Nussbaum, Martha. 2010. *From Disgust to Humanity: Sexual Orientation and Constitutional Law*. Oxford: Oxford University Press.

Perry, Barbara. 2001. *In the Name of Hate: Understanding Hate Crime*. New York: Routledge.

–. 2002. "Hate Crime and Identity Politics." *Theoretical Criminology* 6 (4): 485–91. http://dx.doi.org/10.1177/136248060200600407.

–. 2008. *Silent Victims: Hate Crimes against Native Americans*. Tucson, AZ: University of Arizona Press.

Perry, Marvin, and Frederick Schweitzer. 2002. *Anti-Semitism: Myth and Hate from Antiquity to the Present*. New York: Palgrave Macmillan.

Petersen, Cynthia. 1991. "A Queer Response to Bashing: Legislating Against Hate." *Queen's Law Journal* 16: 237–60.

Puzone, C.A., L.E. Saltzman, M.-J. Kresnow, M.P. Thompson, and J.A. Mercy. 2000. "National Trends in Intimate Partner Homicide, 1976–1995." *Violence Against Women* 6 (4): 409–26. http://dx.doi.org/10.1177/10778010022181912.

Raymond, Janice. 1979. *The Transsexual Empire: The Making of the She-Male*. Boston: Beacon Press.

Rayside, David. 1995. *Disproportionate Harm: Hate Crime in Canada — An Analysis of Recent Statistics*. Ottawa: Department of Justice Canada.

–. 1998. *On the Fringe: Gays and Lesbians in Politics*. Ithaca, NY: Cornell University Press.

Rigdon, Joan E. 1991. "Overcoming a Deep-rooted Reluctance, More Firms Advertise to Gay Community." *Wall Street Journal*, 18 July, B1.

Roach, Kent. 1999. *Due Process and Victims' Rights: The New Law and Politics of Criminal Justice*. Toronto: University of Toronto Press.

Roberts, Julian. 1995. *Disproportionate Harm: Hate Crime in Canada — An Analysis of Recent Statistics*. Ottawa: Department of Justice Canada.

Rose, Nikolas. 2000. "Government and Control." *British Journal of Criminology* 40 (2): 321–39. http://dx.doi.org/10.1093/bjc/40.2.321.

Ross, Jeffrey Ian. 1994. "Hate Crimes in Canada: Growing Pains with New Legislation." In Hate Crime: International Perspectives on Causes and Control, edited by M. Hamm, 151–72. Cincinnati, OH: Anderson. http://dx.doi.org/10.2139/ssrn.2442498.

Rupp, J.C. 1970. "Sudden Death in the Gay World." *Medicine, Science, and the Law* 10 (3): 189–91.

Samis, Stephen Michael. 1995. "An Injury to One Is an Injury to All: Heterosexism, Homophobia, and Anti-Gay/Lesbian Violence in Greater Vancouver." MA thesis, Department of Sociology and Anthropology, Simon Fraser University.

Sepejak, Diana. 1977. "The Willingness of Homosexuals to Report Criminal Victimization to the Police." MA thesis, Centre of Criminology, University of Toronto.

Shaffer, Martha. 1995. "Criminal Responses to Hate-Motivated Violence: Is Bill C-41 Tough Enough?" *McGill Law Journal* 41: 200–51.

Silverman, Kaja. 1983. *The Subject of Semiotics*. New York: Oxford University Press.

Smith, Anne Marie. 1994. *New Right Discourse on Race and Sexuality: Britain 1968-1990*. Cambridge: Cambridge University Press. http://dx.doi.org/10.1017/CBO9780511518676.

Smith, Miriam. 1999. *Lesbian and Gay Rights in Canada: Social Movements and Equality-Seeking, 1971–1995*. Toronto: University of Toronto Press.

–. 2005. "Social Movements and Judicial Empowerment: Courts, Public Policy, and Lesbian and Gay Organizing in Canada." *Politics and Society* 33 (2): 327–53. http://dx.doi.org/10.1177/0032329205275193.

Spade, Dean. 2012. "Their Laws Will Never Make Us Safer." In *Against Equality: Prisons Will Not Protect You*, edited by R. Conrad, 1–12. Edinburgh: AK Press.

Stanko, Elizabeth, and Paul Curry. 1997. "Homophobic Violence and the Self 'At Risk': Interrogating the Boundaries." *Social and Legal Studies* 6 (4): 513–32. http://dx.doi.org/10.1177/096466399700600404.

Staver, Mathew. 2002. "Homosexual Behavior Should Not Be Accorded Special Protection." *National Liberty Journal*, October.

Stein, Gertrude. 1998 [1913]. "Sacred Emily." In *Writings: 1903-1932*, edited by Catharine R. Stimpson and Harriet Chessman, 387–96. New York: Library of America.

Steyn, Mark. 2006. "The Future Belongs to Islam." *Maclean's*, 20 October.

Stingel, Janine. 2001. "From Father to Son: Canadian Jewry's Response to the Alberta Social Credit Party and the Reform Party of Canada." *Canadian Jewish Studies* 9: 1–37.

Stryker, S., and S. Whittle, ed. 2006. *The Transgender Studies Reader*. New York: Routledge

Sumner, Wayne. 2004. *The Hateful and the Obscene: Studies in the Limits of Free Expression*. Toronto: University of Toronto Press.

Suriya, Senaka. 1998. *Combatting Hate? A Socio-legal Discussion on the Criminalization of Hate in Canada*. Ottawa: Carleton University.

Tarnopolsky, Walter. 1971. "The Canadian Bill of Rights From Diefenbaker to Drybones." *McGill Law Journal* 17 (3): 437–75.

Thomas, Kendall. 1993. "Corpus Juris (Hetero)sexualis: Doctrine, Discourse, and Desire in *Bowers v. Hardwick*." *GLQ: A Journal of Lesbian and Gay Studies* 1 (1): 33–52.

–. 2006. "Afterword: Are Transgender Rights Inhuman Rights?" In *Transgender Rights*, edited by P. Currah, R. Juang, and S. Price Minter, 310–26. Minneapolis: University of Minnesota Press.

Tomsen, Stephen, and Gail Mason. 2001. "Engendering Homophobia: Violence, Sexuality and Gender Conformity." *Journal of Sociology* 37 (3): 257–73. http://dx.doi.org/10.1177/144078301128756337.

Toronto Police Service. 1999. *Hate Bias Crime 1998 Statistical Report: Hate Crime Unit, Intelligence Services*. Toronto: Toronto Police Service.

–. 2000. *1999 Hate Bias Crime Statistical Report: Hate Crime Unit, Intelligence Services*. Toronto: Toronto Police Service.

–. 2002. *2001 Hate Bias Crime Statistical Report: Detective Services, Intelligence Support*. Toronto: Toronto Police Service.

Tulchinsky, Gerald. 2008. *Canada's Jews: A People's Journey*. Toronto: University of Toronto Press.

Turner, Victor. 1969. *The Ritual Process: Structure and Antistructure*. Chicago: Aldine Publishing.

Turell, Susan C. 2000. "A Descriptive Analysis of Same-gender Relationship Violence for a Diverse Sample." *Journal of Family Violence* 15 (3): 281–93. http://dx.doi.org/10.1023/A:1007505619577.

"Two-tiered Thought Police." 2008. *National Post*, 19 December, A16.

Valois, Martine. 1992. "Hate Propaganda, Section 2(b) and Section 1 of the *Charter*: A Canadian Constitutional Dilemma." *Revue Juridique Thémis* 26: 373–431.

Valverde, Mariana. 2003. *Law's Dream of a Common Knowledge*. Princeton, NJ: Princeton University Press.

von Krafft-Ebing, Richard. 1905. *Text-Book of Insanity*, trans. Charles Gilbert. Chaddock, Philadelphia: F.A. Davis.

Von Hentig, Hans ([1948] 1967). *The Criminal and His Victim: Studies in the Sociology of Crime*. Hamden, CT: Archon Books.

Walker, Barrington. 2008. *The History of Immigration and Racism in Canada: Essential Readings*. Toronto: Canadian Scholars Press.

Walker, James. 1997. *"Race," Rights and the Law in the Supreme Court of Canada: Historical Case Studies*. Toronto: Osgoode Society for Canadian Legal History and Wilfrid Laurier University Press.

–. 2002. "The 'Jewish Phase' in the Movement for Racial Equality in Canada." *Canadian Ethnic Studies* 34 (1): 1–29.

Walker, Julian. 2010. Section 13 of the Canadian Human Rights Act: Anti-Hate Laws and Freedom of Expression, Legal and Legislative Affairs Division. Ottawa: Library of Parliament.

Wappel, Tom. 1994. *Sexual Orientation': Issues to Consider*, EGALE communiqué, 16 November.

Warner, Tom. 2002. *Never Going Back: A History of Queer Activism in Canada*. Toronto: University of Toronto.

–. 2010. *Losing Control: Canada's Social Conservatives in the Age of Rights*. Toronto: Between the Lines.

Webking, Edwin. 1995. *Freedom of Expression: Hate Literature*. Calgary: Alberta Civil Liberties Research Centre.

Weinberg, George. 1972. *Society and the Healthy Homosexual*. New York: St. Martin's Press.

Wilke, Mike. 2001. "Commercial Closet: Controversy Dogs Gay Marketing Research." *Gay Financial Network*, 8 November.

Williams, Patricia J. 1992. *Alchemy of Race and Rights: Diary of a Law Professor.* Cambridge, MA: Harvard University Press.

Cases

R. v Ahenakew, 2009 SKPC 10

R. v Andrews, [1990] 3 SCR 870

R. v Atkinson, Ing and Roberts (1978), 43 CCC (2d) 342 (Ont. CA)

Boucher v The King, [1951] SCR 265 (SCC)

R. v Buzzanga and Durocher (1979), 49 CCC (2d) 369 (Ont. CA)

Canada (Human Rights Commission) v Taylor, [1990] 3 SCR 892

Canada (Human Rights Commission) v Warman, 2012 FC 1162

Citron v Zundel (2002), 41 CHRR D/274 (CHRT)

Dagenais v Canadian Broadcasting Corporation, [1994] 3 SCR 835

The Queen v. Drybones, [1970] SRC 282

Elmasry and Habib v Roger's Publishing and MacQueen (No. 4), 2008 BCHRT 378

Egan and Nesbit v Canada (1995), 124 DLR (4th) 609 (SCC)

Haig and Birch v Canada (1992), 9 OR (3d) 495 (Ont. CA)

R. v Harding (2001b), 57 OR (3d) 333 (Ont. CA)

R. v. Harding (2001a) 52 OR (3d) 714 (Ont. Supreme Court)

R. v Ingram and Grimsdale (1977), 35 CCC (2d) 376 (Ont. CA)

Kavanagh v Attorney General Canada (Correctional Services of Canada) (2001) 41 CHRR D/119 (CHRT)

R. v Keegstra, [1990] 3 SCR 697

M. v H. (1996), 27 OR (3d) 593 (Ont. Gen. Div.)

M. v H., [1999] 2 SCR 3

Montreuil v Canadian Human Rights Commission and Canadian Forces, 2009 CHRT 28

Owens v Saskatchewan (Human Rights Commission), 2002 SKQB 506

Owens v Saskatchewan (Human Rights Commission), 2006 SKCA 41

R. v Safadi (1994), 121 PEIR 260 (PEI CA)

Smith and Lodge v Western Guard Party (Taylor J.R.) 1979 CHRT D 1/79

Vriend et al. v Alberta (1994), 152 AR 1

Vriend et al. v Alberta (1996) 181 AR 16 (Alta. CA)

Vriend v Alberta, [1998] 1 SCR 493

Warman v Lemire, 2009 CHRT 26

Whatcott v Saskatchewan Human Rights Tribunal, 2007 SKQB 450

Index

LAW AND SOCIETY

George Pavlich, and Matthew P. Unger, eds.
Accusation: Creating Criminals (2016)

Michael Weinrath
Behind the Walls: Inmates and Correctional Officers on the State of Canadian Prisons (2016)

Dimitrios Panagos
Uncertain Accommodation: Aboriginal Identity and Group Rights in the Supreme Court of Canada (2016)

Wes Pue
Lawyers' Empire: Legal Professionals and Cultural Authority, 1780-1950 (2016)

Sarah Turnbull
Parole in Canada: Gender and Diversity in the Federal System (2016)

Amanda Nettelbeck, Russell Smandych, Louis A. Knafla, and Robert Foster
Fragile Settlements: Aboriginal Peoples, Law, and Resistance in South-West Australia and Prairie Canada (2016)

Adam Dodek and Alice Woolley, eds.
In Search of the Ethical Lawyer: Stories from the Canadian Legal Profession (2016)

David R. Boyd
Cleaner, Greener, Healthier: A Prescription for Stronger Canadian Environmental Laws and Policies (2015)

Margaret E. Beare, Nathalie Des Rosiers, and Abby Deshman, eds.
Putting the State on Trial: The Policing of Protest during the G20 Summit (2015)

Dale Brawn
Paths to the Bench: The Judicial Appointment Process in Manitoba, 1870-1950 (2014)